PROFESSIONAL VIDEO PRODUCTION

SECOND EDITION

Ingrid Wiegand
with
Ben Bogossian

Knowledge Industry Publications, Inc.
White Plains, NY

KIPI Bookshelf

Professional Video Production, 2nd Edition

Library of Congress Cataloging in Publication Data

Wiegand, Ingrid.
     Professional video production.

     (Video bookshelf)
     Bibliography: p.
     Includes index.
     1. Video recordings—Production and direction.
I. Title. II. Series.
PN1992.95.W54   1993   791.45'0232   84-21323
ISBN 0-86729-311-X
ISBN 0-86729-321-7

Illustrations by Kathleen Pasquale

Printed in the United States of America

10   9   8   7   6   5   4   3   2   1

Contents

List of Figures and Forms iv
Introduction vii

1 Program Development and
Script Preparation 1

2 The Studio and its
Major Components 21

3 Switchers and Other
Studio Equipment 39

4 Shooting in the Studio:
Production 59

5 Shooting in the Studio:
Staff and Crew 77

6 Shooting in the Field:
Equipment......................................89

7 Shooting in the Field:
Production 101

8 Editing: Concepts, Equipment
and Basic Operations 121

9 Editing: Preparation
and Budgets 131

10 Editing: Elements of
the Fine-Cut 141

11 Post-Production Effects,
Graphics and Fixers 153

12 Summary Production
Budgets 167

Technical Appendix 175
Glossary 189
Selected Bibliography 209
Index...213
About the Author 217

List of Figures and Forms

Figure 1.1: Cover page for a program development program 2

Figure 1.2: Standard talent release 5

Figure 1.3: Basic shot formats 7

Figure 1.4: Diagrams of basic camera moves 8

Figure 1.5: Format for a multi-camera script 11

Figure 1.6: Format for a single-camera script 12

Figure 1.7: Audiovisual script format 14

Figure 1.8: Documentary script format 15

Figure 1.9: Symbols used for flowcharting 17

Figure 1.10: Flowchart for an interactive program segment 18

Figure 2.1: Elements of a basic television studio 22

Figure 2.2: Color-separation optics in three-tube cameras 25

Figure 2.3: Television pickup tube configuration 27

Figure 2.4: A filter and target configuration for a single-tube camera 28

Figure 2.5: An Ampex VPR-3 (one-inch Type C) VTR 32

Figure 2.6: Type C one-inch helical-scan system layout 33

Figure 2.7: Two helical-scan videotape recording formats 33

Figure 2.8: Basic component videotape format 34

Figure 2.9: Typical 3/4-inch cassette system tape layout 34

Figure 2.10: 3/4-inch SP 35

Figure 2.11: Hi8: Feeder 36

Figure 2.12: D-2 Studio VTR, the Ampex VPR-300 37

Figure 3.1: Front panel of a typical switcher 40

Figure 3.2: Simplified block diagram of a special effects generator 41

Figure 3.3: Block diagram of typical SEG operation with downstream keyer and double re-entry 43

Figure 3.4: Front panel of a waveform monitor with horizontal video display for color bars 45

Figure 3.5: A horizontal video trace on a waveform monitor 46

Figure 3.6: Front panel of a vectorscope with color bar display 47

Figure 3.7: Basic audio system for a small-format studio 48

Figure 3.8: Polar sensitivity patterns for microphones 49

Figure 3.9: Dynamic microphones 50

Figure 3.10: Condense microphone 51

Figure 3.11: A studio intercom system 53

Figure 3.12: Luminaries used in television production 55

Figure 3.13: Diagram of film/slide chain (top view) 57

Form 4.1: Basic studio production budget 62

Figure 4.1: Flats, risers and cycs 66

Figure 4.2: Lighting setup with softlights and backlights for flat keyless lighting 68

Figure 4.3: Basic three-point lighting 69

Figure 4.4: Basic lighting with wider background and spot lighting 71

Figure 4.5: Lighting setup for limbo and cameos 72

Figure 4.6: Mic setup for dramatic scene 74

Figure 4.7: Mic setup for recording a small group of musicians 75

Form 5.1: VTR Take log 80

Figure 5.1: Script marked for audio operator ...81

Figure 5.2: Studio floor plan showing set, talent and camera moves 82

Figure 5.3: A director's marked script 84

Figure 6.1: Betacam camcorder 91

Figure 6.2: An EFP configuration 92

Figure 6.3: Camcorder with S/VHS recorder 94

Figure 6.4: Portable 3/4-inch VCR 94

Figure 6.5: Condenser shotgun microphone 96

Figure 6.6: Field mixer 96

Figure 6.7: Portable light kit and battery-operated light 98

Form 7.1: Site checklist for remote shoots 102

Form 7.2: Area checklist for remote shoots 103

Form 7.3: Remote production checklist 106
Form 7.4: Remote production budget 108
Figure 7.1: Interior location lighting for
    daylight matching 111
Figure 7.2: Using the sun to keylight and
    fill an interior 113
Figure 7.3: Mic placement at a church
    wedding shot EFP 117
Figure 7.4: Miking speakers and audience
    at a seminar 118

Figure 8.1: An editing system at work 122
Figure 8.2: Functional diagram of a basic
    editing system 124
Figure 8.3: Edit point layouts on tape 127
Figure 8.4: Editing controller 128

Figure 9.1: Original-to-worktape relation-
    ships 133
Figure 9.2: A time-coded "window dub" 134
Form 9.1: Footage catalog sheet 135
Form 9.2: Edit decision list 135
Form 9.3: Edit decision list, rough cut 137
Form 9.4: Post-production budget 138

Figure 10.1: A three-machine system for
    A/B roll editing 142
Figure 10.2: Image transfer on videotape
    for A/B roll editing 144
Figure 10.3: Scenes conformed on A and
    B rolls 145
Form 10.1: Edit decision list 146
Figure 10.4: Setting time code for real
    program time 148
Figure 10.5: Segment on an 8-track tape
    with time code and audio for video 149
Form 10.2: audio track line-up sheet 150

Figure 11.1: Relative proportions for TV
    board graphics 154
Figure 11.2: Setups for graphics cameras 155
Figure 11.3: Editing system for board
    graphics insertion 156
Figure 11.4: Board-based title card with
    dimensions 157
Figure 11.5: Character generator with
    storage device 159
Figure 11.6: Editing system with character
    generator 160
Figure 11.7: The ADO 100 is designed for
    smaller broadcast, post-production and
    corporate video facilities 162

Form 12.1: Summary production budget 170

Figure A.1: CEI graph of the television
    color spectrum 176
Figure A.2: CEI map showing color shifts
    under tungsten 176
Figure A.3: A Y/I Q encoder block
    diagram 178
Figure A.4: S/N voltage ratio on
    a logarithmic curve 180
Figure A.5: Horizontal blanking
    interval on expanded display 182
Figure A.6: Configuration of the vertical
    blanking interval 183
Figure A.7: Vectorscope display 185
Figure A.8: Image from a cross-pulse
    monitor 186
Figure A.9: Cross-pulse monitor blanking
    information layout 187
Figure A.10: Skew adjustment on a
    cross-pulse monitor 188

Introduction

This book is not for everybody. It is not for those who have never used a video camera or for those who don't understand the basic processes of video recording. It was written for those who have acquired some understanding of the basics of television production and for those who work in the medium and need to fill out their expertise.

To help both the student and the professional, *Professional Video Production* provides a great deal of basic information about how video equipment works. It concerns itself with some very basic production procedures—as well as some sophisticated ones. In fact, this book has a great deal of very solid "how to" information because it is truly intended as a guide and a reference source for the serious video professional.

Professional Video Production is set up to provide the information which the producer needs to handle specific situations—such as studio productions, location shoots and edits—because one seldom finds oneself merely with a piece of equipment to operate or a light to set or an audio board to adjust. These are skills that a producer must understand, but he need not excel at any one of them. What a producer must be able to do, however, is to control a complete production—from the planning stage, all the way through production and post-production.

The planning stage includes script preparation. Preparing a script is so basic to all production situa-tions that it is covered in some detail. It may be possible to make a silk purse out of a sow's ear in some mediums, but without a good script, it is difficult to end up with even a decent pigskin of a television program. And because producers often enter the field without a background in scriptwriting, Chapter 1 covers the subject on several levels.

While not everyone can write a script, every producer needs to know how to "read" one for its production potential and how to work with a scriptwriter. The script may be a detailed shooting script that specifies not only the words and actions but also the camera moves and angles. Or it may be a simple outline of places, subjects and topics to be covered while on a location shoot to gather material for a documentary.

Script in hand, the producer needs to be able to work out a budget he can meet. Money committed, he has to hire a director, talent and crew. If he uses a studio, he must know its capacities and limitations. In each case, he needs to be familiar with the equipment he will need, in terms of its ability to deliver the best image possible for the price he can pay. He has to know enough about his audio requirements to decide whether his VTR person can handle them, or whether he needs to hire an audio recordist. The same goes for the lighting: can his camera person handle it or does the situation (and the budget) call for a lighting designer? This book will help with those decisions.

In post-production, the producer needs to know what to expect of each stage in the process, such as how many hours an edit will take and what kind of equipment will be needed. Time and money hang on every decision, and every decision represents a trade-off among the considerations of quality, money and time.

This book should help to demystify some aspects of television. There are many technical terms used by people in TV production, and the producer should be familiar enough with most of them to use them with ease. If a reader of this book is told "the pedestal is too high," he will know to ask, "Can you adjust it from here or do you have to get into the camera?"—rather than look for something lower on which to perch the talent.

Many producers, especially independents, really need to know how to do everything themselves, because their budgets demand it. And all, at some point in their careers, will have to work with much less money than they need and will need to rely on all the "smarts" at their command. This book was written for all those people, and to this end it contains ways to avoid all the mistakes that the author has made—or watched others make.

Professional Video Production is, in any case, dedicated to those who are intrepid enough to become serious producers. Video is a profession in which the best-laid plans hinge on dozens of small things going right for several hours at a stretch. Video equipment is temperamental at best and, because video production is a collaborative process that requires a number of talented (and often edgy) people to work together under pressure, the serious producer must also be prepared to deal with a wide range of human temperaments.

For those who make it into the profession and stay there, the personal and financial rewards can be very big. A good producer can take a small budget and make a good mid-sized program or he can take a mid-sized budget and make a program "big." He can put together the right people, equipment and locations, set up a workable schedule, shepherd the production through each of its stages and come up with a program that leaves a lasting impression on its audience. Whether it is entertainment, a documentary, a training tape, a news program or a quiz show, a good producer can make it better than it would have been without him. Making it better is what *Professional Video Production* is all about.

Finally, readers should note that the generic "he" is normally used throughout this book to keep the language simple. Nevertheless, the producers for whom this book is intended are definitely and equally he or she. The makings of a first-rate video producer are intelligence, patience, professionalism, wit and the ability to assume authority gracefully—qualities without gender.

Editor's Note

When this book was published in 1985, it was welcomed by the industry as one of the few resources available for the nonbroadcast video producer—a book that explained in careful detail the techniques, the equipment and the technology available to the professional nonbroadcast video producer. *Professional Video Production* has also been a steady resource for hundreds of students each year in college-level courses in media production. The first edition remained remarkably up to date, despite the numerous changes in video technology, because it was not product-specific, or even technology-specific. The concepts and explanations, about both programming and technology, remain valid today.

However, so much new technology has been introduced that major shifts occurred in the industry, in the facilities and in the practices used by producers. The second edition therefore includes increased coverage of new technology including video formats, desktop video and updated chapters on post-production and graphics, and studio, field and editing equipment. Almost all chapters have been at least slightly revised and the glossary and bibliography have been updated. We hope this second edition continues to provide readers with the basic information they need about how video equipment works and how this affects production procedures.

Ellen Lazer

1 Program Development and Script Preparation

Every television program gets its start when someone says, "Hey, let's make a program about ....!" This is true whether the idea comes from a sleek network executive in a three-piece suit, a tousle-haired Hollywood gogetter in dark glasses or someone conceiving his first show on a slow winter afternoon.

The difference between those shows that reach a public on the TV screen and those that never get beyond the idea state has less to do with money and power than with presentation of the program's concept. It is true that many ideas simply have no merit or have been done better by others, and that national television outlets are not easily accessed. But as we near the end of the twentieth century, when literally hundreds of cable, home video and other programming distribution markets are looking for viable material, it doesn't take genius or influence to get a show on the tube. What it does take is a little program development.

PROGRAM DEVELOPMENT

The process of developing a program involves taking the original idea and working out the problems that stand in the way of making it a reality. In that process, certain basic but vital questions must be answered. These include: What is the show really about? What will its format be? Who will be in it? Who will want to watch it? What is its

market? If rights are not cleared, what will it take to clear them? How much will it cost?

The answers to these questions form a proposal (see Figure 1.1) that will make it possible to raise the money needed to produce the program, to get the go-ahead from a boss or client, or to get a producing organization to commit staff and funds to the project. Following is a rundown of the various elements a program proposal might contain.

Content and Format: The Treatment

A treatment is simply a description of a proposed film or television project, whether it is a major motion picture or a cable talk show. The treatment can be preliminary to getting the go-ahead on a script, or it can be part of a development proposal. Its purpose is to let investors and participants know how and why the idea will work as a show.

Although the descriptions of various kinds of programs (drama, documentary, etc.) are very different in their handling of content, all have to be very specific.

Dramatic Treatments

It is not enough, for example, to say that the program is a feature-length film based on the leg-

1

Figure 1.1: Cover page for a program development proposal.

```
Development Proposal and Treatment

            for

     YOU ARE WHAT YOU EAT

A half-hour nutrition and health

    magazine for television




       ©1984 by Ingrid Wiegand
          WIEGAND VIDEO

       All rights reserved


Note: This treatment was registered
with the writer's Guild of America,
East, on January 12 1984
```

end of Dracula. While we know the story, we would have no reason to produce another version unless the information contained in the treatment is much more specific. For example, will the story be set in the past or present? Will it be a horror story, a comic takeoff or a dramatic allegory? Will it be farce or high comedy? How will the vampire angle be handled? Will we use effects and makeup, or will a transformation be suggested, rather than shown?

Presumably, if such a familiar theme is being used, the producer intends to introduce a new angle, for instance, making Dracula a contemporary comedy. In that case, it is necessary to tell why the proposed story will be funny. What in the events and style will make people laugh? For example, we might describe a scene in which Dracula finds himself at the dentist.

The treatment for a dramatic show should thus cover all the major scenes that are essential to the progress of the story. Each of them should be described separately in a paragraph that tells how the scene starts, where it takes place, how it develops and how it leads into the next scene. A treatment for a 60- or 90-minute feature might be as short as 10 pages or as long as 25. Shorter shows should have proportionally shorter treatments.

Documentary Treatments

Documentary treatments always start with a statement of the purpose of the documentary. While such a statement is useful for any nonfiction production to ensure agreement between the producer and his client, for the documentary it is also a necessity.

Let's use a typical subject for a feature documentary—nuclear power accident at Three-Mile Island—as an example. A documentary might show the effect of the accident on the use of nuclear power and explore any resulting patterns of energy development. Or, the documentary could show how the accident was used by the anti-nuclear movement. It might instead focus on the impact of the accident on individuals who live near Three-Mile Island. Same subject; three totally different documentaries.

An institutional documentary designed to be used as a promotional tool also presents a range of possibilities. Is the program to address the organization's founders and funders or its stockholders? Will it also address the public at large? Will it be shown to employees? Is the object of the program to get approval for existing policies, to raise additional funds, to encourage stock purchases, to gain public approval, to promote products, or several of these? Clearly, a documentary-style annual report for stockholders will be written rather differently from one that is shown to new employees, even if similar (or even identical) footage is used for both.

A documentary treatment identifies the central structure that will hold all the disparate locations, people and images together. The program can, for example, be a single interview in which all the material that will be covered visually is discussed. The interview then sets the structure from which the sequences depart, and to which the program returns. It might be a journey that someone takes, which strings together a series of locations. It might be "a day in the life of . . . ," or a personal, corporate or other history.

Once a viable central structure is selected, the rest of the treatment is relatively easy. The different people to be interviewed or otherwise shot are described. The different locations to be used are specified, and the material that will be gathered at each is explained.

Other Types of Programs

Descriptions of the content of nondramatic programs should also be quite specific and illustrative, but the emphasis will be on the format. If it is a talk show, will it feature a panel of experts, like the reporters of "Washington Week in Review"; a lineup of celebrity guests, like "The Tonight Show"; or a broad range of guests and audience participants, like "Donohue"? (Celebrities for shows, of course, are not confined to those in Hollywood and Washington. A show on bowling might interview a series of national, regional and local champions, bowling-alley owners, competition sponsors, equipment manufacturers and the like. All of these are celebrities to the bowling fan.)

News shows, game shows, travel shows and the like have the potential for accommodating a great variety of formats, many of which have yet to be invented. Describing the format in some detail and providing a treatment for hypothetical segments will make the show seem more real, and boost the chances that potential backers will find it worth considering.

The Talent

If there's no talent, there's no show. The success of dramatic and other programs, despite the best writing and presentation, depends on having just the right people on camera.

Although there are many very talented "unknown" actors who would do a first-rate job with a dramatic script, it is unlikely that a producer will "sell" a dramatic script, with their names listed as proposed talent. Whether or not major actors are ever really under consideration, it behooves the writer of a treatment to suggest well-known film and television talent for the lead roles. Whether these people are ultimately used does not matter.

Suggesting well-known talent in a treatment serves two important functions. It helps the reader visualize the characters and the action, and it communicates the idea that the writer is conversant with the industry in which he works.

In documentary treatments, the subjects should be described in some detail so that those who do not know them personally can learn why they would be interesting on camera. Readers of proposals also like to see the name of a potential narrator—preferably a name they recognize. Although many documentary producers would rather have their subjects speak for themselves, the narrator seems to be with us more often than not.

It is important to remember that the proposal should suggest one or more suitable candidates for each major role. The producer's friends and family (unless the name is Marx, Redford or the like) should not apply.

But whether the talent is a cast of actors or a single host, a letter from the talent (or an agent), indicating interest, is an enormous asset.

Audience and Market

Occasionally, a show will be produced for the love of it, or for a tax advantage. But most programs are produced to make money. Since a show will only turn a profit if people watch it, it is necessary to define its potential audience. Even when a program is made for public television, a producer has to convince underwriters and other funding sources that his or her program will attract a substantial number of PBS viewers. Once the audience is sketched out, the producer can also decide the market in which the program will be released.

Defining the Audience

• *The audience for similar shows.* Statistics for the viewing audiences for many television shows are not all that easy to come by, but bits and pieces can be picked up from publications that discuss television in any of its forms. One would think the Nielsen rating would be useful, but because the Nielsen company sells its ratings information for tidy sums, such data have to be obtained by most small producers by less direct routes that provide less concrete information. Nevertheless, when related shows exist, a bit of research can usually turn up some information. Where hard figures are not available, often articles discussing interest in this or that type of show can be found.

• *The audience for the subject.* Much more information is available on the number of people interested in a given subject. The audience for horror films should support a project with a Dracula theme; and there is always an audience for comedy. Statistics for more specific subjects are fairly easy to come by. There are any number of organizations and publications for almost every subject or sport that a producer might like to explore, from bowling to bridge or black magic. Such sources are only too glad to give optimistic estimates of their numbers, and to give positive support (often in writing) to programs dealing with subjects near and dear to their hearts.

• *The show as inherently interesting.* Whether or not there are similar shows and pre-sold audiences, every producer should be able to present a strong and heartfelt argument as to why a show is inherently interesting and will find its own audience.

Finding the Market

Only a very limited number of programs are suitable for broadcast to a large television audience, and even fewer actually get on the air. Public television may be more open to some types of shows than the networks are, but it makes few buys from independent producers because of limited funds and program interests. A great many more producers have learned that their programs can succeed in the smaller, but not insubstantial markets offered by cable television and home video—not to mention markets opened by even more recent developments, such as Direct Broadcast Satellite (DBS) and Low-Power Television (LPTV).

Access to these markets varies enormously by type and region, and changes are constant. There are as yet no hard-and-fast rules a producer can follow to tap these markets; it is probably wise to get the help of a professional distributor. However, if a series is proposed, one way to establish an audience and reach those who might buy it is to put the programs on public access television. If the series is professionally produced and consistent, the interest of a syndicator may put the producer on the road to distribution.

Rights

If a program is entirely original, there will probably be no problem with rights to its material. The important word is "probably," because the area of rights is a hotbed of legalities that keeps a horde of expensive lawyers employed. For example, if music is playing on the radio during an interview, and if it is a complete, identifiable piece, the producer may need to obtain a release—and may even have to pay royalties. If the music is commented on, or used purposely as background, this would almost

certainly be true. On the other hand, a release would probably not be necessary if the music is very much in the background and is not commented on.

If rights have to be obtained, the cost can vary from zero to considerable sums, depending on the audience (the bigger the audience, the more the money); the current popularity of the material (a recent release by a popular recording artist will be expensive); the commercial potential of the program (a non-profit venture may not have to pay anything); and how reasonable the copyright holder is (some rights are priced solely for the big spender).

Releases, unlike rights, are granted by those who appear, speak or perform on a program. Some details on clearances, rights and releases follow.

Music

There are several types of music clearances. If a recording is used, the rights will have to be obtained from the recording company. The rights may be priced by the "needle-drop"—which means that the fee applies every time a part of the music is used, whether it is on for five seconds or for its whole length. It may also be priced by the minute.

If published music is used, but the producer hires the musicians who perform it, the producer pays the publisher of the music directly. To find the publisher, the producer can call Broadcast Music Inc. (BMI) or American Society of Composers, Authors and Publishers (ASCAP) and ask for the Index. These two organizations (to which all professional musicians belong) will provide the name and address of the rights holder. Releases from the musicians who are hired to perform the music for the show will also be needed.

Finally, music which has been recorded solely for use by radio and television producers can be bought from companies specializing in it. These companies can provide shorter or longer recordings of specific works, or music "in the style of" different composers. They, too, sell by the minute or the needledrop, and vary the price depending on the program's market.

Text

Unlike music, for which substitutions may often be found, rights to a text may be central to a show. If the program is a presentation of a published work, or based on a published text, the right to use it in the way the program intends must be

Figure 1.2: Standard talent release.

PRODUCER'S LETTERHEAD

TALENT RELEASE

I, _____ (name) _____ , of

_____ (address) _____

hereby permit the producer, _____(name of person or company)_____ to record my performance on

videotape for use in the program,_____(title)_____ , and to distribute

this program, edited as the producer sees fit, for presentation via broadcast, cablecast, pay-television, direct-broadcast satellite and on closed circuit television, including home video, in the United States and other countries (although I understand that the producer does not guarantee any or all such exhibition) for a total consideration of _____ .

Agreed to and signed by me this_____ day of_____ 19__ .

_____ (performer) L.S.

_____ L.S.
(Performer's parent or guardian, if under age)

Witness _____ L.S.

---

obtained and in the producer's hand before a proposal can be taken seriously. In most cases, the rights can be obtained directly from the publisher.

If the program is based on a newspaper story in which living people are involved, it may be necessary to get rights to the story from those individuals. This is difficult territory, in which good legal advice is needed.

Releases

Everyone who appears on camera as an identifiable individual, or whose voice is recorded, should sign a release. A release, as shown in Fig-

ure 1.2, is a signed and dated statement with which the signer permits his image and his voice to be used in a specific program or series, and includes an acknowledgment of the compensation (if any) that he has received for this appearance. The release may also give the producer the right to exhibit the program in certain markets (e.g., closed circuit) without further compensation or specifies the compensation required (see Figure 1.2).

In deciding if a release is required, it may be helpful to determine if the performers or subjects appear as distinct individuals, rather than as anonymous faces in a crowd. For example, if someone offers an opinion in response to a question from an interviewer, a release is needed. If the opinion is clearly unsolicited, a release may not be required.

The person's involvement in the program need not be verbal, however. If someone is sunning himself in a park, and the camera focuses on his face, hands and feet, a release may be in order. The subject, although in a public place, was not participating in a public event.

If someone *is* participating in a public event, such as a demonstration, he may be fair game, and not require a release.

The subject of releases is endlessly complicated and not at all clear-cut. A dancer, performing at a public celebration, can be photographed as part of a program on the celebration. However, if that dancer's performance constitutes a substantial part of the show, a release may be required. Needless to say, all actors, hosts and others who have a part in a program (paid or unpaid), should sign a release. The producer should get the release before he records the subject, and certainly before he pays the talent. Afterwards, it becomes much harder to obtain.

Budget

Before production on a program can start, the producer must work out a fairly accurate estimate of what the project will cost.

In addition to the costs incurred for talent and rights, the producer will need to consider what parts of the program will be produced in the studio, what will be produced in the field and what the post-production process will involve. Separate budget forms for studio and remote production are provided and explained in Chapters 3 and 4; a budget for all the stages of post-production appears in Chapter 5. In addition, a summary budget form, suitable for a budget projection, is provided in Chapter 12.

ELEMENTS OF A SCRIPT

When we talk about scriptwriting for television, we know that television (or film, for that matter) is made in the international language of moving images. It is a language that every person who has watched his or her quota of film or television can "read." To write strong film or TV scripts, we have to be able to use this language consciously.

When we talk about the "language" of moving images, we mean that we manipulate the images on the screen so that they make sense to us—as viewer or creator. Take this example: a camera at a football game pans the crowd from left to right. Because we are familiar with the language of moving images, we know that it is the camera and not the people who are moving. But a very young child or a person unfamiliar with the "language" will only see a mass of people floating from right to left across the screen.

Similarly, when a camera zooms in on a part of an image—such as a knife on a table or a knob on a machine—we immediately accept two things: one is that it is the camera mechanism which is bringing the image toward the lens, not the object that is floating toward the camera; and also that the knife or knob is important to what follows.

These images form the basic unit—the "word"—of moving-image making: the shot, cut or edit (depending on whether the context is shooting or editing and whether the medium is tape or film). But the syntax or grammar that makes these words into coherent thoughts is provided by the transitions between shots, and the way shots are grouped into shot sequences. Defining shots and the transitions between them differentiates scriptwriting from other forms of writing.

Since this book is primarily concerned with the elements of program production, it will not deal with the discipline of writing per se (how to develop a story, write credible dialogue and define characters). Writing is partly a gift and partly experience. The best place to learn it, next to doing it, is in a creative writing course. Some useful books on the basics of scriptwriting are listed in the Bibliography, and may prove helpful.

This chapter is intended for those who have written for other media, such as theater, and for those who do not write professionally, but wish to familiarize themselves with scriptwriting.

Calling the Shots

In many types of scripts, the scriptwriting "calls the shots." Writers of commercials prepare their material as *storyboards,* using preprinted paper with blank frames (similar to a comic book) in which an image and its transitions are sketched. Many television shows (and films) are shot from shooting scripts prepared by writers, in which each shot and the transitions between shots are specified. (Steven Spielberg "storyboarded" every shot of *Raiders of the Lost Ark*.)

The scriptwriter normally starts with an outline. It specifies the action for the major sequences of the program, describes the talent (age, sex and type of person), and indicates the location and settings. After this outline is approved (where approval is needed), the writer prepares a script that indicates the action and the dialogue. Although the action will always be visualized in terms of shots and shot sequences, the script format required will determine whether the shots are specified (as discussed in detail in the next section).

The writer, therefore, has to deal with three basic shots (long, medium and close-up), their variations and an increasing number of transitions. In terms of the camera, we are dealing with shots ranging from telephoto to wide-angle. See Figure 1.3.

The *long shot* (LS) includes any shot from the horizon to the point where the frame is human scale. Sometimes film makers omit these "establishing shots." Doing so forces viewers to piece the situation together for themselves. This keeps them on their psychological toes and can sometimes be a very effective technique. But omitting establishing shots is tricky business and is not for the novice.

The point at which the frame approaches the human scale is a *medium shot* (MS), which also begins to focus the viewer's interest. Closer to the subject (within conversational distance) is the *medium close-up* (MCU), which draws more intense interest. To get really intimate, we use a *close-up* (CU).

The viewer can get even closer with an *extreme close-up* (ECU). ECUs are reserved for small details of inanimate objects, or for very intense viewing of a face. It would not do, for example, to use an ECU to present the president of a company to his employees, although a documentary critical of the industry in which he works might do this deliberately to get uncomfortably close to him. A shot does "speak," and it can say a great deal.

Basic Camera Moves

Shots also have the potential of being viewed from a special angle or from a moving camera (see Figure 1.4). The writer may call for a *tilt*. A tilt *down* (providing the view from above), is the view of a superior over an inferior, especially if an

Figure 1.3: Basic shot formats.

Long shot (LS)

Medium shot (MS)

Medium close-up (MCU)

Close-up (CU)

Extreme close-up (ECU)

Figure 1.4: Diagrams of basic camera moves.

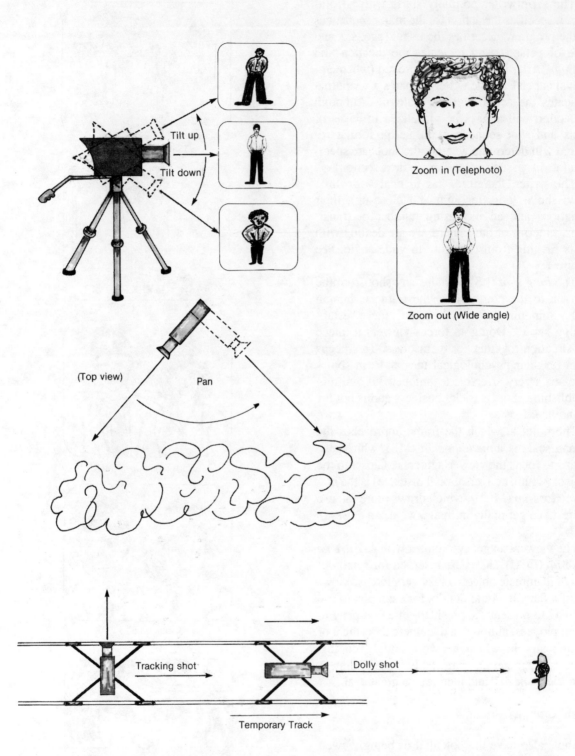

MS or CU is used. On the other hand, it provides a God-like view (a Hitchcock favorite) when a high camera tilts down for a long shot. A tilt *up* offers a worm's eye view of the world (an Orson Welles favorite). It makes the viewer feel small.

Camera movements include the *pan,* where the stationary camera pivots over an arc between right and left. When the camera covers the same view while moving smoothly along a track *parallel* to its subject, it is a *tracking* shot. When a camera on the same track points and moves *toward* the subject, it is called a *dolly* shot. Both tracking and dolly shots enable viewers to feel as if they are moving through space.

There are, of course, the zooms—*in* to telephoto; *out* to wide-angle. Zooms are also high-energy devices, because they strengthen the viewer's sense of participation—moving in relation to the subject. Because they are easy to do, they are greatly overused by novices who consequently give their viewers vertigo.

Basically, a *zoom-in* demands that the viewer's attention be rapidly focused. If used occasionally, it keeps the viewer awake and adds to the visual excitement. A *zoom-out,* on the other hand, is a relaxing device that re-establishes the setting and gives the viewer a breather to reflect on what he has just been looking at. In a dramatic context, of course, the effect of a pull-back can also be reversed to reveal a forest that was lost to the trees; for example, when tight shots of action on a battlefield yield to a slow, widening view of the carnage that remains.

The *crane shot* is always grandiose. Mounted on a multi-jointed crane, the camera and its operator can move in any direction to create a three-dimensional view that is unlike ordinary conscious viewing. The crane shot is a favorite of Fellini, who sometimes uses it for close-ups (but then, he can afford to).

Basic Shot Transitions

The real integration of a program is achieved in the way all these shots are put together. The place where one shot is joined to another is called a *transition.* The basic transition is called a *hard cut,* or edit, in which the last frame of the previous shot is butted to the first frame of the next shot. The hard cut is the most basic and powerful tool of any program, educational or dramatic. By simply linking images with cuts, we can relate those images in a meaningful way in the mind of the viewer.

A classic example is a sequence suggested by Sergei Eisenstein, the Russian film director, who first articulated the language of moving images in the 1920s. Starting with footage taken of a small boy walking home from school, the writer intercuts it with separate footage of a shabby-looking man with his hand in his pocket (CU of hand in pocket). Start with a slow take of one of the subjects. Cut to a slow take of the other. Cut to a slightly shorter take of the first, and a still shorter take of the other. Make the shots increasingly shorter until the cuts between the man and the little boy are rapid. Even without an eerie synthesizer score, the viewers are on the verge of jumping out of their seats. That is the power of a good script, using nothing more than hard cuts.

However, the writer also has at his call the *dissolve,* where the previous shot fades out as the next shot fades in. Because they overlap, this is called a *lap dissolve.* Conventionally, very long dissolves (say, 5 to 10 seconds) evoke a nostalgic mood, or indicate a passage of time or change of location. Changes of time or place can also be indicated by a *cross-fade,* where a fade-to-black is immediately followed by a fade-in. Short dissolves merely provide a softer effect than hard cuts. An intermediate effect is provided by a *soft cut,* a 6- to 10-frame or half-second dissolve that is not really perceptible to the viewer as such, but softens the impact of a cut. Cutting or dissolving so that the direction of movement from one image to the next is continued or interrupted creates, respectively, pleasant or abrasive effects.

The television scriptwriter can also use the *wipe,* which, at its simplest, can bring in one image— say, from the left—to "wipe out" the preceding image. Sophisticated video equipment provides dozens of wipe formats, both hard- and soft-edged, but like any dramatic effect, wipes need to be used judiciously, so that the viewer does not become more aware of the cleverness of the writer or director than of the subject of the program.

One of the few "rules" that has to be observed, when using any transition within a scene, is that the viewer's "right" and "left" must be maintained. This means that when a person on-screen is facing left, he must be shown to be in that position in all shots—long, medium and close-up—unless a move by the performer or the camera is made during a shot to permit the viewer to change his perspective. In film, this is dubbed the 180° rule, because it is as if there were a line drawn across the action over which the editor cannot step, unless the action or camera movement permits it.

Of course, all of the transitions discussed can be used in combination, as can the numerous trick shots and transitions—swish pans, mirror shots, rack focus and the like—that are the province of the accomplished professional. Because these techniques have been well developed for film, those interested can read books on film technique to learn more about them. (Some sources are listed in the Bibliography.)

A vast array of transitions are available for television by means of digital effects devices (discussed in Chapter 11). These devices can manipulate the image in an infinite number of ways by shrinking, expanding, twirling, folding and multiplying it. Options are limited only by the user's imagination and the size of the budget. But at this point, we are a long way from such intricacies. In the following sections, some practical considerations for preparing a script for a variety of situations will be covered

PREPARING A SCRIPT

There are only a few script formats that are used in the industry, and a professional who wants to be taken seriously will cast his script in the appropriate form. There are two basic formats currently in use in the broadcast industry: the "three-camera" format and the "one-camera" format. The three-camera format is used for a live-cut production, no matter how many cameras are used. The single-camera, or "teleplay" format is virtually identical to that used for the motion picture screenplay. It is designed for shots taken from one perspective at a time. These formats have been codified by the Writers Guild of America*, and their specifications are used in the industry. A different format, standard in the audiovisual field, is acceptable for most industrial television productions. Less standardized formats are used for documentary and interactive scripts.

Script for a Multi-Camera, Live-Cut Studio Shoot

A live-cut studio production requires the use of multiple cameras and a special-effects generator,

*See Jerome Coopersmith, *Professional Writer's Teleplay/ Screeplay Format* (New York: Writer's Guild of America, East, 1983).

with a director who will call the shots—and, in many cases, will decide what the shots are to be. For this reason, scripted productions that are shot in the studio generally use a very simple but specific script format that has become the standard throughout the broadcast industry. A facsimile is shown in Figure 1.5.

The format's principal characteristic is that only the left two-thirds of the page is used, so the right third is available for the director's notes. In this portion, he enters his handwritten notes to himself, his assistant director (AD), his technical director (TD) and whoever else might need to know.

In this space, the director notes the point at which he calls each shot, or "take," the point at which he instructs the TD to set up the shot and how he readies the appropriate production personnel—the camera, audio and sound effects persons, the floor manager and the other equipment operators. (To find out more about these people and their roles, and to see what a director's notes look like, see Chapter 5.)

Since the director makes these decisions, the camera and talent directions provided by the writer include only those that are needed to clarify the action. Because of the intense pace of live-cut television, even the writer who will direct his own script will find that it is much easier to identify these directions when they are written in this space, than when they are buried within the script.

The live-cut script is also typewritten in a certain style specified by the Writer's Guild of America as follows:

• All the writer's directions are in solid caps, single-spaced and in parentheses. They start at the margin, which is located 20 (24) units from the edge of the paper, and run no more than 35 (42) units wide, to leave at least a 2½-inch margin for the director to use.[1]

• Names of characters above the dialogue are in caps, and are located 42 (50) units from the edge of the page.

• Only the actual dialogue is typed in upper and lower case letters. It is indented 29 (35) units from the left margin, and runs no more than 25 units per line, to allow for the director's margin.

[1]All spacing is given in picas (or 10-pitch); the numbers in parentheses give the spacing in elite (12-pitch).

Figure 1.5: Format for a multi-camera script.

FADE IN

(A SUPER MODERN LIVING ROOM WITH
COMPUTER TERMINAL AND LARGE
SCREEN, THE APARTMENT OF JACK AND
ANNE WARREN. JACK STANDS IN HALL
DOORWAY.)

                    JACK

    Come on. We're late.

(ANNE ENTERS FROM OTHER DOOR,
WEARING SLIGHTLY FUTURISTIC
CLOTHES. AS SHE CROSSES THE ROOM,
THE SCREEN LIGHTS UP AND THE
COMPUTER EMITS A SERIES OF TONES.
ANNE TURNS TO LOOK AT IT.)

                    ANNE

    Who is it?

                    JACK

    I don't know. I don't recognize the code.

(STARTS TOWARD TERMINAL, THEN
CHANGES MIND)

    Oh, let the comp take it. We'll check
    it out when we get back.

(A MAN APPEAR ON THE SCREEN,
GESTURING URGENTLY, BUT WITHOUT
SOUND. ANNE POINTS)

                    ANNE

    No! Wait! Look! Who is that?

(JACK TURNS TO LOOK)

                    JACK

    I don't know. It's probably some kind of
    salesman.

                    ANNE

    That doesn't look like a salesman to me.

(DASHES OVER TO TERMINAL)

    He's in some kind of trouble.

(TOUCHES BUTTON ON TERMINAL. A
VOICE BOOMS OUT)

                    VOICE

    Can anybody hear me? Answer please.
    We're in danger. All of us. Terrible
    danger. Please respond.

• Parenthetical instructions within the dialogue relating to a character's actions are given in caps.

• Transitions called for by the writer are in underlined caps, but these start at 55 (61) units. (At 55 units they appear in the director's margin, but as they are his business, this is the proper place for them to be.) FADE IN appears at the left margin.

• The page number at the top right corner is at 75 (90) units.

• Top and bottom margins should be large, about 1¼ to 1½ inches.

• Everything but the writer's instructions is consistently double-spaced. (These rules also apply to scripts prepared with word processors.)

This basic format is used for sitcoms and soaps, as well as for news programs, all of which are shot in studios. If a writer is preparing a script for an ongoing show, or for a production company, it is important to get that organization's script format specifications. However, if they are unavailable, the writer will produce a professional-looking script by following this format.

When a scripted program is to be made with a single camera, a different style of script prevails.

Script for a Single-Camera Shoot: The Teleplay

Shooting with a single camera is the basic technique of traditional filmmaking. The entire structure of professional film production is based on the idea that a scene is shot from one position at a time. Even today, a program shot with a single camera on videotape is still described as having been shot "film style." It is not surprising, then, that a professional script for this type of production follows the standard format for a screenplay (as illustrated in Figure 1.6).

As can be seen, the writer's descriptions and instructions, single-spaced, run across the normal typed width of the page, starting at a margin of 17 (20) units and going up to 75 (90) units. As in the script for a live-cut production, the dialogue is indented from the left margin (at 28 (33) units), but it is also indented at the right to form a column about 30 (36) units wide. The character's name above the dialogue is in caps and indented 43 (51) units. Parenthetical remarks regarding the speaker's

Figure 1.6: Format for a single-camera script.

FADE IN:

A SUPER-MODERN LIVING ROOM WITH A SMALL BUT SOPHISTICATED COMPUTER
TERMINAL WITH A FAIRLY LARGE SCREEN AGAINST ONE WALL. IT IS THE
APARTMENT OF JACK AND ANNE WARREN. WIDE SHOT FROM APARTMENT HALL
DOORWAY. LATE AFTERNOON.

Jack, speaking from camera position.

JACK

Come on. We're late.

Anne enters from another door, dressed in slightly futuristic
clothes. As she crosses, smiling, toward the camera, the screen
lights up and the computer emits a series of tones.

ANNE

Who is it?

CUT TO MEDIUM SHOT OF JACK, STANDING IN DOORWAY.

JACK

I don't know. I don't recognize the code.

(Starts to walk toward
terminal, then canges
mind, goes toward door)

On, let the comp take it. We'll
check it when we get back.

As Jack reaches the door, where Anne is standing, CUT TO MEDIUM 1/4
SHOT OF SCREEN, on which the figure of a man appears, gesturing,
urgently, but there is no sound. CUT TO TWO SHOT. Anne points
to screen. Jack turns

ANNE

No! Wait! Look! Who is that?

CUT TO SCREEN. Man appears to be pleading anxiously.

JACK

I don't know. It's probably some kind of salesman.

ANNE

That doesn't look like a salesman to me.

(Dashes over toward the
terminal as CAMERA FOLLOWS)

He's in some kind of trouble.

(Touches a button on terminal. A voice booms out.)

CUT TO SCREEN.

MAN'S VOICE

Can anybody hear me? Answer please.
We're in danger. All of us. Terrible
danger. Please respond.

A beam of light appears to move toward the man on the screen
from his right. As it reaches him he screams and dissolves
into an intense bright nebula as the screen goes blank.

actions are single-spaced and indented from the dialogue margin, at 35 (42) units.

The distinction between what is in solid caps and what is in upper-and-lower case is more subtle. Basically, anything that concerns the talent—e.g., how a line should be spoken, where an actor should move—is in upper-and-lower case, including the parenthetical directions within the dialogue. All camera directions, however, are in caps. By themselves, they are pulled out to start flush left, at the margin. Transitions (not shown in the example) are also in caps and at the right, at 66 (79) units—except FADE IN, which is at the left margin, as for a live-cut shoot. All speeches and directions are single-spaced. The spaces between them, under names and before and after scene transitions, are double-spaced.

Why is this single-camera format so different? There are good reasons that were developed over time. Certainly, the performers' material is clearly defined by identation and type, so that they can concern themselves with it. Similarly, the shots for the director and cameraperson are always given in unindented caps, to be readily accessible. The same is true of the information for the setting, which is the concern of the set designer. Since each shot may require a separate take, the director can easily locate and number it. However, since a single line or gesture may be the entire subject of a take, he has plenty of time to plan the shot before the film or tape starts rolling.

This format also assumes that the director does not have to call upon his notes to set up one shot while another is in progress, as the director of a multi- (three-) camera shoot must. Accordingly, he can use the direction appearing in the script, and the script can cover the entire width of the page.

When submitting a script (especially a dramatic script) to a producer, this is probably the best format to use, because it is the most general.

For the world of industrial television, however, still another format is frequently used.

Standard Audiovisual Scripts

Because industrial and educational television programs were first produced by audiovisual specialists, most scripts for this sector are still written in "AV" style, which separates the visual and audio content into two columns, as shown in Figure 1.7. It is used for both single- and multi-camera productions in the industrial and educational fields.

As can be seen, all descriptions, shots and transitions are placed in the left column under VIDEO, while all speeches, sound effects, intonations and pauses are placed under AUDIO. Simultaneous events are lined up horizontally. For example, "Cut to MS of JACK" occurs simultaneously with Jack's line, "I don't know." All material is double-spaced.

These are the complete specifications of this format. Unlike the other two formats, which are fairly well codified, the industrial format is not very strict. Names, shots and other matter may or may not be in caps. Nonverbal audio cues may or may not be placed in parentheses to separate them from the dialogue or narration, depending on the requirements of the producer or the writer's preference. The basic concept behind the format is that the audio and video people have very different concerns and technology, and that it is easier for each of them if the two parts of the script are separate. Nevertheless, the talent and the director must be aware of both sides, and so must the producer.

As nonbroadcast television develops, adaptations of the major broadcast script format are becoming more common. Nevertheless, the two-column format will undoubtedly be in use for some time, so it behooves producers to be familiar with it.

Documentary Scripts

At first thought, the concept of a documentary script seems to be a contradiction in terms. A documentary is a documentation of a person, a place, an institution—who cannot be given lines to speak or actions to perform. That is why the documentary script is a hybrid. It is part outline, part treatment and part shooting script and, where narration is used, part dialogue, although the final narration is not usually done until the editing process begins. In fact, the only true "script" a documentary ever has is its editing script (which is discussed in Chapter 9).

Most producers will at some time be called on to make a documentary of one sort or another. Even if a producer does not create a classic documentary that shows, for example, social or environmental impact, he may well produce a travelogue, a portrait of a person or group, or a document of an event, an institution or a company. In

Figure 1.7: Audiovisual script format.

VIDEO	AUDIO
FADE IN. A super-modern living room with a small but sophisticated computer terminal with a fairly large screen against one wall. It is the apartment of Jack and Anne Warren. We see a camera-eye view from the hall doorway, JACK is at camera position.	(Silence and then the sound of high-heeled footsteps moving back and forth.)
ANNE enters through a door on the camera right, wearing slightly futuristic clothes. As she crosses toward JACK, the screen lights up and the computer emits a series of tones. ANNE turns to look at it.	JACK: Come on. We're late. (The footsteps approach the room.) ANNE: Who is it?
Slow zoom past ANNE toward the screen.	
CUT to MS of JACK.	JACK: I don't know. I don't recognize the code. (Pauses)
Starts toward terminal, then changes mind. CUT back to wide shot from door, and start zoom to screen again. A man appears on the screen, gesturing urgently, but without sound. ANNE points to screen	. . . . . . Oh, let the comp take it. We'll check it when we get back. ANNE: No! Wait! Who is that?

one respect, these latter programs are the easiest to do, because they implicitly dictate a single point of view—one that is *for* the subject, and minimizes or avoids material that casts shadows on it.

As was discussed earlier in this chapter, a documentary needs to be built around a central structure that will hold its disparate locations, people and images together. In our example (Figure 1.8), a page from the script for the annual report produced on videotape for the Good Health Foods Company, the central structure is an interview with its CEO, Jim Barnes. The script for the interview would probably be prepared after a detailed treatment for the documentary report was completed, so that the interview can be used to provide introductory segments for each part of the program. The sample script shown in Figure 1.5 starts with such a segment, but any number of variations is possible. For example, one could use the history of the organization, supposing it has a history. One could follow the development of a product (here it might be a loaf of bread) from conception to the end-user, and tell a great deal about the company.

While this process is similar to that used in the development of other scripts, in the documentary it is not as obvious, because there are so many more variables than exist in other script formats. For the documentary format, furthermore, the alternate script format in which the video and audio are separated into columns is particularly suitable. This is true because the video with sync sound is usually shot separately from the voice-over material that accompanies it. As Figure 1.8 shows, it is handy to list together the shots that will be gathered at a given location, and separate them from (for example) a series of interview questions. On documentary shoots, the main concern is that there will be no regrets in the editing room. It is the writer's job to anticipate the possibilities.

Scripting Narration

It is here that a discussion of narration is in order. Aside from being written to be said, good narration fits the program's style; it is brief and it never steals words from the people on camera.

Different styles of programs lend themselves to different styles of narration. Thus, narration for a program on endangered species may be somber and apocalyptic. For a program about a technique or technology, it may be terse and tutorial, while a program encouraging a particular attitude may require some charm in the narration.

Aside from brevity's usual virtues, in television there is the virtue that silence gives the viewer time to look and the on-camera subject time to speak. It is also important to remember that the camera is, in a sense, "talking." The primary ob-ject of good narration in a well-made program should be to give just enough information so that the images—perhaps assisted by sync sound—can speak for themselves.

Speaking for themselves is something that on-camera people generally do very well. Stealing their words is bad form, like dropping the punch line to someone's joke. All of us have watched programs where the narrator said something like: "When his friend died, he felt as if he were somehow responsible." Immediately after, the subject came on and said, "When my friend died, I felt as if I were

Figure 1.8: Documentary script format.

ANDOVER PLANT SEGMENT

VIDEO	AUDIO
Jim Barnes interview	Start with J.B. interview segment dealing with Andover plant.
DISSOLVE TO:	
Andover plant exterior RAPID CUTS of plant exterior, including long and medium shots of different parts of plant interior: mixers, ovens, conveyers, packaging operations, personnel.	
DISSOLVE TO Ray Dines, plant manager. Mix shots during interview or RD only.	Ray Dines interview. Record questions audio only.
With RD in dough mixing room. Shot of ingredients being loaded, mixers mixing, dough forming. For CU's:	Interviewer: What kind of breads are made here?
	RD: Answer
1. Have RD pick up handful of flour.	I: Can you tell us more about the plant? Its size, production quantities, that sort of thing.
2. Zoom in on ingredients forming into dough.	RD: Answer
3. Shot of risen dough being kneaded down by machine.	I: What is happening here?
	RD: Answer
	I: Tell us about the quality of your ingredients.
	RD: Answer
	I: How does the machine know when to stop stirring?
	RD: Answer, describing equipment capabilities.

somehow responsible." The doubling of words makes both the narrator and the subject sound foolish. The television or film writer must constantly ask, "How much of what needs to be said is already there?"

Choosing the Narrator

Choosing a narrator is a tough proposition, unless one wants the standard style—a deep, extremely professional and authoritative male voice, which many actors unconsciously imitate when they read narration. This type may be ideal for a number of programs, but other voices and styles of narration can add a great deal. Where would *Masterpiece Theater* be without an urbane Briton to introduce it?

There are, of course, no hard-and-fast rules for choosing narrators, but suitability to the subject matter is a solid criterion. Having an urbane British narrator present an American working class show, or having a high-class cultural subject presented by a narrator with a distinct working-class accent, may create a comic effect. Unless a comic effect is desired, it is best not to break any ground in this area.

The narrator should be invisible—not only visually, as he or she in fact is, but also to the consciousness of the viewer. For this reason, the narrator's delivery, while expressive, should be on the cool side. When it is said that television is a cool medium, it means that it works best when the emotional intensity of a speaker is restrained. Without going into the theory behind this, we can say that in general, a "laid back" narration seems to work best. To get the right tone, actors who have done narration are probably a producer's best bet.

First-person narration often works when the speaker is (or appears to be) the experiencer of the events shown. If the subject appears on camera, then he or she can be used to do all the narration. Even when the visible subject does not speak on camera, first-person narration can still be done by a third person—such as an actor. In this case, of course, the narrator should be the same sex as the subject, and match the subject in personal style. Otherwise, gender should not be an issue.

Another approach that is sometimes fruitful is using two or more narrators, when they are the subjects of the program. This may work if, for example, the program presents the work of a husband-and-wife or other kind of team, but it is

tricky. If the narrators are not kept distinct, you will get a "Russian novel effect," where the viewer will spend more effort keeping track of who is talking than of the action. If a third narrator is introduced, one of the three must be the lead narrator who controls the focus of the narration.

Interactive Video Scripts

There is a considerable mystique surrounding the making of interactive video programs. Some of this is due to the proprietary nature of a few of the methods used. But most of the mystery exists merely because the processes involved are new to video producers, who are not entirely sure of what they are doing in this area. In fact, interactive video uses techniques that were developed earlier for the programming of computer-assisted instruction (CAI). So, although these techniques may require a great deal of work to integrate them with video material, they are relatively easy to understand.

In conventional (linear) video production, a program is made to be viewed from beginning to end by an audience of several people. The viewer is asked to do nothing more than watch the screen, and—if possible—to integrate what he has seen and heard into his store of information. The producer's job is to make the program as entertaining and as smooth as possible, so that there will be no point at which the viewer's attention wanes.

With interactive programs, the object is to address a *single* viewer at a time and to *interrupt* the flow in order to give the viewer a chance to choose the particular segments he will view. He may take a test, repeat what he has just seen or perform an exercise that uses the information he has just learned. The viewer's mode of selection can be anything from touching a START, STOP or PAUSE button on a remote VCR control, to using a "touch screen" or electronic "palette" to point to a desired item on a display. (In one American Heart Association program that teaches cardiopulmonary resuscitation (CPR), the viewer even gets a wired, pressure-sensitive practice mannequin. Its outputs are integrated into program, so that the video segments that appear are responsive to the student's actual performance at any given point.)

An interactive video program, accordingly, is nonlinear and relies heavily on graphics (lists, questions and instructions) as well as graphic images. Nevertheless, at some point the text must be written; a script must be prepared. To get to that point in interactive program preparation, there is an extra step—the creation of a program flow chart.

A flow chart is a map of the program that shows all its elements and all the possible routes that a viewer can take through them. This kind of diagram uses a number of symbols derived from computer programming, and several that have been devised to specify video functions. Some of these symbols are shown in Figure 1.9; Figure 1.10 illustrates how they can be used.

Figure 1.10 shows a segment of a typical interactive learning program in flowchart form. A student begins with a live-aciton segment made like a

Figure 1.9: Symbols used for flowcharting.

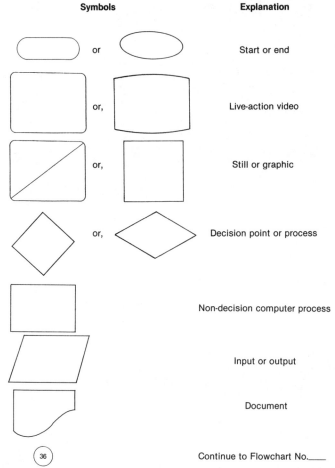

Symbols		Explanation
or		Start or end
or,		Live-action video
or,		Still or graphic
or,		Decision point or process
		Non-decision computer process
		Input or output
		Document
36		Continue to Flowchart No.___

conventional videotape. It contains a person speaking and demonstrating the material to be learned and various close-ups and graphics. The segment is edited as is a linear program.

When the segment is completed, however, it is followed by a graphic which presents a test. The test may be a single question, a set of questions, a task or a task sequence. In this example, it is a set of questions. If we are dealing with a simple videotape and programmable-controller type of system, the student will put his answers on paper, and the "evaluation" step will be a series of still frames; one or more will give the answers to the test, and one will tell the student how to grade himself and which segment to access as the next step.

However, if we are dealing with an integrated computer-interactive system, or one with a microprocessor with sufficient data-handling capability, the student will input his answers, and the system will grade him and access the next appropriate segment for him. In either case, the diagram indicates that if the student scores more than 85, he is sent on to the next learning unit. If he scores 70 to 85, he is given the segment to review and the test to retake.

If the student gets more than 50 but less than 70 on his first try, it is probable that a review would be insufficient, and he is given, or is sent to, a remedial segment. This may explore the lesson in greater detail or present it in simpler terms. Upon completion of the remedial segment, he is sent to retake the test. If, on the first try, a student scores less than 50, he is brought out of the program. Clearly, he is not ready for the material, and he is directed to a teacher or to a text or workbook, as the situation requires.

If the student retakes the test, there is a second evaluation (a process with which a number of interactive video systems can deal). If he scores more than 85 on this second round, he is sent on to the next learning unit. However, if after review or remediation he still cannot score 85, the program shuts down and directs him to a teacher or text. This segment could also, of course, be designed so that if he gets between 70 and 85 on his second try, he is rerouted to the first teaching segment and given a third chance to score 85 and move on. (In most cases, however, two runs through the same material are enough to establish learning capability on a given day.)

As can be seen, the flow chart contains a great deal of information. When he creates it, the writer

Figure 1.10: Flowchart for an interactive program segment.

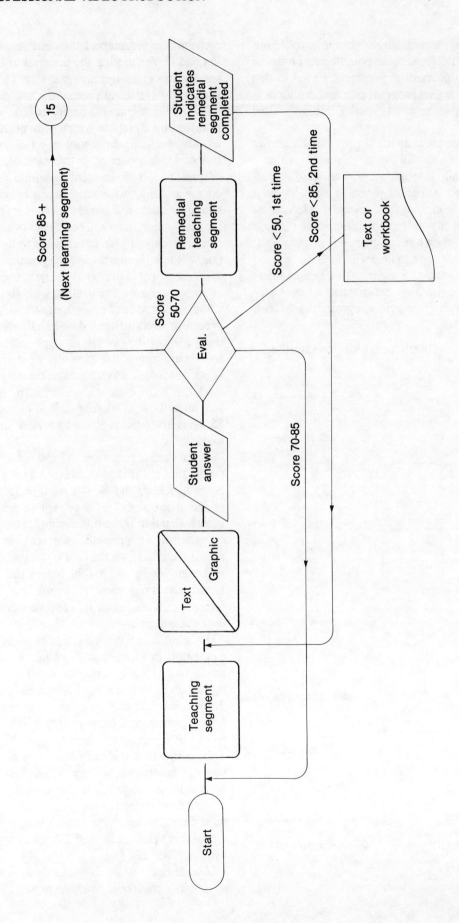

defines the producer's job, because the flow chart is an implicit part of the script. The learning segment and the remedial segment are live-action video programs and are written to be produced in a conventional manner.

With an interactive program that is made to be used with videotape or disc equipment only, the word and picture graphics are designed to fit on a video frame, as are instructions to the student. With a computer-driven videodisc or tape program, tests and instructions can be designed as computer graphics.

The kind of routing information the writer incorporates into the program depends on the particular characteristics of the computer or other input device used. To generate the routing data requires either the use of an authoring program or a computer programmer familiar with the video-interactive process. In all cases, the programmed instructions that determine how the user proceeds from step to step are as much a part of the script as are the live-action segments, whether they are written as graphics incorporated into the video or as computer-programmed instructions invisible to the viewer.

The flow chart segment in Figure 1.10 represents only one type of interactive program. The same process can be greatly enhanced by the use of a variety of taped live-action responses to different user actions, by using video to present the problems as real-life simulations, and by increasing the frequency of user interactions. As the possibilities of interactivity expand, so, of course, do its complexities. But this format is the future, and even in its present stage, it works.

2 The Studio and Its Major Components

While portable equipment has opened the world outside the studio to on-location videotape production, the studio is still an important part of producing video programs. Although working in a studio places certain limitations on the range of settings and actions that can be accommodated, the studio provides for complete control of the environment. Studio productions still demonstrate the medium's technical possibilities and help to set standards for what can be achieved working in a controlled environment. The large studios of yesteryear have been replaced with "insert" studios. These smaller studios provide a place for shooting program transitions while being more cost-effective than large studios. For productions that require a large stage area it is usually more cost-effective to rent a facility.

The material presented here is intended for the producer who needs to set up or manage his or her own studio and who must ensure the technical quality of a production. Much of this chapter will also be useful for producers who rent studios, because they need to be aware of the elements that make studio productions go well. This chapter, along with the next, can also serve as an introduction to the inner workings of production equipment.

Many of the terms discussed in this chapter (and others) are defined in the Glossary at the end of this book. For those who want further information, a Technical Appendix and Bibliography are also provided.

ELEMENTS OF A BASIC STUDIO

Until the late 1970's, a person setting up a television studio had only two choices in terms of quality: high technology (broadcast) and low technology (industrial/nonbroadcast). The last few years have seen the difference between high-tech and low-tech equipment become very fuzzy. It is no longer just price that determines the category that equipment fits into. "High tech" was very high in both quality and cost; "low tech" was relatively inexpensive and made acceptable color images, if the material shot was not required to hold up under the stress of post-production (i.e., editing). Broadcast equipment (high technology) is still expensive, involving not only substantial purchase prices, but high maintenance costs, including considerable engineering support. The alternatives in the industrial/nonbroadcast range of video technology, however, are no longer low in anything but price. There is now a broad mid-tech range of equipment that provides excellent images with relatively low maintenance cost and little need for in-house engineering support. (The format of a basic studio using such equipment is illustrated in Figure 2.1.)

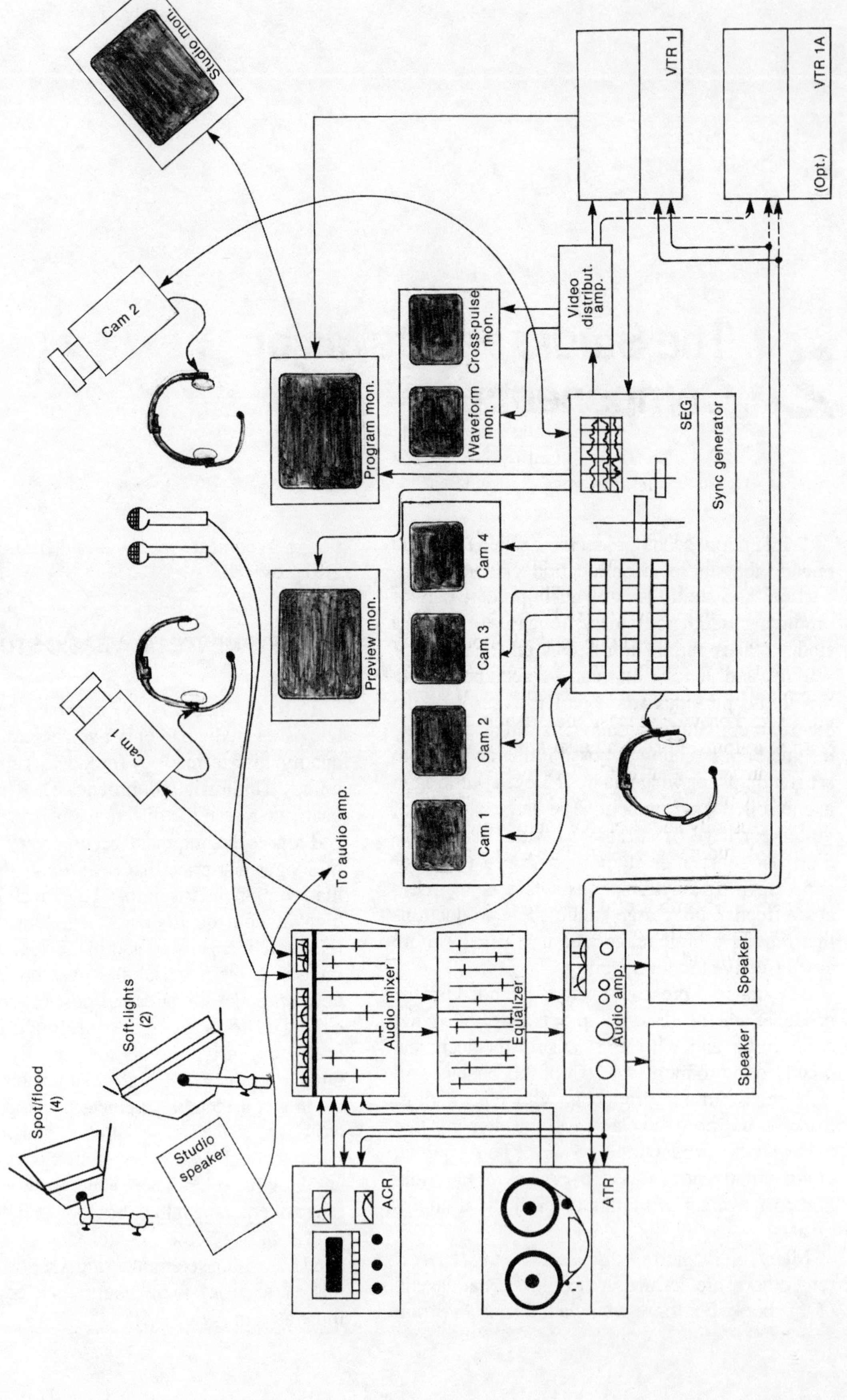

Figure 2.1: Elements of a basic television studio.

The basic studio shown in Figure 2.1 includes two cameras. It is designed to handle up to four cameras, but two are more than adequate for most applications. When in-house productions require more than two cameras, others can be rented on a per diem basis. This approach prevents investing the better part of a capital budget on equipment that will be outdated long before its useful life is finished. Such logistics are at the heart of the approach to cost-effective production which is presented in this book.

The brain of the studio system, the special effects generator (SEG), is more commonly referred to as the switcher. It is called a switcher because it evolved from the basic camera switcher and because one of its functions is to route video from any source to any connected destination. The term should not lead the reader to confuse this use of the word switcher with video routing switchers, which are separate units designed solely as video switchboards.

While image quality depends primarily on the cameras, the capability and flexibility of the studio depends primarily on its switcher. A typical small-format studio switcher should be able to handle four cameras and one genlock input. (The latter is used to synchronize all elements of the system.) The switcher must be able to dissolve and key and provide at least one preview and two program outputs. For the smaller studio, it should contain an internal NTSC (National Television Standards Committee) sync generator, four phase shifters, plus tally and intercom capability. A more substantial studio may have separate equipment to provide these capabilities. The switcher would also provide a number of different wipes, preferably with both hard and soft edges.

The studio videotape recorder (VTR) and/or videocassette recorder (VCR) can consist of a lower format (¾-inch, ½-inch or 8 mm) system and should have full one hour tape-handling capability. A higher-format (1-inch or component ½-inch) system is desirable, especially if the final product is a VHS duplicate of a multi-generational edit master.

In determining whether a studio warrants a higher- format deck, a good rule of thumb is that the cost of the VTR should not exceed that of one studio camera. It is also important to note that the studio control room equipment often serves as the basis for the post-production system in educational and corporate facilities. If dual purpose capabilities are needed the choice of recording decks will reflect this. A second, optional deck is used to make safety copies of all material recorded during production. An emphasis on safety, and the maintenance of technical quality, should be integral to all video production. By these means, excellent results may be obtained from using industrial equipment.

For viewing, nine monitors are needed: one large studio monitor, four camera monitors (which can be black-and-white [BW]), two color monitors (one to preview effects or switching and one to show program output), and two test signal displays (including a waveform monitor and vectorscope). The preview and program monitors must be the most precise because they are used to make critical decisions on the final look of the program, while the other picture monitors serve for general reference.

In terms of audio equipment, it is most cost-effective to use high-quality balanced components for mixing and recording, in conjunction with microphones of professional quality.

An audiotape recorder and audiocassette recorder, both with stereo capability, are included in the basic studio, as both source and record units. A compact disc (CD) player rounds out the sources. The basic microphones needed for studio recording are two cardioids, one omni, and from two to five lavaliers. The rest of the audio complement includes several headsets and three reference speakers.

The lighting requirements of the studio depend primarily on the kinds of programs that will be produced (which is true for all equipment discussed). Most smaller studio productions require a relatively small area to be lit for each scene. To do this, two 2000-watt soft lights and four adjustable 500W to 1000W spot/floods are needed. After that, the possibilities can go any direction; up to a multi-watt klieg, or down to the 200W "inky."

A complete studio cannot function without such staples as tripods and distribution amplifiers. A film/slide chain and a character generator can extend its capabilities. All are dealt with in more detail in Chapter 3.

VIDEO CAMERAS

A studio's cameras are its primary feature, since they determine, in great part, the quality of the images produced. To help the producer choose the proper camera for a particular application, a crash course in some basic camera parameters follows.

Although all cameras are fundamentally alike, the more sophisticated cameras have better components and circuit designs. They also require more technical sophistication on the part of the camera operator since more operating parameters are accessible and designed for user adjustment. The reverse is also true. Less sophisticated cameras usually have fewer features, and these are factory set. Despite these limitations, however, some less expensive cameras are capable of producing acceptable images for broadcast, provided the signals are kept at their best technical quality during post-production. These cameras are also quite versatile and can be handled by people with less technical savvy.

Regardless of its cost and complexity, no piece of equipment requires as much involvement from the user as the camera does. A camera needs frequent attention to perform optimally in various shooting situations, especially outside the studio. This is why selecting cameras, whether for purchase or rental, requires an informed decision. (See the technical Appendixes for information on a number of camera parameters that are pertinent to selecting and using cameras.) The following section describes the functional elements of the video camera and discusses how an image is converted into video information.

In order of function, the camera consists of: a lens that collects and focuses the light of the image; an imaging element that transforms the light of the image into an electrical signal and provides information regarding the position of each image element; an encoding system that transforms the brightness and color aspects of the image into coded electrical signals that all video equipment can handle; circuits within the camera that refine and amplify the video signal; and a miniature picture tube, the viewfinder that displays the image the camera "sees."

Camera Optics

The camera's optical system determines how faithfully the original image is focused on the target (the image forming element of the pickup tube or CCD [charge-coupled device] chip). In the single-imaging device camera, the lens brings the image into the camera and focuses it onto the target directly. In a multi-imaging device camera, the lens is followed by an optical system that splits the image into its green, red and blue components.

Lenses

Video production cameras are usually outfitted with zoom lenses, ranging from 6:1 to 10:1 ratio. In lower-priced tube cameras, the number of lenses that can be used is usually limited, sometimes to the one lens that comes with the camera. This is because the lens to target distance varies in the different cameras, as does the target size. Most tubes designed for single-tube cameras are 1-inch tubes, while most multi-tube cameras use ¾-inch tubes. But whether it is a matter of distance or target size, the lens must match the camera configuration (lenses on portable cameras are discussed in Chapter 6). More expensive cameras are designed to accept a number of lenses standard in the film and television industry, and these are specified by the manufacturer. Before straying beyond the range of lenses specified, it is well worth testing alternate lenses to make sure they work properly. Selecting and using different lenses to record moving images is a skill that requires the expertise of a specialist. For most producers (and productions), the lens that comes with the camera is more than suitable.

Prism and Mirror Systems

Prism optics can be found in the better multi-imaging units, while dichroic mirror systems appear on lesser multi-imaging models. As shown in Figure 2.2, both systems perform exactly the same function.

Prism systems are superior, because there is less light loss in prism systems than in mirror systems. There is also less registration error, because the system is not vulnerable to vibration. But the prisms that accurately divide the light into its primary colors are expensive, as are the required hard and flawless glass and the precision process involved in the manufacture of the system.

Dichroic mirror systems are less costly to manufacture because the demands on glass quality are lower and they are more easily assembled. However, they are more likely to generate registration errors. The dichroic mirror system is also more vulnerable to dust than the prism system and requires one additional F-stop of light compared to prism optics. Sealed optics is a distinct advantage in both prism and mirror systems.

Choosing between a prism and dichroic mirror optical system has become less of a issue, since

Figure 2.2: Color-separation optics in three-tube cameras.

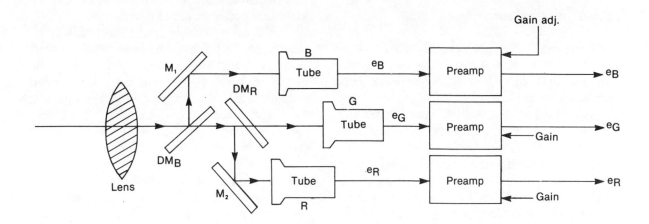

Dichroic mirror system

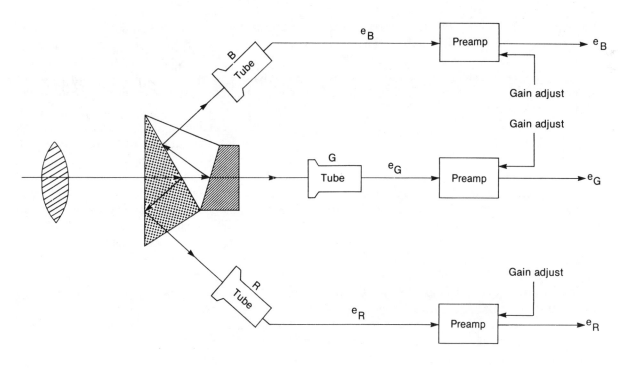

Prism optics

the cost of prism optics has dropped dramatically over the past few years and manufacturers now routinely use the prism system.

Video Camera Filters

To correct for differences in the color temperature of light by which television images are illuminated, optical color filters and white balance adjustments are used.

Selecting the proper color temperature filter is the first step in getting correct color. Color temperature filters are provided on a filter wheel, so that appropriate filters can be rotated into the light path. Typical filters include a 6000°K filter, which corrects light in very bright or hazy outdoor conditions; a 4500°K or 4700°K for ordinary sunlight and fluorescent lights; and a 3200°K filter for tungsten illumination (the basic studio setup). It should be noted that while fluorescent lights don't have standard color temperature, the 4500°K to 4700°K filter is close to correct when no alternative filters are available. Since this lighting condition is normally found in the field, it is covered more fully in Chapter 4.

Better cameras also include neutral density (ND) filters, panchromatic filters that simply cut down the level of light entering the camera. ND filters are primarily used in bright sunlight conditions such as bright sun on water, snow or sand. They are graded by the percentage of light they cut out, such as 25% or 50% and can be obtained as over-the-lens screw-on filters.

Imaging Elements

The imaging device is a primary factor in determining camera cost, quality and the look of its images. Traditionally the imaging device for all video cameras was the cathode-ray tube (CRT). Recently the charged-coupled device (CCD), an integrated circuit chip, has gained wide usage by camera manufacturers for both studio and portable cameras. Currently the CCD is most popular for use in portable cameras, but as CCD technology improves, its use in studio cameras will increase.

The cathode-ray tube is similar in principle to that used in a television set, but has a layer of photoconductive material on its face, called the target (see Figure 2.3). This photoconductive surface changes its electrical resistance at each point in proportion to the amount of light falling on it. The amount is determined by the pattern of the image focused on the target by the camera optics. The pickup tube converts an image into video information and delivers it to the camera circuits as a continuous signal, as follows.

The electron beam generated at the back of the tube is controlled by a horizontal and vertical beam deflection system. This system moves the beam from left to right and vertically, so that it can scan the target in a series of lines that form the video raster (the 525 lines that make up the image). Each time the 525 lines are scanned, at the rate of 30 times per second, a frame of video is completed.

However, the 525 lines are not scanned at once, from top to bottom, because the 30-times-per-second frame rate is too slow for the human eye. To prevent the image from appearing to flicker, the raster is scanned in two interlaced fields.

Each field consists of 262½ lines, half of the 525 lines per frames. The first field consists of even lines; the second field, all the odd lines. At the end of the second field, after the 525th line, a new frame starts. Thirty frames, and therefore 60 fields, are generated each second in the pickup tube.

Before it reaches the target, the scanning electron beam is focused and modulated by additional electrodes so that it scans the target at a precise point. As the beam reaches any given point on the target surface, the energy of the beam, and the photoconductive response of the surface illumination at that point, determine the electrical output of the surface at that moment. The more light there is on a point, the stronger the output from that point will be. Thus, in creating the lines of the raster, the beam makes a continuous electrical record of the amount of light reaching the target. How accurately each part of each line reflects this amount of light is called the horizontal resolution of the image, and it determines how faithfully the original image has been stored.

Types of Pickup Tubes

Camera tubes include Vidicons, Newvicons, Saticons™ and Plumbicons™ (in general order of cost and quality).

Vidicons are basic, general-purpose tubes that are somewhat lacking in sensitivity. They have low signal-to-noise ratios and excessive lag, but are relatively inexpensive and viable under a wide

Figure 2.3: Television pickup tube configuration.

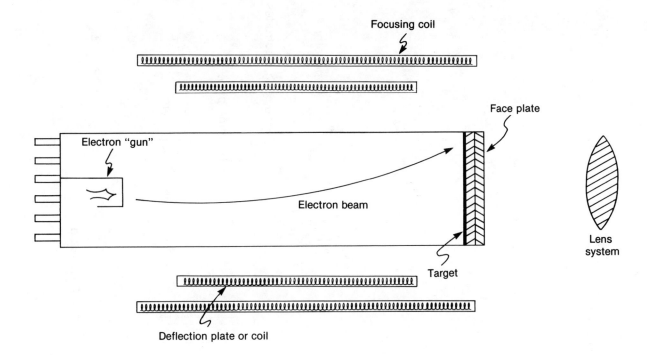

range of lighting conditions. They are ideal for applications where a "good" rather than a "great" image is acceptable, and nonprofessional or semi-skilled camera operators are used.

Newvicons are much more sensitive than Vidicons and have higher signal-to-noise ratios, but require carefully controlled lighting for optimum image production. They are especially useful in very low light conditions, such as those found in certain industrial situations, or in the recording of, say, theatrical performances without additional illumination. Newvicons and Vidicons are still used for closed circuit applications. However, with the use of CCD cameras for all applications, Newvicons and Vidicons are slowly being phased out.

Plumbicons are the long-standing aristocrats of pickup tubes and are priced accordingly. They were the first to provide low lag and low noise with high definition and sensitivity. Diode-gun Plumbicons were developed more recently and offer even less lag by requiring less beam current, thus permitting faster recovery of the photoconductive surface from exposure to intense illumination. Today other tubes match Plumbicons in performance for less cost.

Saticons utilize a complex oxide with characteristics comparable to those of Plumbicons, but they are considerably lower in price and have a longer life. A diode-gun Saticon is also available. Accordingly, either a Saticon or Plumbicon tube is a logical choice when a high-quality image is desired. There are not only differences between each tube type, but also within, as each is graded according to industry specifications. There are "industrial quality" Plumbicons, as there are "broadcast quality" Saticons. The difference is that broadcast-quality tubes of any type are virtually flawless, while different grades of industrial quality tubes are distinguished by flaws of a certain number and size, which reduce resolution and/or sensitivity.

It is important, therefore, to know not only what kind of tube a camera uses, but what grade of tube is involved.

Pickup Tube Design for Single-Tube Color Cameras

Single-tube color cameras are smaller, lighter and less expensive than three-tube cameras, but tend to have less horizontal resolution. In these

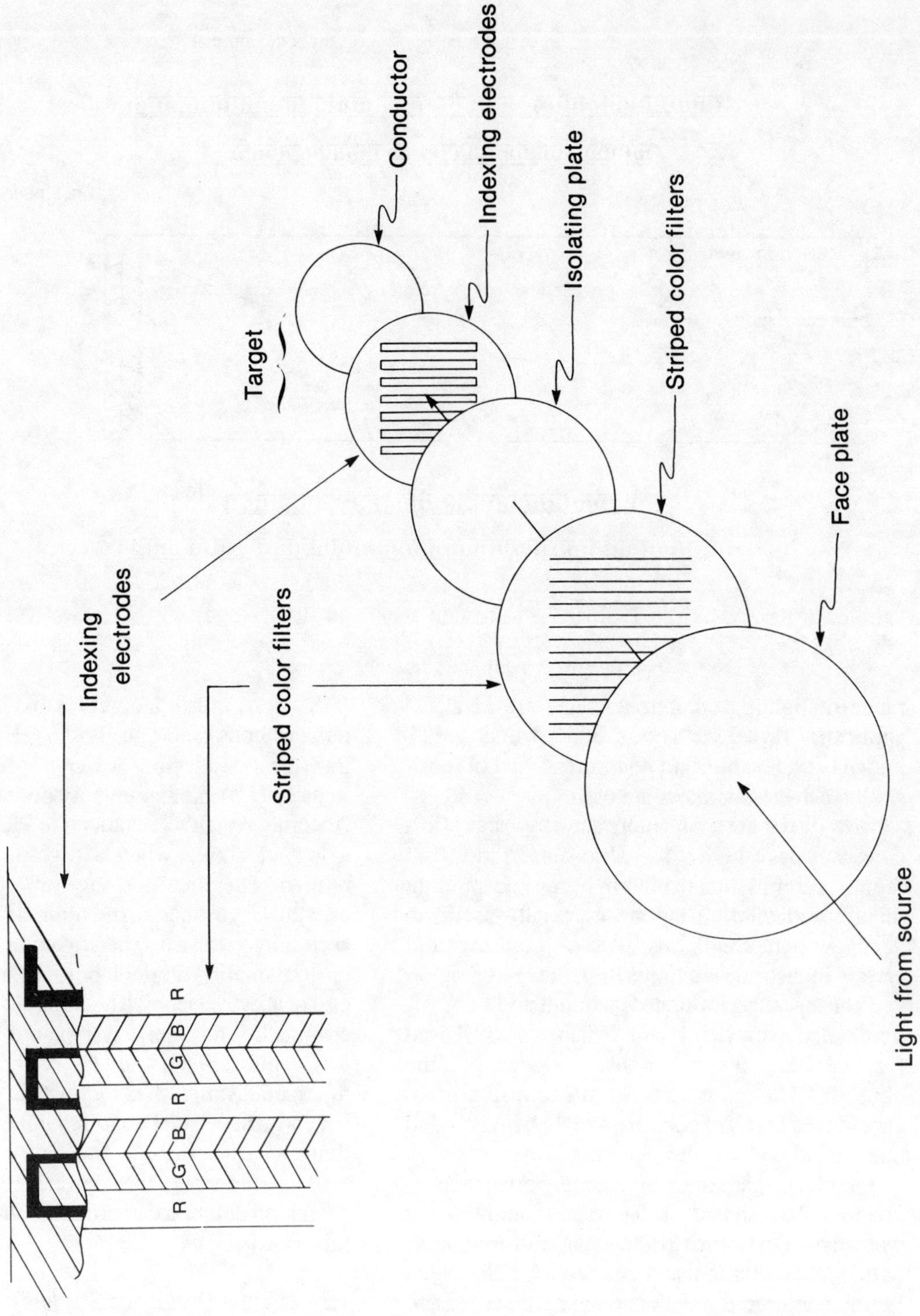

Figure 2.4: A filter and target configuration for a single-tube camera.

Indexing electrodes

Striped color filters

Indexing electrodes

Striped color filters

R G B R

R G B R

Target

Conductor

Indexing electrodes

Isolating plate

Striped color filters

Face plate

Light from source

Fig 2.4

cameras, color is discriminated by a color filter made up of red, green and blue filter stripes in a vertical array, as shown in Figure 2.4. The filter is part of a sandwich on the face of the tube; it includes an insulator and a transparent striped electrode, whose stripes are aligned with the filter stripes. The photoconductive imaging surface (the target) is positioned behind the electrode plate.

Therefore, any point of the image reaches the target through a filter segment. The color of each point is deduced by logic circuits that relate luminance to the color of the filter at the point. To do this, the striped electrode generates a reference signal for each color of the filter, which is sent along with the video signal. When the video signal is ready for color encoding, this reference tells the logic circuit which color strip filtered each pixel.

Solid-State Imaging Elements

The pickup tube configuration previously discussed has existed since the beginning of television. The next generation of image transducers are photosensitive solid-state chips. They include arrays of charge-coupled devices (CCDs) and metal oxide semiconductors (MOS). Two CCD transfer methods are offered, Frame Transfer and Interline Transfer. Both CCD and MOS units consist of grids of photosensitive material, which are charged in proportion to the amount of light falling on each sector of the grid. This pattern of charges is then read out sector by sector (as a digital register is read out bit by bit) to generate a television signal that is a very accurate record of the image.

Since the response of the solid-state surface to light is read out directly, it provides a far more consistent record of the image than does the conventional pickup tube. It is not subject to lag, comet-tailing, registration and geometry errors or burn-in from overexposure to intense light sources. Solid-state imaging elements are also much smaller than pickup tubes, and therefore make lighter and smaller cameras possible. However, as these arrays are positioned in the camera at the plane where the target in a pickup tube would be located, the general configuration of a solid-state camera is not very different from that of cameras with tubes.

The CCD camera represents an important step toward generating the image in digital form, because each pixel, or picture element, is a discrete unit of information. However, the pixel is not yet truly digitized, because the information about its brightness is recorded by varying the amplitude of the electrical pulse generated for each pixel. Nor is the information about the red, green and blue color components of each pixel in digital form. Even if it were, television recording and transmitting systems, as well as the signal-handling circuits in the camera, are not currently designed to operate as digital units.

Therefore, the information from the solid-state imaging elements is transformed into a conventional analog television signal, a continuously varying voltage for each of the 525 lines of video. From then on, it is handled as if it had been generated in a conventional pickup tube.

Like tubes, CCD and MOS chips are graded according to industry specifications, with "industrial quality" chips and "broadcast quality" chips. The difference is that broadcast-quality chips of any type are virtually flawless, while different grades of industrial-quality chips are distinguished by flaws of a certain number and size, which reduce resolution and/or sensitivity.

It is important, therefore, to know not only what type of chips a camera uses, but also their grade.

Single versus Multi-Element Cameras

It is important to be aware that an imaging element in a color camera never "sees" the television picture as a multicolored pattern. Each imaging unit is a monochrome device, recording only the brightness of the image presented to it. In a three-tube camera each tube reads only brightness information. The color of the information it transmits is identified only as an input from a red, green or blue channel to a logic circuit (the color encoder). In a single-tube camera, each element "sees" the output from a given color filter stripe, or from a precoded combination of stripes. In any case, the information the sensing element yields directly regards only the brightness of a point. The color of that point is recorded by an encoding system.

Encoding and Color Adjustment

The three color images, red, green and blue (R, G and B), that a camera "sees" are encoded into Y, I and Q outputs to conform to the American NTSC television standard. The encoder uses the output of the imaging elements after it is passed through preamplifiers. It is a fairly simple logic circuit that takes the color information and turns it into a form that is compatible with both the old American monochrome standard and the American color standard. As a result, a color program can be viewed on either black and white or color television sets.

Y stands for "luminance," the brightness level of the video signal, and is indicated by the amplitude of the output of each imaging device. The Y encoder abstracts a percentage of each of the three color signals to form the total Y output from the image. By itself, the Y output can be used to generate a black and white version of the video image.

I and Q, the transmission primaries, are more complex than Y. Each is a mix according to a specific formula of the three primary colors: red, green and blue. I stands for "in-phase subcarrier" and represents a color range from cyan to orange. Q, the "quadrature subcarrier," represents a range from yellow/green to magenta. This I and Q information is used to modulate different sidebands of the color subcarrier (a frequency of 3.579545 MHz), while the Y information is used to modulate the primary carrier. The difference in phase between this color subcarrier and the transmitted I and Q signals provides color information for each point of the image. Since the subcarrier reference frequency is so critical, it is carried as a color burst signal that is repeated before the start of every line of color video. (A more complete discussion of color encoding and phase relationships is included in the Technical Appendix.)

A subcarrier phase adjustment is performed when two or more cameras are matched. However, even the more sophisticated cameras adjust only the color phase of the red and blue information. This is because the encoding formulas have been designed so that the green information we see can be derived directly from the decoded Y, R and B information. For the same reason, only the R and B gain and the R and B black level are adjusted at the camera control unit (CCU). The CCU provides a remote method of adjusting the camera's operating parameters. Traditionally the CCU housed the sync broads and other encoding devices, but current field and studio cameras house all the electronics in the camera head, with the CCU serving as a remote panel for camera adjustments. Moreover, some cameras offer R, G and B

outputs, either from the CCU or through a special camera cable. These options have become important features in choosing cameras for your specific application.

Digital Cameras

Recently digital signal processing (DSP) has made its way into video cameras. DSP cameras offer producers some distinct benefits: they are easy to setup; provide a simple way of matching multiple cameras; and, because DSP eliminates moving parts, they have increased reliability and stability. These benefits add up to improved picture quality with greater operator flexibility.

In selecting a camera for purchase, it is useful to "road-test" it. To do this, the camera can be rented for a preliminary shoot and tested in the producer's typical shooting environment to see how it performs.

VIDEOTAPE RECORDERS

The quality of the videotape recorder (VTR) determines to what degree the image quality produced by the camera is retained on tape. As a critical element of the production process, it is worthwhile to understand how VTRs work and what the different tape formats have to offer.

Recording begins with the tape passing through a slip-ring assembly on a shaft to a pair of rapidly rotating video heads. These heads transform the video signal (a stream of video and synchronizing information which is used to modulate a RF carrier) into magnetic flux which varies constantly in proportion to variations in the modulated RF. As the tape passes over the heads, the flux changes the magnetic orientation of the oxide particles on the tape so that they reflect the intensity of the signal at each instant. In this way, the tape "stores" the original signal.

In playback, as these oxide particles on the tape move across the heads again, their movement regenerates the original signals as magnetic flux. The flux in the heads is transformed back into an electronic RF signal. When the RF is demodulated, the original video signal is restored. Unless subject to another magnetic field, the oxide particles maintain their orientation on videotape for years and can be read many times without disturbing the information they contain.

This general description is true of any videotape recording. But the videotape technology most popular today is helical scan recording used on 1-inch, ¾-inch, ½-inch and 8mm videotape equipment. To appreciate the importance of helical scan systems, it is useful to take a brief look at the "quad" videotape recording systems that were the broadcast recording standard until the late 1970's.

These 2-inch tape recorders can record the full bandwidth of the broadcast color television signal, but they do so in a segmented manner. The video signal is recorded on quad tape by means of four heads mounted 90 degrees apart on the outside of a drum. The heads rotate in a circle, perpendicular to the tape path and to the tape surface. Each head describes a track across the width of the tape that records 16 lines of each 525 line frame. The parallel tracks that result are slanted only to the degree that the tape has moved during the pass of each head. However, direct still framing and pause viewing for cueing and editing are not possible when the tape is stopped, because the signal track that is read with the pass of each head covers only a small part of the image.

This is why the videodisc was first developed as a frame storage device for broadcast television and why computer editing was created as a necessity, rather than a luxury, for the broadcast market. It is also the reason why a more versatile and smaller "high-band" format succeeded quad in the broadcast field. In the United States, that "high-band" format has been 1-inch Type C, and most recently D2 and D1.

Another major problem with quad systems was their enormous cost, which limited their use to broadcasting and major corporations. The price of a fully equipped tape deck ran to six figures. In response to this problem various smaller, "low-band" formats were developed. Today these formats include ¾-inch, ½-inch and 8mm.

A third-range format is available, superior to the low-band formats but similar to the high-band systems in quality. This is ½-inch component video recording. Nevertheless, this format, as well as all the others used today, uses helical scan recording.

Helical Scan Videotape Recording Systems

While there are differences in the way video information is recorded by the different helical scan formats, in all of them, the video recording heads trace a sharply diagonal path across the tape. While the tape is winding its way around the heads, this path forms a segment of a helix (hence, "helical" scan). The earlier Type A and Type B recorders actually moved the tape in a spiral, while Type C recorders do not completely wrap tape around the cylinder.

Still-Frame and Pause/Review Capability

Although there are different helical scan formats, all record an entire field with one pass of a recording head. This means that it is possible to still-frame or pause/view an entire image without special equipment. As long as the heads are aligned with a video track on the tape the rotating heads will continue to read out the image. The ability to view a specific image while the tape is stopped makes it possible to perform basic editing operations without frame storage or computer assistance.

Control Track

The control track is a separate track that is recorded by a stationary head onto the edge of the videotape for the first video track of each frame. The control track thus consists of a single pulse positioned at the start of each frame of video. It is triggered by the vertical sync that starts each frame. Its purpose is to provide a clock, or timing signal, by which the speed of the videotape across the heads can be regulated. The function of the control track is similar to the sprockets in film.

Tracking and Tracking Error

To "read" the video that has been recorded, the heads must move over the exact path in which the track was originally laid down. Videotape recorders use a guard band, the space between tracks, to isolate one track from the next and to minimize "tracking error." Tracking error occurs during playback if the head path across the tape does not line up precisely with the track of video. As the head-to-track alignment is reduced, the image starts to show horizontal breakup.

The Capstan Servo and Tracking Correction

To correct tracking error, the tape must be moved so that each track arrives at the video head

Figure 2.5: An Ampex VPR-3 (one-inch Type C) VTR.

Courtesy Ampex

as the next video head rotates into position to read it. To provide this alignment, the period between control track pulses is used to adjust the capstan servo. The "capstan" is a small rotating drum that, paired with a pinch roller, pulls the tape along and sets actual tape speed. The servo makes constant fine corrections in the rotational rate of the capstan, so that correct tracking is maintained. Additional correction of head-to-tape alignment is provided by another servo located on the head drum. If a previously recorded tape has a slightly different track angle (which might be caused by tape stretch), an additional manual tracking adjustment can be used to correct for this. In the record mode, the capstan speed is timed by the sync rate of the recorded video, ensuring that the video tracks are laid down at precisely spaced intervals.

High and Low Band

These are terms that describe the bandwidth of the modulated carrier used for videotape recording, and should not be confused with the bandwidth over which television signals are transmitted for broadcast purposes. As noted before, video signals are not recorded directly, but in the form of a frequency modulated RF carrier. This is necessitated by certain technical requirements of magnetic videotape recording. The high-band recording method is the broadcast standard and is used by all 1-inch equipment as well as D2 (explained later in this chapter). It uses a 3 MHz bandwidth, over the 7 to 10 MHz range, for both luminance and chrominance. High- band recording maximizes signal-to-noise ratio and resolution. Low-band recording, popular in smaller formats, uses a narrower band (4.3 to 6.8 MHz) at lower frequencies. Luminance is recorded over a 2.5 MHz band and chrominance over only 1.0 MHz. Low-band recording results in significantly lower signal-to-noise ratio, which significantly limits the number of generations (copies) that can be made from an original recording.

One-Inch Type C

Due to the development of appropriate magnetic tape characteristics, head design technology and sophisticated micro control circuits and transducers, Type C systems (see Figure 2.5) record in the high- band mode, providing high resolution, low noise and excellent color. In the Type C sys-

Figure 2.6: Type C one-inch helical-scan system layout.

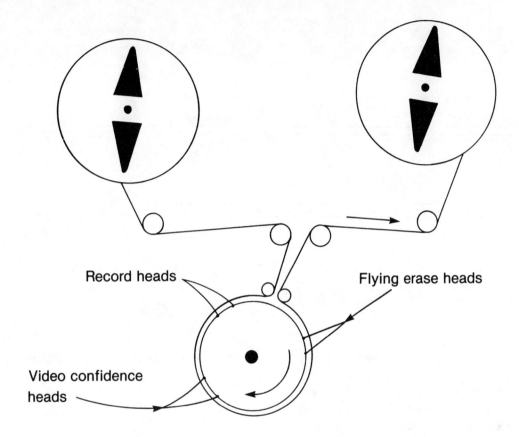

Record heads

Flying erase heads

Video confidence heads

Figure 2.7: Two helical-scan videotape recording formats.

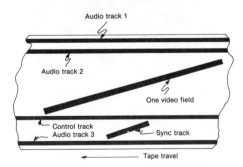

One-inch Type C tape recording format

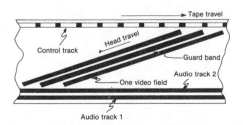

Three-quarter-inch tape recording format

tem, the tape is wrapped 344 degrees around the head drum to form the helical track (see Figure 2.6).

The system uses only one head to record video, but it also uses a second head to record the vertical sync. This second head is necessary because the signal head system fails to record 10 lines as it transits from the end of one track to the beginning of the next. While these lines are well within the blanking interval and normally carry no information, it is likely they will do so in the future. Type C VTRs that do not incorporate a sync head are designed to accept one as an option.

To ensure compatibility among different manufacturers' Type C VTRs, the layout information on the tape adheres to the standard shown in Figure 2.7. As can be seen, this format requires a separate sync track.

Type C specs also call the three audio tracks, two for stereo recording capability and a third for time code. Time code is a audio signal that gives each recorded frame a unique code, or address. During editing, controllers with the ability to read time code can edit accurately within a frame.

Figure 2.8: Basic component videotape format.

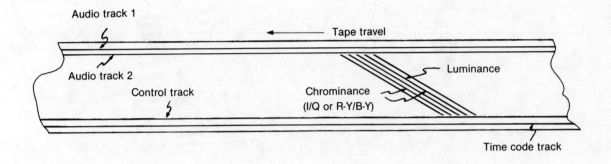

Component Videocassette Recorders

For many years, all video information was recorded as "composite video," containing both luminance (Y) and chrominance (I and Q) information, as well as synchronizing signals. Composite video recorded at full bandwidth occupies a great deal of tape space. The compromise, low-band video, permitted the use of narrower tape formats but produced inferior images. This situation led to the development of "component video" recording systems.

Component recording techniques eliminate interaction between chrominance and luminance by separating the luminance and two chrominance components (R-Y and B-Y) in three different locations on the tape (see Figure 2.8). Component recording provides greater flexibility by not incurring significant picture degradation before six generations.

The two component systems available are Betacam[R] and MII. Even though they follow the same general format, these two systems are incompatible because they differ in track angle and spacing.

The primary impetus for the development of component video has been the need for high-band in-camera recorders (see Chapter 6, Camcorders). However, since component video studio decks

Figure 2.9: Typical 3/4-inch cassette system tape layout.

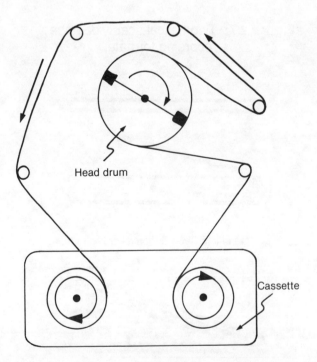

Figure 2.10: 3/4-Inch SP

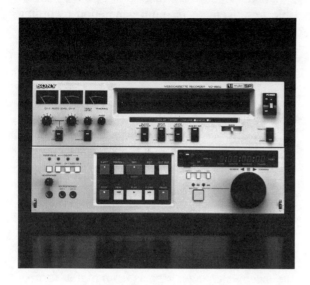

Courtesy Sony Corp.

and editing systems became available, more and more facilities have turned toward a mix of component and composite equipment. Because component images are close to 1-inch performance and cost less to produce, this format has become a desirable alternative for some producers.

Three-Quarter-Inch Videocassette Recorders

There are many similarities between the Type C 1-inch and ¾-inch systems. Both record a full frame of video with each pass of the head in a single diagonal across the width of the tape (see Figure 2.6). Moreover, both use flying erase heads.

The difference lies in the use of two video heads, each of which records alternate fields. The information to the heads (in "record") or from the heads (in "playback") is switched from one head to another during the vertical blanking interval. The result is a shorter video track. Nevertheless, the shorter track works because the ¾-inch recording system uses a lower bandwidth, and therefore has to record less detailed picture information. (See Figure 2.9.)

The lower bandwidth, however, limits the resolution these systems are capable of attaining. Lower bandwidth also means reduced signal-to-noise (S/N) ratio, and therefore fewer viable videotape generations.

Sony has enhanced the ¾-inch format by offering ¾-inch SP (Figure 2.10). This improvement over standard ¾-inch U-Matic provides increased FM carrier frequency without destroying compatibility. It represents an effort to keep the ¾-inch format appealing and competitive. SP tapes are metal based and are both upward and downward compatible. It is important to note that significant improvement only occurs if SP recorded tapes are played in SP units.

Half-Inch Videocassette Recorders

This format is used by most producers for distribution of the finished program and has not gained wide use as a production format. While the format shares most of its specifications and methods for signal recording with ¾-inch, it is severely limited by its narrow bandwidth. Recently, the Super VHS (S/VHS) format has made its way into the production arena.

S/VHS follows the VHS format, but offers improved picture quality, including greater horizontal resolution and improved S/N ratio. Further improvement in picture quality is achieved by employing separate luminance (Y) and chrominance (C) terminals for both input and output. S/VHS provides 400-line resolution by raising the FM carrier frequency of the Y signal from 3.4-4.4 MHz band for standard VHS to 5.4-7.0 MHz for S/VHS. The result is increased detail and clarity. Separating the Y/C inputs and outputs paves the way for high-resolution monitors, cameras and editing equipment all allowing the signals to stay in their purest forms.

S/VHS video tapes are metal based and can be recorded and played back on standard VHS recorders only in Standard VHS mode. S/VHS recorders are downward compatible, allowing the recording and playing of standard VHS format. For playback the S/VHS units automatically select the correct mode, S/VHS or VHS.

8 mm Videocassette Recording

This format, like VHS, is used for distribution of the finished program and has not gained wide

Figure 2.11: Hi8: Feeder

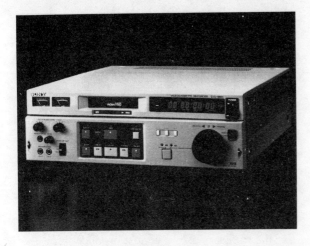

Courtesy Sony Corp.

use as a production format. Again like VHS, this format shares most of its specifications and methods for signal recording with ¾-inch.

Recently the 8 mm format was improved with the introduction of Hi8 (Figure 2.11). This format has made its way into the production arena, offering improved quality over standard 8 mm. Hi8 uses a metal tape of magnetic material higher than that of standard 8 mm metal tape. The orientation of the metal particles is more uniformly vertical. This allows Hi8 tape to provide a higher output and higher frequencies.

To increase horizontal resolution to 400 lines, the luminance carrier frequency has been shifted from 5 MHz in standard 8 mm systems up to 7 MHz. This provides for the recording of more detailed visual information.

Hi8 insures upward compatibility with the standard 8 mm system by having Hi8 equipment automatically switch to recording in the standard 8 mm format when sensing standard 8 mm metal tape. It is important to note that standard 8 mm equipment will not play back Hi8 recordings.

Digital Video Recording

Digital video recording (D1) offers considerable improvement in multi-generation recording over the analog recording systems previously discussed. The digital video recorder (DVR) uses sophisticated processing techniques to encode video signals to digital codes. Digital recording, unlike analog recording, results in very little signal degradation over time. What is recorded today remains intact for many years. The only limitations are those placed by the medium, i.e., the physical tape will deteriorate with time.

The D1 component recorder operates in an all-digital environment and by definition is able to produce 20 digital generations before signal degradation. The D2 recorder is designed to operate in an analog composite environment and although digital interface ports are provided for dubbing, the machine changes signals from digital form to analog form and vice versa with each recording.

The D2 format (Figure 2.12) uses the standard "D" cassette, but with play time increased approximately three times over that of the D1 format. The D2 format does not use a guard band between helical tracks. Instead, azimuth recording is used to reduce interference from neighboring tracks. The rejection of interference is most effective when long wavelengths are not recorded.

The D2 format offers superior multi-generation performance, reliable operation, and compatibility with the current composite environment. D2 gives the producer the opportunity to store images and sound using the advantages of digital technology while still being able to interface with existing facilities.

Videotape

When television began, videotape did not exist. Unless a program was simultaneously recorded on film, it was gone forever. The development of videotape, to store the images generated and to regenerate them for playback, makes modern video production possible.

Videotape consists of a thin layer of flexible plastic, usually mylar, on which a layer of fine, evenly-sized oxide particles is deposited in a binding medium and covered with a protective coating. Each microscopic oxide particle is polarized, so that it acts as a micro magnet. On new videotape, the particles are evenly but randomly ar-

Figure 2.12: D-2 Studio VTR, the Ampex VPR-300

ranged, and that is what creates the dancing black-and-white "snow" on the screen and generates the hiss of "white noise" when it is played. But when video and audio information is recorded on the tape, the electrical signal from each point of the image orients the particles passing under the recording heads at that moment. The stronger the signal, the more the particles are aligned and until they are remagnetized, they stay in position. In this way, they provide a record of each image, with an accuracy that is limited mostly by the quality of the equipment used to record it.

Although contemporary tape is relatively tough, it still needs careful handling. Knowing that the particles are magnetic makes it clear why tape must be kept out of magnetic fields, such as those generated by motors. But it is also important to avoid extreme temperature and humidity conditions. If a tape has been left in cold temperature condition, it is essential to let it warm up—up to two hours if the temperatures are in the 40°F range. Near or below freezing, the tape may be damaged permanently. Similarly, tape cannot be allowed to get too hot. Tapes left on radiators, in the sun, or stacked on top of operating equipment may have their plastic components deformed, causing distortion of the image. If tape has not been "cooked" in these ways but has been stored at temperatures over 90°F, it must be allowed to adjust to the operating environment. However, if the operating environment is going to be a problem—as for example if the shoot is at a desert location—the tape has to be kept in thermally insulated containers and brought out and returned as needed.

Accordingly, the videotape supply must be stored in a clean and dry area, where the producer can count on fairly stable levels of temperature. There, and wherever tapes are stored, they must be set on end, like books, rather than stacked.

The producer cannot always control the recording environment but decisions can be made to avoid certain situations. Low temperatures cause winding of the tape to loosen, which may result in cinching. High temperatures increase pack tightness, which increases dropouts and distortion leading to potential interchange problems. It is a good practice to acclimate the tape for 24 hours to the environment you are shooting in.

Tapes should be stored in an area that has acceptable levels of heat and humidity. This area must be clean and dry and the tapes should be kept upright, never stacked upon one another.

To safeguard your production investment, be sure to label and catalog each tape. Nothing is more frustrating than not knowing what is stored on a specific videotape.

INSERT STUDIO

Because of the great expense of creating a studio or even of renting one, the producer may consider creating an insert studio, even if a full studio is available to him. An insert studio is a small space in which shots required to cover or fill in were omitted in production can be made. Reaction were shots, where the interviewer is shot listening, or reacting to the interviewee, can be taken here, as can "table-top" shots, as when an equipment or procedure is being described in closeup. It can easily be large enough for two-person interviews to be shot in their entirety. This may be especially useful for the corporate producer who works with confidential material or whose talent does not have time to travel to off-site locations. But it will be useful to any producer who is handling multiple productions and tight schedules.

CONCLUSION

In the constantly changing world of professional video, understanding the latest video formats and technologies has become a very complex and time-consuming process, but an important one. These questions may have very different answers for the in-house producer than they do for the creator of a studio for a school or college, or for a production house. To make wise choices, the guiding factor must be the studio's objectives—how it will be used and who will use it—because these issues will determine the interaction between level of quality and cost. Remaining clear about these objectives will enable the producer to choose among competing products.

3 Switchers and Other Studio Equipment

The camera and record deck are the two essential tools used to capture an image on tape. To create a more sophisticated product, switchers (special effects generators) and other studio production equipment are used.

SWITCHERS

Switchers are essentially editing devices that are used in the production as well as the post-production processes. In production, switchers control transitions among cameras and various auxiliary devices, including film chains, videotape recorders containing prerecorded material, and character generators. When a switcher is used extensively in production, most of the editing decisions are made on the spot. Television sitcoms and soap operas, for example, are created mostly by live-cutting each sequence within a specific studio set, making all transitions between shots with a switcher. Later editing is thus constrained by the production sequences, and usually post-production primarily involves the assembly of these sequences into a program. In such cases, the switcher is the means by which the creative editing is done. A typical small format switcher is shown in Figure 3.1.

Time Base Considerations

For a switcher to create transitions among the different images generated by two or more pieces of equipment, the images must arrive on the same "time base." That is, they must be perfectly synchronized, so that the sync intervals of the lines and frames generated by each piece of equipment all start at the same time.

To do this in production, all image sources are "genlocked" to the sync provided by one source, such as the sync from one of the cameras, or from a sync generator. Thus, to fade from Camera A to Camera B presents no problem, because the start of a frame from A can be mixed with the start of a frame from B without changing sync. If a video-tape recorder is used as an image source in a studio, the VTR must be equipped with a time base corrector (TBC). (For a discussion of VTRs and TBCs, see the section on "Effects" in Chapter 11.)

Switching and Mixing

Once the time base issue is understood, a great deal becomes clear about switchers and their capabilities. All contemporary switchers are vertical interval switchers that can transition cleanly from the end of the last frame of one source to the beginning of the first frame of another.

When the video sources are connected to the inputs of the switcher, their outputs can be related via buses—lines to which they have a common connection (Figure 3.2). To get a mix, for example, between Camera 2 at Input 2 on A Bus, and Camera 3 at Input 3 on B Bus, the image from

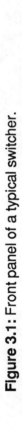

Figure 3.1: Front panel of a typical switcher.

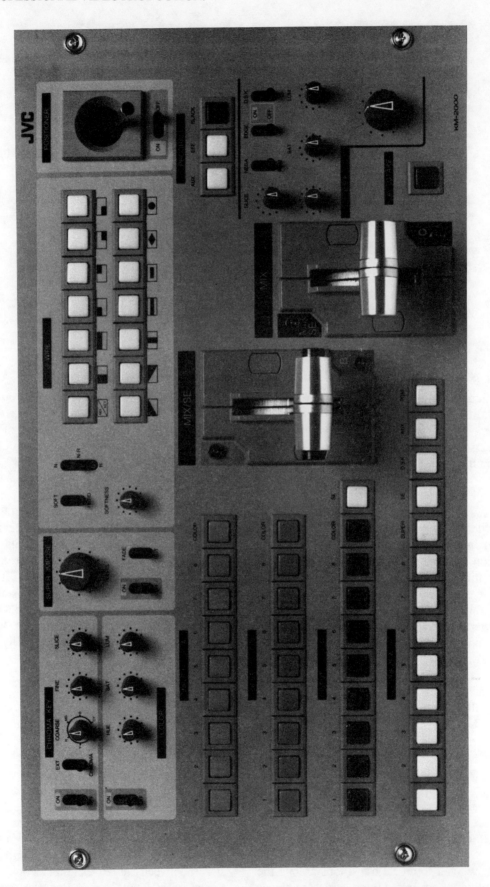

Model KM-2000, Courtesy of JVC AMERICA, Inc.

Figure 3.2: Simplified block diagram of a special effects generator.

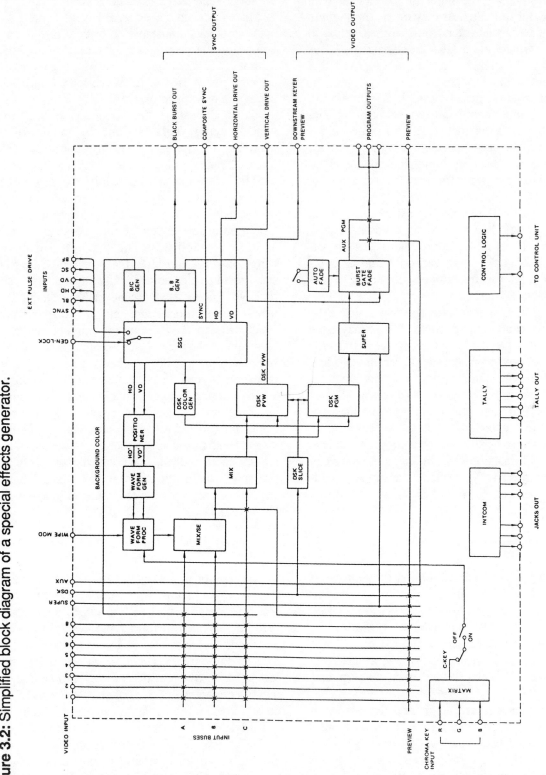

Courtesy of JVC AMERICA, Inc.

Camera 2 goes through the system and out via the PROGRAM outputs. To get a clean dissolve, the MIX handles are moved at the correct moment from A Bus to B Bus. As they move, the strength of the video signal taken from A Bus (Camera 2) decreases in the amount that the signal from B Bus (Camera 3) increases, leaving a completed dissolve to Camera 3 video.

While cuts and dissolves are the staples of film, wipes are more common to video, primarily because they are much more easily performed in this medium. Wipes are essentially graphic effects made when one image is transformed into another along the edges of a pattern. This can be a vertical edge moving from left to right, as in a simple horizontal wipe. It can also be a complex, expanding chevron pattern, which the new image takes as it "wipes" out the existing image. More than 100 wipe patterns are available. However, only a dozen or so constitute the vast majority of wipes used in professional television.

Almost all switchers offer soft wipes, where the edge is a continuous dissolve. Wipes may have borders that are dark, light or colored, and they may be spotlit or shadowed. Adjustable shadow edges are used to make titles or credits stand out against image backgrounds. Wipes can also be reversed. For example, a circle wipe which appears in the center and expands can also bring in the new image by starting at the edges and shrinking the old image inward. In addition, wipes can be positioned so that the circle starts in any quadrant. Wipes can be rotated or modulated so that they appear to pulse.

Keys and Mattes

Keying is an electronic relative of wiping. But where wipes bring a new image in at specified edges, keys bring in the new image in specified areas, defined by luminance or chrominance. Mattes can be used as background or to fill a border or a key. In another words, a person or object can be placed (keyed) over a background (matte).

Most switchers are luminance keyers. These are used to create subtitles which are generated against a black background and superimposed over the action. The black background is ignored by the keyer, while the bright letters supersede the image where they appear. However, where the luminance of the keyed letters is equal to that of the image,

the letters become unreadable if they are not shadowed or bordered. External inputs to these keyers are usually character generators.

Mattes are another external key. A matte generator provides adjustable color control that can be used to colorize the keyed source to any hue, saturation or luminance level. Matte generators are commonly used to fill white letters on black backgrounds with color.

Video also offers the possibility of chrominance keying. This is done by means of a chromakeyer that uses a specific hue to key an image. Traditionally, chromakey blue has been used for this purpose, because this color contains a minimum of flesh tones. However, chromakeys using green and other hues are also available.

Chrominance keying offers endless post-production possibilities. For example, using a chromakeyer set to blue, the image of a person standing in an area covered with blue material can be keyed onto a street scene in New Delhi. By means of the chrominance unit, the image of the street will appear wherever the original image is blue, so that the person will be surrounded by the New Delhi image. For another example, an actor in a commercial—who appears to be walking among a series of gigantic cookie boxes—is actually shot with one camera while moving around a carefully designed route in a chromakey set constructed with box-shaped structures. A second camera is focused on the actual cookie boxes carefully positioned to match the chromakey set. These cookie boxes provide the environment onto which the actor is keyed.

Upstream, Downstream and Re-Entry

The position of the keyer in the circuit is important. A keyer may be upstream, between the effects/mix amplifier where the image keyed can then be subjected to further processing, such as wipes and dissolves. Alternatively, a keyer can be located downstream, where, in effect, it has the last word, as when a title is keyed into an image that has undergone a series of effects and remains on the screen after the "effected" image has been faded out.

The effects stages in the operations of an SEG with a downstream keyer in a production situation are illustrated in Figure 3.3. We take, for example, a slide (from the film/slide chain) of the Capitol in Washington, DC. (The image could also come

Figure 3.3: Block diagram of typical SEG operation with downstream keyer and double re-entry.

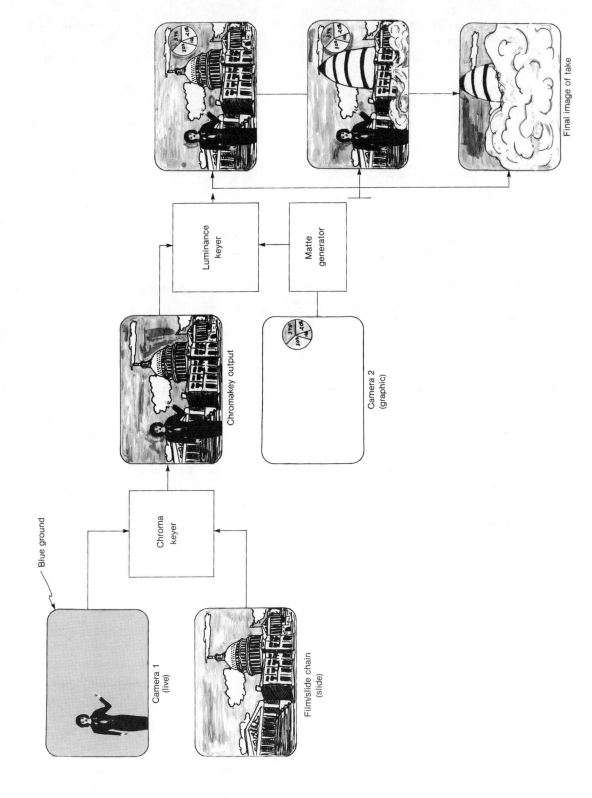

from a VTR.) Camera 2 is on a television reporter standing in a chromakey area in the studio, framed to the left of the picture area. When these two images are mixed in the chromakeyer, we get a single image of the reporter standing in front of the Capitol, framed to the left of the total image area. Now we take Camera 2, which is holding on a pie chart depicting allocation sectors of the congressional budget. The graphic is positioned so that it is in the upper right quadrant of the Camera 2 image, and by using an upper right quadrant wipe, we now wipe the pie chart into the program image of the reporter standing before the Capitol. If we have a positionable wipe, we can frame the graphic so that it sits more tightly in the quadrant, as shown in the illustration.

With a downstream keyer, we can elaborate on this image structure further by introducing another element. Let us say that in this case we will "segue" (lead into) a segment that starts with the image of a missile being fired, while the reporter discusses the military expenditures. Since ours is a luminance keyer, the whiteness of the burning missile fuel will appear first. As we key in the entire image of the rising missile, the keyed image supersedes all other effects, so that we end up with an image of the missile rising and the reporter voice-over.

Alternatively, we might use the same system to chromakey the commentator over the Capitol and then dissolve to the missile, using the downstream keyer to superimpose the congressional budget allocation graphic from Camera 2 over the missile, assuming that the graphic is suitable for luminance keying.

Each point at which we can impose an effect over an existing effect is called a re-entry. If we did not have the second re-entry point at which we could dissolve, then we would have to switch; no effects could be set up after the first one until the switch was completed. Clearly, in designing a program, the capabilities of the special effects generator to be used must govern all but the most basic decisions the director makes.

Other Effects Considerations

Special effects can also be automated. The switcher circuits can be activated by instructions stored in an electronic memory, providing an auto-take of the sequence of effects that is stored in it. This is particularly useful when a fast or elaborate sequence of effects is desired. With an auto-take, a series of effects can be executed at dazzling speed without error.

Effects can be either previewed or programmed. When an effect is previewed, it is simply shown on the preview monitor, which is connected to the preview output of the switcher. This enables the director to check his effects options without committing them to tape. On the other hand, the program output can be connected directly to the recording device.

VIDEO TEST EQUIPMENT

For the small-format studio, two of the producer's best tools are his waveform monitor and vectorscope. Once very high-tech items, these pieces of test equipment are now available at lower prices or as combination units (with one monitor operable in both test modes) and in portable configurations.

The Waveform Monitor

A video waveform monitor (Figure 3.4) is an oscilloscope designed to display the video signal as a linear trace. It is both an operational and measurement tool that is used to determine the electronic integrity of the image that is being (or has been) recorded.

The screen of the waveform monitor is marked by a grid generally referred to as a scale or graticule. The grid divides the face of the tube vertically into units of measurement called IREs. The horizontal scale of the graticule is used to mark time divisions, to determine the duration of electronic pulses.

The first step in reading a waveform monitor is to understand that video is comprised solely of horizontal lines. Although we refer to "vertical" sync and blanking, these are recorded on horizontal lines. In video, all verticality is created by the stacking of horizontal lines, and the only vertical movement is the movement of the electron beam that "writes" the image from one line to the next and from the bottom to the top of the image. Since the basic element of video is the horizontal line, control of the line quality and timing is essential for a quality product.

Figure 3.5 displays a video signal on a waveform monitor. Illustrated is the horizontal blanking interval, in which the horizontal sync and

Figure 3.4: Front panel of a waveform monitor with horizontal video display for color bars.

Courtesy of Tektronix, Inc.

color burst signals are included (also see Technical Appendix Figure A.5). The horizontal blanking interval is an "off" period that gives the beam in the camera or television tube time to get from one side of the screen to the other (and from the end of one line to the beginning of the next) without leaving a trace. The horizontal sync pulse is an electrical pulse of a specific form and duration that marks the start of the blanking period and thus indicates the start of each line. It is important that this pulse be clear and strong so that all horizontal lines start at the same time and stack up one over the other in the same way they were written.

The burst of short pulses that follows the sync pulse is the color burst. Color burst is a reference signal of a specific frequency (3.5 MHz) that sets a standard for the colors in the image. The ragged (grassy) signal that follows the burst is the video signal that creates the image. It consists of two video fields of 262 ½ lines each, superimposed on each other. Their height indicates the "video level"

or luminance of the image. (A more detailed discussion of video image parameters and waveform monitor use is given in the Technical Appendix.)

The Vectorscope

Vectorscopes are designed to check the color, or chrominance, relationships within a video image. Color has two aspects—hue and chroma—which describe the actual color (hue) and its intensity (chroma, or chroma level). In production, vectorscopes enable two or more cameras to be matched or balanced and to check that the signal being recorded displays both correct chroma and hue.

Matching cameras involves checking that each is set for the same color relationship. If this is not done, there can be noticeable differences in the color of the same scene shot with different cameras. For example, in the image from one camera, the skin tone may be slightly pink because it con-

Figure 3.5: A horizontal video trace on a waveform monitor.

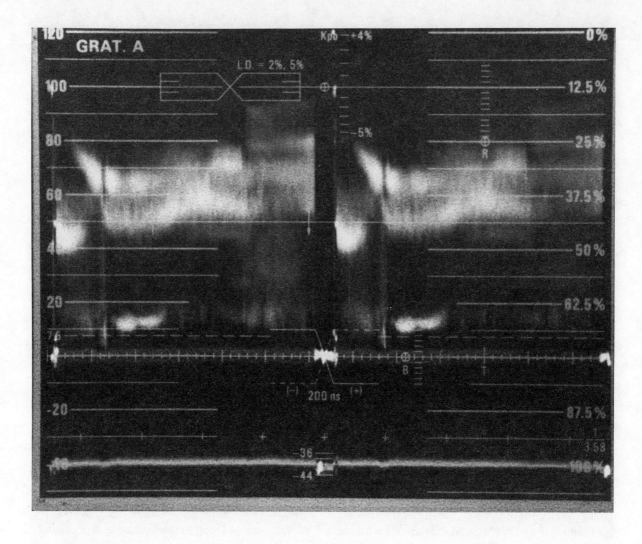

Courtesy of Tektronix, Inc.

tains more blue tones, while in the image from the second camera, the skin tone may be slightly more orange because the color balance is shifted toward yellow. If the two cameras are matched, the differential between the two can be minimized or eliminated entirely. However, when they are not, the entire scene will look off-color whenever there is a switch or dissolve from one camera to another.

A vectorscope with a display from a typical video image is shown in Figure 3.6. In this illustration, the video signal is displayed in cross-section, as if it were flowing toward the viewer through a pipe. The chrominance level, or "saturation," determines the radius of this "pipe," and the

hue, or "chrominance phase," determines the pattern of color spots around the center.

Different colors appear as spots at specified positions around the circle. The graticule is calibrated to locate the precise phase angle and amplitude angles of the primary and intermediate colors. When the hues and their saturation are correct, the primaries (red, green and blue) and their intermediates (magenta, yellow-green and cyan) fall at specific angles around the circle and into small squares on the vectorscope graticule.

In post-production, the vectorscope is also used to check color, primarily the color bars that should have been recorded at the head of each tape during production. The color bars will indicate precisely how much color phase adjustment is necessary to provide a color-correct master (assuming a time base corrector or other equipment is available). In dubbing, the vectorscope can be used to check the color bars on the master to ensure a correct color dub.

THE AUDIO AND INTERCOM SYSTEMS

Today quality audio is recognized as an important element of producing effective programs. While audio recording is a discipline that commands its own technology and expertise, there are some important concepts and concerns a producer should be aware of.

Whether you are using an outside or in-house studio, the following concerns are applicable. If sources recorded outside the facility are to be incorporated., it is necessary to make certain that formats are compatible. Moreover, audio requirements should be detailed so as to allow matching of microphones and feeds. This provides a method of determining what additional equipment maybe needed. Audio requirements should be discussed with as much detail and concern as the video setup.

The intercom system for a small studio need not be sophisticated. Its prime function is to enable the director to communicate with the crew and talent.

A typical audio system based on stereo capabilities is presented in Figure 3.7. In addition to microphones and audio recorders, there is provision for using other audio sources. The latter may include sound from a prerecorded videotape, perhaps the genlock video-source, a phonograph recording, and an audio synthesizer, or computer with audio synthesizing capability.

Figure 3.6: Front panel of a vectorscope with color bar display.

Courtesy of Tektronix, Inc.

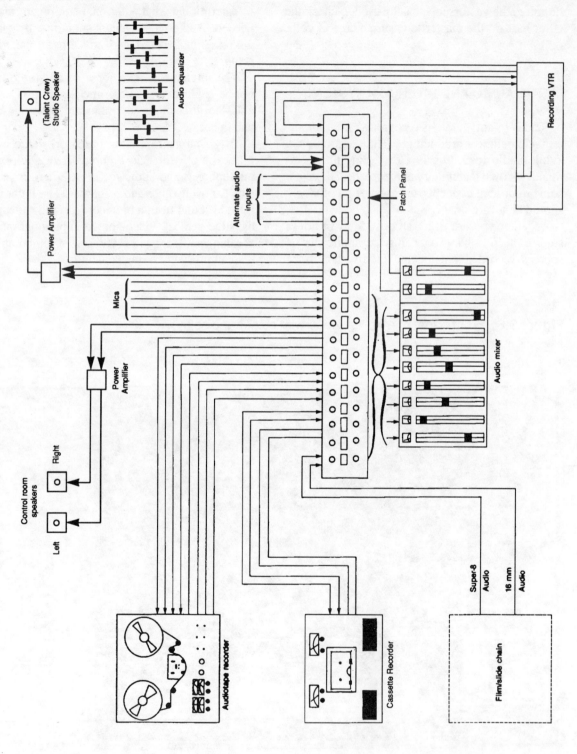

Figure 3.7: Basic audio system for a small-format studio.

Microphones

Choosing the proper microphone for a given situation is not easy for the video producer who has to work without an audio specialist. An understanding of how microphones pick up sound and some experimentation greatly aids in choosing microphones that best meet the application. The basic microphones needed for studio recording are two cardioids, an omni and from two to five lavaliers.

Polar Patterns

Microphones are defined not only by their "polar patterns" but also by the format of their transducers, applications and configurations.

A variety of common polar patterns for microphones is shown in Figure 3.8. The shaded part of these diagrams indicates how each type of microphone responds to the sound around it. In the diagrams, the microphone is at the center, pointing in the direction of 0 degrees. The larger the gray area, the stronger the mic responds on that axis.

It is important to note that polar patterns are run in an anechoic (echo free) chamber and they represent performance in an ideal acoustic environment: one without walls, ceiling or floor. Common to all specifications, polar patterns are for reference use. Actual pick-up patterns are only verified through practical use in your given situation.

Omnidirectional Microphones

An omnidirectional (or all-directional) microphone has virtually equal sensitivity over 360 degrees. This means that the mic responds as strongly to an audio source behind it as it does to a source directly in front of it. Omnis are general-purpose mics, most often used to capture ambience. Ambi-

Figure 3.8: Polar Sensitivity patterns for microphones.

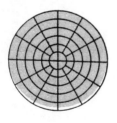

a. Omnidirectional

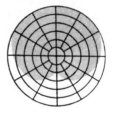

b. Cardiod

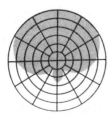

c. Supercardiod

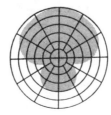

d. Hypercardiod

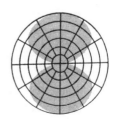

e. Bidirectional

ent noise is the overall sound produced by an event, such as the sounds of conversation, tinkling of glasses and the clink of silver on plates at a dinner party.

Cardioid Microphones

The cardioid microphone has a "heart-shaped" pick-up pattern. This is the second basic pattern of mic sensitivity and, by far, the one most used. Microphones of this type are much more sensitive to sounds in front of than they are to sounds behind the mic head. Cardioid mics, when pointed directly at the source, are used to focus a sound out from its ambience. Mics used on shotguns and booms (see the following section) are cardioids.

Various types of cardioid microphones are available. Microphones of the super-cardioid and hyper-cardioid type offer sensitivity that is even more directional toward the front and greater attenuation (poor sensitivity) toward the back. An important consideration when using these microphones is the requirement that the talent stay directly in front of the microphone (on mic).

Microphone Transducers

Microphones are also distinguished by the design of their transducers—the mechanisms that convert sound waves into electrical signals. In general the basic types used for television production are dynamic and condenser mics.

Dynamic Mics

Dynamic mics (Figure 3.9) use a coil of wire that is compressed by sound waves. As the coil vibrates in a magnetic field, an electrical signal proportional to the volume of the sound and at the same frequency as the sound is generated in the mic. This is a fairly rugged design that can withstand a lot of handling. Therefore, hand-held mics often use dynamic transducers.

Condenser Mics

Condenser mics (Figure 3.10) use a transducer with two electrically charged plates, like a capacitor. As the sound waves move one of the plates, the electrical signal varies accordingly. This design provides excellent sound quality but is more sensitive to shock than are dynamic mics. A varia-

Figure 3.9: Dynamic Microphone.

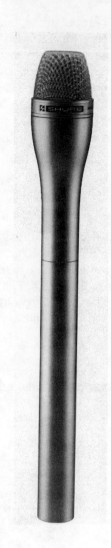

Courtesy Sheve Brothers, Inc.

tion of this format is the electret condenser mic, which uses a plate that is permanently electrostatically charged. It requires less battery power to operate the head than do other mics.

Other Transducer Types

Less common formats include ribbon mics and pressure-zone (or piezoelectric) transducer mics. Because ribbon mics are extremely sensitive, and pressure-zone transducer mics are placement dependent, they are best left to the audio specialist.

Figure 3.10: Condenser Microphone.

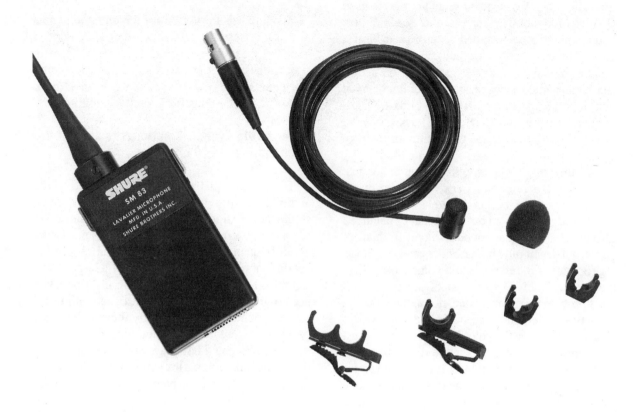

Courtesy Sheve Brothers, Inc.

Microphone Formats

Various microphone formats are available to suit a range of production situations, such as standard, lavalier or shotgun mics.

Standard microphones include hand-held mics as well as those used on mic stands. This type has a mic head (or "capsule") mounted on a handle. The handle usually holds batteries and a solid-state preamplifier. These are generally designed for a very flat response over the range of frequencies of the human voice.

With lavalier mics only the capsule is worn by the performer while the power source is at the other end of the mic wire. Originally the term lavalier was used for a microphone hung around the neck of the performer. Today it is also used to describe lapel mics, very small devices that can be clipped to a performer's clothing. These mics are

usually designed with better response at the higher voice frequencies than at the lower. This enables them to suppress resonances from the performer's chest.

Shotgun and wireless mics are primarily used on remote productions. Shotguns are super- or hyper-cardioid mics that have extremely long pickup heads, and can operate over a much longer distance than conventional cardioids can. Wireless mics contain small transmitters in their handles, allowing the performer to enjoy greater freedom of movement.

The Audio Mixer

The audio mixer, often referred to as the "board" or "desk," allows a variety of audio sources to be selected or combined and then fed into a videotape recorder or other audio equipment. Boards designed for video production differ from those used in audio recording studios. Audio produced for video places less importance on fold back and special effects. Consequently, audio mixers used in video production do not offer these capabilities. If the sound to be recorded requires capabilities more like those of audio recording studios, the sources should be recorded separately on audiotape by an audio specialist, and a carefully planned mix should be performed at a sound-mixing facility. In such cases, only a reference track should be recorded on the videotape at the time of the production.

Whether mixing a complete program or just laying down a reference track, the audio mixer used for video production should have the following features. The mixer must have balanced (grounded) inputs and outputs to prevent hum or buzz from developing because connectors are floating (operating in reference to a voltage other than the zero volt level of the rest of the system). It must provide a reference tone, normally 1000 Hz, for setting levels in all channels and to provide a reference tone for the color bars. The mixer must have correct impedances for the different sound sources to be used. It should provide power for condenser microphones through the microphone cable (phantom powering). Finally, the board must have an adequate number of lines. These should include at least four mic inputs and at least four line inputs (preferably with the ability to switch all inputs between line and mic) to mix prerecorded audio from the audio tape, audiocassette and videocassette recorders.

Audiotape Recorders

Even small studios should have separate audio playback and recording units, with stereo capabilities. They can serve as sources of prerecorded sounds or as audio recording devices.

Traditionally, reel-to-reel audio recorders provided the most flexibility and quality in recording audio. However, with the advent of digital sound and the perfection of techniques that allow small analog cassette formats to perform at reel-to-reel quality, the small studio now has many more choices.

Synchronization is now possible on many reel-to-reel units, some cassette units and a few digital tape (DAT) recorders. If future synching is provided by recording time code on one of the audio

tracks, it is a good practice to place time code on a outside track. Time code is recorded at very high amplitude which to prevent bleed onto the next track of audio.

The important criterion for the unit and or format you choose for audio recording may depend on where the post production process is performed. If outside services are used for audio sweetening and general audio work, your facility must have access to similar units for interchangeability.

Other Audio system Components and Accessories

The audio equalizer (EQ) unit built into the audio mixer provides enough control for most studio applications; thus outboard EQ units are not required. The equalizer provides control over given frequencies: for example, it can reduce the "boom" of a room and the gravel of a large voice. EQ must be used judiciously; care must be taken not to limit frequency response and eliminate wanted sounds. If used properly the equalizer can be a valuable audio production tool.

The audio patch bay plays an important role in providing maximum flexibility and adaptability for the studio. It is a panel or box fitted with carefully labeled and mounted female audio connectors to which all audio equipment is input. Each input connector at the back is connected to another connector at the front. By means of the patch bay, audio sources can be quickly and easily connected to each other, to VTRs or to other audio recorders. However, if a patch bay is used, all connectors must be connected to a common ground (a balance wiring scheme is preferred).

The rest of the audio complement should include several monitoring headsets, three reference speakers and such items as audio amplifiers, mic stands and headphones.

Audio amplifiers are needed to drive the reference speakers. Because clean audio is desired, the chosen amplifiers should not introduce any unwanted hiss or noise.

Mic stands include both floor and table models, which should take the same heads (mounting devices). The basic boom is comprised of a dolly base, telescoping post and arm assembly. The mic stands and boom are tools for mic placement and controlling sound pick up during a production.

Headphones provide audio personnel a method of monitoring which is not influenced by room acoustics. Headphones should be of the closed ear type, to provide good isolation from ambient sound.

The Intercom System

The intercom system (shown in Figure 3.11) is separate from the studio audio system and exists solely to permit communication among the pro- duction team in the various parts of the studio. Its primary function is to allow the director in the control room to communicate with camera and floor people through their headsets and to studio talent through a loud speaker.

Program audio can be fed into one line of the headset to make personnel aware of the program audio with one ear and intercom audio with the

Figure 3.11: A studio intercom system.

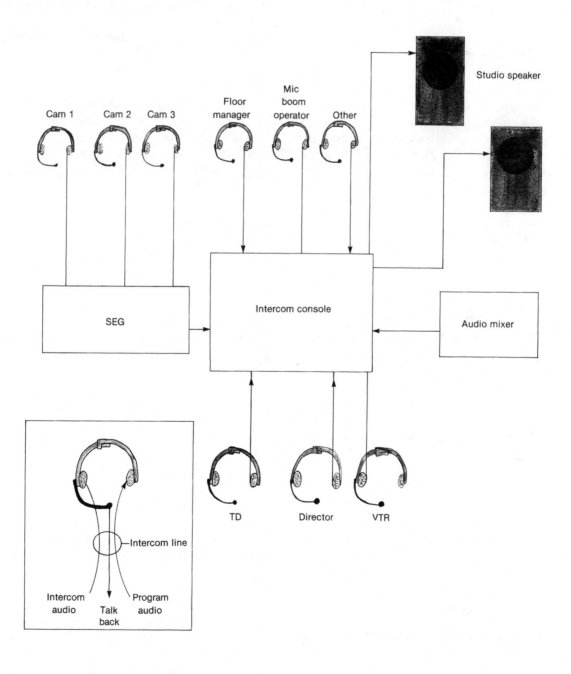

other. The studio speaker is switched off during shooting but is used to address talent and crew during set-up and rehearsal.

While intercom systems need not provide the same audio quality required for recording, they must have enough flexibility and clarity to accommodate the changing demands dictated by the different types of programs produced. Generally, a separate intercom system is required. However, intercom connections provided through the cameras and switchers may be adequate for smaller studios.

THE STUDIO LIGHTING SYSTEM

This section blocks out the basics of a small studio lighting system. Outlined will be the basic types of studio lights, or "luminaries," and some of the equipment associated with them. Techniques for using this equipment are discussed in Chapter 4. Emphasis has been placed on providing the reader with an overview and does not address the more complex systems found in larger studios.

Types of Studio Lights

A common lighting package for a small studio includes two floods, or broads, and four adjustable lights that can act as floods or spots, providing at least 6000 watts of illumination at 3200° Kelvin. Although not all lights may be used during particular scenes, for the greatest flexibility and ability to adapt to scene changes more lights prove useful, especially the smaller units.

Several types of lighting units are illustrated in Figure 3.12, though there are many more variations than shown. The flood provides a large, diffuse pool of light. At least one of the floods should be 2000 watts, so that it can be used as a key when high key lighting is required. "Soft lights" are floods with built-in diffusers. They are an excellent adjunct when flat, diffuse lighting is required.

While floods provide the base or main illumination for a set, the more focused lights create the lighting character and balance. Spots may be fix-focused by reflectors, but more often they are adjusted to focus at a particular distance by moving a simple fresnel lens nearer to or farther from the light element. These lights usually vary from 500 to 1200 watts, although more powerful spots are available.

Lighting Stands and Grids

Lighting stands are versatile and usually adequate for a small studio, although they can be expensive. Before choosing a lighting stand the following should be considered: working environment, weight capacity and height extension (at least 10 feet).

Lighting grids are very expensive, but they reduce the clutter of light stands on precious studio floor space. Grids can be purchased in prefabricated sections and adjusted for size. They are frequently made from ¾-inch or 1-inch pipe. The pipe diameter depends on the size of the space. In either case, it is a fairly expensive proposition, requiring a studio area with a ceiling height of at least 15 feet. Moreover, the room structure must be able to support the additional weight of grid and lights. While much in the small studio can be built and installed in-house, the lighting grid is an exception. Because of the structure and weight issues, the grid system should be installed by a lighting contractor.

Studio Lighting Accessories

If a lighting grid is used, extenders are needed. These include poles to reach lights and adjusting poles or "pantographs" that enable the lights to be directed. Safety lines that provide backup in case of clamp failure should also be used.

Other accessories may include color gels to add a feeling of warmth, coolness, cheer or gloom to a scene; pattern generators to create shadow and flicker, such as the light of a fire or the lights from the windows of a passing train; and a variety of "flags" and "gobos"—squares and circles of metal that can shade the spill from lights. Larger gobos are black curtains of material that can be hung to block larger spill areas.

The Lighting Board

At its simplest, a lighting board can be an assembly of power dimmers mounted on a wooden board to which all the lights are connected. Once lights are positioned, their level of illumination is controlled from the board. At its most sophisticated, the entire lighting sequence (combination and levels of lights operating at a given moment) is computer-controlled from the board. Many small studios use commercially produced boards that

Figure 3.12: Luminaries used in television production.

a. Scoop
(Courtesy Colortran, Inc.)

b. Adjustable flood/spot
(Courtesy Lowel-Light Mfg., Inc.)

c. Ellipsoidal spot
(Courtesy Colortran, Inc.)

d. Broad
(Courtesy Colortran, Inc.)

e. Portable reflectors light
(Courtesy Lowel-Light Mfg., Inc.)

f. Cyc strip elements
(Courtesy Colortran, Inc.)

g. Soft-light, set
(Courtesy Lowel-Light Mfg., Inc.)

offer computer control for small systems. The lighting board should be bought with the lighting grid, forming a complete lighting system.

OTHER STUDIO EQUIPMENT

Other studio equipment includes video monitors, a film/slide chain and tripods. Accessories include patch panels, distribution amplifiers and cables.

Monitors

For a four-camera studio, six picture monitors form the basis for the video monitoring system located in the control room. A seventh picture monitor located on the studio floor provides studio crew and talent a means of watching a playback as well as following the taping process.

The studio video monitor needs to be the largest and typically averages 19 to 20 inches (measured diagonally). This monitor only serves as reference for talent and crew. Because it is not used to make technical decisions, it does not need to be studio quality.

In the control room, the image appears on a set of camera monitors. There is one monitor for each camera. They are usually black and white with five- to eight-inch screens. To minimize space usage, they are offered in banks of four or three rackmountable units. In conjunction with these, two 12-inch color monitors are needed, one to preview images (preview monitor) and the other to show program output being recorded (program monitor). These two monitors are what the final images are judged by and should be of the finest quality. They serve to check set-up of the cameras and positioning of effects and graphics. These monitors should provide underscan and cross-pulse capabilities.

Film/Slide Chain

The ability to incorporate a variety of images from different media is an important feature for small studios that produce "live-type" programs. These programs generally do not use post-production, but tend to utilize the "switched" program feed. In nonbroadcast programs they often take the form of training programs that must be produced quickly in order to meet current demands.

To best exploit all the resources available, a method for incorporating existing program information is essential. This is especially true for the corporate producer who interfaces with other in-house media departments that work in traditional A/V media (slides and film).

The traditional film chain (see Figure 3.13) comprises an optical assembly that takes the image from a projector and positions it on a mirror so that a video camera's lens can pick it up. Drawbacks of this system include the need for exact lens alignment as well as precise positioning of camera and projector.

Recently, CCD technology has been mated with film and slide projectors, producing a transfer system that does not rely on external mirrors and cameras. Those transfer units provide a signal that is hooked in to the switcher and can be timed so that incorporation into the switching system is possible. They do not suffer from alignment difficulties and take up less room than traditional film chains.

With the advent of computer-based slide programs, many producers can now incorporate slides directly from the computer. The most common method involves using a PC board that fits in the host computer and transforms the signal into composite video signals.

Tripods

In most small-format studios, tripods on dollies are used. The hydraulically operated, counterbalanced pedestals used in large studios are designed for heavy broadcast studio cameras and are not necessary for most nonbroadcast productions.

The mounting head and the tripod itself should be matched to the weight of the cameras used in the studio. If the camera is too heavy for the head assembly it will cause premature wear of the head. In addition it will not safely hold the camera or work smoothly. Conversely, if the camera is too light for the head it will not be properly balanced, impeding smooth movement.

Fluid-head tripods use oil-cushioned, counterbalanced, spring-loaded mechanisms that compensate for the small irregular movements of the operator to achieve a smooth camera motion. Although they are relatively expensive, it is difficult to achieve a professional look without them. However, it should be noted that fluid heads must be properly balanced to work effectively.

Figure 3.13: Diagram of film/slide chain layout (top view).

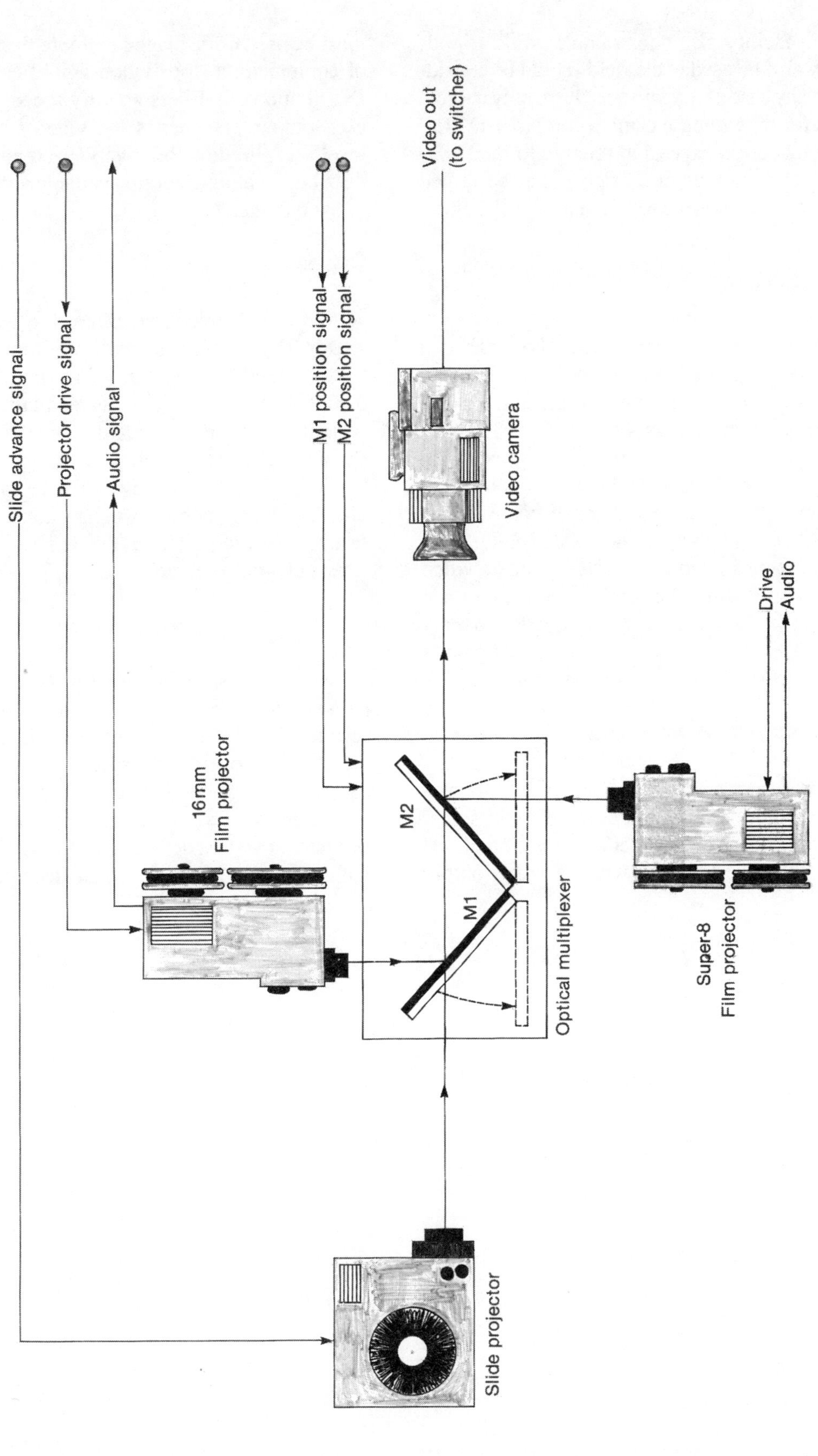

If the facility also does remote work, tripods that can also be used in the field should be considered. In any case, the studio need have only enough tripods for the in-house camera complement. Tripod rentals are inexpensive relative to their purchase price, so additional tripods can be rented when more cameras are required for special situations.

Patch Boards

Video patch boards (or patch panels) are needed to provide flexibility in studio set-up. Video patch panels are identical in format to the audio patch bay discussed earlier in this chapter; they simplify the interconnecting of production equipment. By keeping all signal inputs and outputs centralized, units can be easily connected and disconnected as required, without going to the back of equipment. They are constructed with BNC or other video connectors. Whether the patch panel is pre-made or built in-house it must use only quality connectors so as to ensure that no signal degradation is introduced through the patching system.

Video Distribution Amplifiers

Video signals must always maintain a full one-volt amplitude. Even a fractional drop in signal level can result in substantial deterioration of image quality. Accordingly, when a video output must be used or displayed by more than one piece of equipment, a distribution amplifier is needed. Distribution amplifiers amplify the signal so that each output line carries the video signal at full level (amplitude). Relatively inexpensive video distribution amplifiers are available with from two to ten outputs.

Cables

Audio and video cables are the veins of the studio. They provide signal flow from the source (i.e., camera) to the destination (i.e., VCR). Although often overlooked, cables play a very important part in making quality sound and images. For the studio, built-in house cabling represents a "major expense." The key to ensure success is to plan for change and to compare notes with other facilities before purchase (this holds true in every aspect of studio design).

CONCLUSION

Because the studio is the sum of many complex parts, each piece of equipment must be carefully selected in relation to other units. It is essential, therefore to consider the effect on the system of each part. Many studios that employ state-of-the-art equipment have produced programs with inferior audio due to a defective audio patch panel, or with an inferior image due to an inadequate tripod.

4 Shooting in the Studio: Production

A day in the studio is very expensive, and a great deal needs to be accomplished every hour. Even a modest production, in a modest studio, will cost hundreds of dollars per day, which add up fast. Accordingly, a studio shoot has to be planned, budgeted, set, lit, miked, staffed and directed with skill and concentration.

All these steps are discussed in some detail in this chapter. Again, as in the rest of this book, the material primarily addresses the independent and industrial producer, and therefore does not deal with budgets that allow for large staffs and salary structures.

PLANNING A STUDIO SHOOT

Good planning is not only the straight road to economy, but it is also the way to maximize the quality of a production. A well-planned shoot does not stress the talent and the staff needlessly, and therefore gets the best out of everyone, even though every studio hour is made to count.

Analyzing the Script

Planning begins, of course, with the script which dictates the sets, the talent and the action. By knowing these, the producer can determine the size of the studio required and how long it will be

needed. These conclusions are not casually arrived at. Before the studio is reserved, each shot or shot sequence will be analyzed for the following:

- the set and props required;
- the talent required;
- the lighting setup;
- setup time;
- the number of takes that may be required; and
- the duration of the shot.

From this, working lists can be prepared that itemize the following:

- sets and props;

- lighting setups (from which light plots can be made);

- studio time estimates (taking into account shot duration, number of probable takes and setup times, while allowing liberally for errors and breakdowns);

- talent time requirements (for each member of the cast); and

- production footage (the amount of tape needed).

59

The director's shot sheet, with each shot sequence identified and numbered in the order in which it will be shot, must also be prepared.

The only major facet of production left off this list is direction, which is entirely in the director's hands. Clearly, the lighting setups will be determined by the sets, action and camera moves—all of which are constrained by the director's handling of the script. (The director's functions and relationship to the rest of the staff are explained in Chapter 5.)

Determining the Shooting Sequence

One of the critical elements that determine how efficiently a production will be done is the shooting sequence. In a studio setting, the sets normally govern the shot sequences because setting up and lighting a specific set usually take the most off-camera time. Therefore, once a set is up and lit, it is most economical to shoot all the action that will take place on that set, making lighting adjustments as required during the course of different shot sequences.

However, the availability of talent may also be a consideration. If an important talent is only available for a specified part of the shooting time, the most efficient sequence may have to be reordered to accommodate him or her. Or, for example, if an actor appears only at the beginning and end of a show, it may be possible to shoot both scenes on the same day, so that he does not have to be paid for more than one day.

A major decision in a studio production is whether to cut the show on the SEG, or shoot footage that will be assembled in post-production. If a program includes remotes, it may be wiser to go for post-production assembly because it is difficult to match the "look" of the live-cut studio scenes with edited scenes assembled from footage shot on location. However, if the production is shot entirely in the studio, it may be most economical to cut the program to minimize post-production costs.

Of course, live-cut shows require planning, although not as much as live, on-air shows (which are now pretty much confined to news programs and some talk shows). The secret is to shoot in three-to-five minute segments, so that the pitch of the performance need only be sustained for short bursts by both talent and crew. This system is used regularly for sitcoms and soaps, where an entire show has to be shot in one day. Of course, these shows operate with from two to five standard sets per program and with a full complement of expert (and highly paid) staff, crew and talent that are accustomed to working with each other. While the average producer making a single program cannot expect that kind of readiness, he can still plan his way toward it.

Choosing the Studio

The producer ensures that everything and everybody that will be needed are present, and that the studio is ready for the production. If he is not dealing with an in-house studio, it is his job to choose the studio to be rented.

If the studio is to be rented, one feasible choice is a sound stage; this is a large, almost bare area that should have good acoustics and be well insulated from exterior sound. Sound stages are usually equipped with a lighting grid and can supply adequate power to meet television lighting requirements. Some have lights and a lighting board, dressing rooms and standard sets, like kitchen and living room sets. However, virtually all sound stages are set up for film, which is shot single-camera, and therefore do not have the control rooms required for multi-cam video. Since this may leave the director calling his shots from inconvenient places so that his voice will not appear on the audio track, a sound stage is usually rented with a mobile van for multi-camera video productions. The van serves as the control room, and all the equipment is set up and run from the van via "umbilical cords." The lower cost of the sound stage, therefore, has to be balanced against the high cost of bringing in the equipment.

More often, an equipped television studio is the best choice, especially when the basic rate includes virtually all the equipment that will be needed, and an engineer. In this case, an important variable is the cost of extra equipment that might be needed, such as an additional camera, teleprompter or graphics generator. The studio's policy with regard to overtime costs should also be checked.

Generally, better rates can be found at studios located away from major cities, but the costs of getting the talent and staff there may cancel any savings. In addition, the availability of qualified crew is usually more limited in suburbs than it is in the heart of town.

Once the studio is chosen, the rest of the production plan, including the budget, can be refined.

THE BASIC STUDIO PRODUCTION BUDGET

The budget form in Form 4.1 is basic; suitable for a small to mid-size production. Unless the producer is dealing with a major production for which he must separate above- and below-line costs, this form will suffice.[1] If any category exceeds the spaces provided, the relevant information can be listed and totaled on a separate page and the final figures entered in the appropriate place. This form deals solely with the direct costs of the production; it does not include overhead or profit. Nor does it include costs or fees for work done prior to the production (such as script development and writing), although some of these costs can be built into the staff time and spelled out under the catch-all, "other." (For these items, see the summary budget in Chapter 12.)

In any case, the budget form presumes that the producer has a script, has selected a studio and has done a lot of homework using some of the considerations discussed elsewhere in this book. If the studio is rented, he must know how much it will cost per day for setup, rehearsal and production. (The cost per hour or per diem is usually different for each stage.) He must also know the equipment and personnel included in the studio price, as well as the auxiliary facilities, such as dressing rooms, that are available.

The form starts with charges for the studio, and continues with additional equipment that will be needed. For example, the studio may provide two cameras, with a third costing extra. If the producer rents a sound stage and decides to rent a fully equipped mobile van, this cost is itemized in the budget form.

But whether the studio comes equipped, or a van is added, the production may still require such extras as a teleprompter, character generator, film/slide chain, graphics camera or graphics generator. Section 2 of the budget provides for these.

The third section of the budget includes set construction, which requires a sub-budget from which only the total is included here. Prop costs can be tallied from the prop list. "Graphics" includes anything that is prepared at additional cost, such as illustrations, photographs, slides or film. It can even include the cost of preparing electronic graphics, although these are usually introduced in post-production. Costumes may also require a sub-budget, if they are not supplied from a single source. While the makeup artist (who is usually part of the crew) generally provides the makeup, special items, such as wigs, masks or plastic blood for "wounds," would fit here.

For the small producer, the division between staff and crew need not conform to the categories used for the "above-" and "below-line" system employed for large productions and within corporate structures where accountants prevail. Rather, it is the division between those who work with the producer on a continuing basis and those who are hired on a per diem basis (usually for the mechanics of the actual production). Thus, the "staff," accounted for in the fourth section of the budgeted form, may include (besides the producer and director) the assistants to the producer and director, production assistants and the scenic and lighting designers, as well as other artistic personnel. If, however, the scenic or lighting designer comes with an extra per diem charge from the studio, he or she may be considered as crew. Whatever distinction is made between staff and crew, it should meet the user's needs and follow some logical parameters. However the crew (itemized in Section 5) is defined, there must be one person for each position—or at least for each major piece of equipment.

The talent is, of course, whoever appears in front of the camera. It may be one or more staff members of an industrial client, or it may be a group of professional actors. In the first case, this sixth section will be blank. In the second case, the budget might contain not only actors fees, but also a fee to their unions.

Local travel may include transportation of sets, props and supplies, as well as personnel—although the staff, talent and crew can usually be expected to get to the studio on their own. Nevertheless, there may be extra taxi or car runs for replacement items and people. The amount of videotape needed (budgeted for in the eighth section) should be augmented by some spare reels or cassettes—just in case. Supplies that don't seem to fit in elsewhere can go in this section.

---

[1] For large productions, the standard budget form developed for feature filmmaking by the American Society of Cinematographers (ASCI) may be useful. See the reference in the Bibliography.

Form 4.1:   Basic studio production budget.

Program title _____

Item	Qty	Item per day	No. days	Item total	Total
1. Studio fees					
Pre-Light _____	___	___	___	_____	XXXXXXXX
Rehearsal _____	___	___	___	_____	XXXXXXXX
Production _____	___	___	___	_____	XXXXXXXX
Knockdown _____	___	___	___	_____	XXXXXXXX
Mobile van _____	___	___	___	_____	XXXXXXXX
Studio subtotal	xxxx	xxxxxx	xxxxxx	xxxxxxxxx	$
2. Additional equipment					
Cameras _____	___	___	___	_____	XXXXXXXX
VTRs _____	___	___	___	_____	XXXXXXXX
Lighting _____	___	___	___	_____	XXXXXXXX
Audio _____	___	___	___	_____	XXXXXXXX
Accessory equipment ___	___	___	___	_____	XXXXXXXX
Other _____	___	___	___	_____	XXXXXXXX
_____	___	___	___	_____	XXXXXXXX
_____	___	___	___	_____	XXXXXXXX
_____	___	___	___	_____	XXXXXXXX
Equip. subtotal	xxxx	xxxxxx	xxxxxx	xxxxxxxxx	$
3. Sets, props, graphics					
Sets (from set list) _____	___	___	___	_____	XXXXXXXX
Props (from prop list)	___	___	___	_____	XXXXXXXX
Graphics _____	___	___	___	_____	XXXXXXXX
Costume _____	___	___	___	_____	XXXXXXXX
Makeup _____	___	___	___	_____	XXXXXXXX
Subtotal	xxxx	xxxxxx	xxxxxx	xxxxxxxxx	$
4. Staff					
Producer _____	___	___	___	_____	XXXXXXXX
Director _____	___	___	___	_____	XXXXXXXX
_____	___	___	___	_____	XXXXXXXX
_____	___	___	___	_____	XXXXXXXX
_____	___	___	___	_____	XXXXXXXX
_____	___	___	___	_____	XXXXXXXX
_____	___	___	___	_____	XXXXXXXX
Staff subtotal	xxxx	xxxxxx	xxxxxx	xxxxxxxxx	$
5. Crew					
Tech. director _____	___	___	___	_____	XXXXXXXX
Camera _____	___	___	___	_____	XXXXXXXX
Lighting _____	___	___	___	_____	XXXXXXXX
Audio _____	___	___	___	_____	XXXXXXXX
VTR _____	___	___	___	_____	XXXXXXXX
_____	___	___	___	_____	XXXXXXXX
_____	___	___	___	_____	XXXXXXXX
Crew subtotal		xxxxxx	xxxxxx	xxxxxxxxx	$
Page subtotal	xxxxxxxxxxxxxxxxxxxxxxxxxxxx				$

Form 4.1: Basic studio production budget (cont'd).

Item	Qty	Item per day	No. days	Item total	Total
Balance carried forward	xxxxxxxxxxxxxxxxxxxxxxxxxxxxxxxxxxxxxxxxxxxxxxx				$
6. Talent					xxxxxxxxxx
					xxxxxxxxxx
					xxxxxxxxxx
					xxxxxxxxxx
					xxxxxxxxxx
					xxxxxxxxxx
					xxxxxxxxxx
					xxxxxxxxxx
Talent Subtotal		xxxxxx	xxxxxx	xxxxxxxxxx	$
7. Local travel					
Van					xxxxxxxxxx
Car Rental					xxxxxxxxxx
Other					xxxxxxxxxx
Travel subtotal	xxxx	xxxxxx	xxxxxx	xxxxxxxxxx	$
8. Supplies					
Videotape					xxxxxxxxxx
Other					xxxxxxxxxx
					xxxxxxxxxx
					xxxxxxxxxx
					xxxxxxxxxx
Supplies subtotal	xxxx	xxxxxx	xxxxxx	xxxxxxxxxx	$
9. Commissary					
Meals	xxxx				xxxxxxxxxx
Catering	xxxx				xxxxxxxxxx
Commis. subtotal	xxxx	xxxxxx	xxxxxx	xxxxxxxxxx	$
10. Insurance					
Production ins.	xxxx				xxxxxxxxxx
Other	xxxx				xxxxxxxxxx
Subtotal	xxxx	xxxxxx	xxxxxx	xxxxxxxxxx	$
11. Other					
					xxxxxxxxxx
					xxxxxxxxxx
					xxxxxxxxxx
					xxxxxxxxxx
	xxxx	xxxxxx	xxxxxx	xxxxxxxxxx	xxxxxxxxxx
Subtotal					$
Budget subtotal	xxxx	xxxxxx	xxxxxx	xxxxxxxxxx	$
Contingency (%)	xxxx	xxxxxx	xxxxxx	xxxxxxxxxx	$
Total studio budget	xxxx	xxxxxx	xxxxxx	xxxxxxxxxx	$

The commissary, item nine, is one of the givens of film and television productions. The old Hollywood studios found that it was a lot cheaper to feed their expensive personnel on the lot than wait for them to get back from what could be a very long and "liquid" lunch. Feeding people simply but well on the set also makes good sense because people take their meals and coffee breaks more seriously than they will admit. The investment a producer makes in catering (within reason) to a variety of dietary preferences is returned—with interest—when the production resumes.

Insurance includes policies that cover everything from equipment breakdown, to the lead talent's shingles, to small, specific two-day policies for specific equipment. "Other" is everything else, such as music fees, for example (if the music is inserted during production). The contingency fee is usually 5%, and covers unexpected problems that invariably crop up and add costs; for instance, the essential prop that breaks and has to be replaced, the extra money paid a last-minute stand-in and, above all, the overtime costs that are incurred while the whole production waits for these problems to be resolved.

SETS AND SETTINGS FOR TELEVISION PRODUCTION

When the average person thinks of sets, he thinks of the theater, the lavish sets of the Hollywood film or the garish sets of television game shows. These sets, through which people move, are made of wood, plastic, cloth and other solid materials. But television can do with very little of such sets, because the medium does not necessarily take place in "real space." Rather, the images on the screen, even when the contain people, exist in a different dimension: "videospace."

Videospace and Television Sets

A classic set for television is the "void" or "limbo," in which a person is seen against a gray or beige background of seemingly infinite depth. This type of set is often used for talk shows and interview segments and is achieved by lighting the subject from the front and back, leaving the background in shadow. The effect is most easily achieved when the background is a pale cloth that absorbs light evenly, but any non-white material can be used, providing the lighting is correctly set

and the talent is placed away from the background. A variation on this kind of set is the "cameo," where a black background is used to obtain a very high-contrast effect.

Limbo is just one type of video space; there are many other options available to the producer. "Chromakey space," for example, enables the producer to put his talent practically anywhere on earth—and off it—at the touch of a button, merely by providing the appropriate image for the chromakey. The studio "set" is then a chromakey drop, which need be nothing more than blue or green seamless photographers' paper—depending on the color on which the chromakey unit operates. TV commercials regularly make use of this creative device, putting actors in remote mountain valleys or dwarfing them among the boxes of a product. Dramatic and other productions can also take advantage of chromakey, especially when the talent does not have to interact with the set. When interaction is necessary, chromakey can be used to provide a background, as effectively and less expensively than rear projection (such as the view of a city behind a small rooftop set).

An extension of the key is provided by the various frame-store and raster manipulation devices that can "squeeze," position, rotate, border and even mix any television raster, and incorporate it into a program. Such devices are regularly used on a number of news programs, to permit people from various geographic areas to appear on a program at one time. While this type of video effect seems to be far from the subject of sets, it is not. Consider the contemporary television news set; it is usually almost monastic in its simplicity, because the real set for the television news program is the world.

Sets may also be generated as computer graphics, like the computer sets of the movie *Tron*. While this form of image generation is expensive, and still in its infancy, its potential for imaginative settings is enormous. Considering the sizable graphics capabilities of microcomputers costing only a few hundred dollars, it is an area for producers to explore. (See the note on computer/video interfaces in Chapter 11.)

Other Set Considerations for Video

The making of physical sets for television requires a good knowledge of the techniques of stage and film set design, and sources are listed in the Bibliography. However, television studios use three items that are not standard for other media: risers, flats and cycs.

• *Risers* are low platforms of plywood set on a frame of two-by-fours or two-by-sixes (see Figure 4.1a). They are designed to raise the talent above floor level, so that they can be shot straight on instead of from the slightly higher camera angle required by most studio tripods and camera platforms. That is why risers are almost invariably used for talk shows, where the talent is seated. Risers are usually heavily carpeted, not only for cosmetic reasons, but also because they are hollow, and therefore noisy.

• *Flats* for small television studios are usually made on 8' x 4' frames reinforced with a crosspiece and corner braces (see Figure 4.1b). These can be assembled into larger units with clamps, or hinges with removable pins. Flats are basic units for the creation of nonelectronic backgrounds, as almost any kind of graphic background can be prepared and attached to them. When set at angles to one other, a wall of flats becomes self-supporting.

• *Cycs, ground rows and strip lights* are other devices used to create studio sets. Cycs, short for "cyclorama," are floor-length curtains (usually of beige or very pale blue) that are hung from a track (see Figure 4.1c). When the pale tone of the cyc is reasonably matched by the color of the studio floor, the use of a "ground row" that obscures the bottom of the cyc, creates the effect of a deep and borderless space. The ground row is 12" to 18" high and runs the width of the extended cyc. To light the cyc evenly from the bottom, "strip lights" are used. These may be white, or colored for specific effects. Sections of the cyc can be used as rear projection screens, and the whole cyc can be used for different lighting effects, from realistic changes of daylight to abstract effects. (Lighting the set and leaving the cyc unlit is one of the ways to create an effective limbo.) One of the fringe benefits of the cyc is that it absorbs sound, so it is helpful to keep it in place even when it is not part of the set.

Because the construction of elaborate sets is normally more expensive than shooting on location, they are reserved for large-budget productions. For such sets as are needed on small-scale productions, simple materials such as paper, cardboard and styrofoam, will accomplish a great deal if carefully worked. Furnishings, as well as most other props, can be rented on a daily or weekly basis from second-hand furniture stores that cater to the theater and television trades. Provided there are no gross breaks, tears or stains (and extreme closeups of the furniture are avoided), television can make old furniture look a lot better than it really is.

What to Avoid in Sets and Costumes

• Avoid anything with large areas of red. The American television standard (NTSC) has trouble with red, and tends to smear large areas of it—particularly on second and later generations of low-band format video.

• Stay away from large areas of black or white. The camera will make the blacks blacker or the whites whiter to compensate, sending both white and black video levels to the moon.

• Avoid complicated checks and stripes; they cause the generation of moving moire patterns that can distract the viewer.

Remember that the most important word for sets—as for everything in video—is K.I.S.S.: Keep It Simple, Stupid!

LIGHTING THE SET

The bottom line for television lighting is enough light to enable the camera to record the scene at optimum specifications. When an area of the set is underlit, the blacks and darker grays get very noisy, and the scene in general has an "underwater" look. As a rule, lower-end cameras need more light than do expensive models to generate acceptable images.

Good lighting is invisible, just like good direction. Lighting sets the mood, and it reinforces the feeling that the scene needs to convey. It also focuses the viewer's attention on the main point of a shot, whether it be the talent, the background or a detail.

To light well and creatively requires much more than simply learning the rules. But there are ba-

Figure 4.1: Flats, risers and cycs.

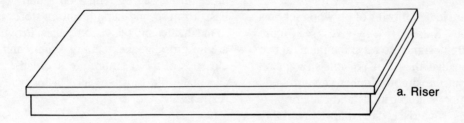

a. Riser

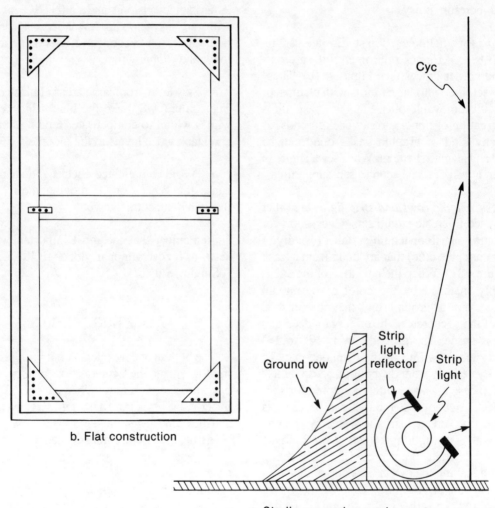

b. Flat construction

Cyc

Ground row

Strip light reflector

Strip light

c. Studio cyc and ground row

sics—standard television lighting considerations and a few lighting setups—that form a useful structure from which to work.

General Lighting Considerations

Baselight

Baselight is the standard illumination level for which television cameras are normally rated. Most color cameras are rated for a standard illumination of 200 footcandles (fc) at an aperture setting of f/4. Were a set to be evenly lit so that wherever the camera pointed it would see 200 fc of illumination, then the set would be, in effect, lit by baselight. Actually, simple, flat baselighting is not uncommon, especially since it has been made so easy with the introduction of the softlight—a professional luminaire that provides a diffuse 500, 1000 or 2000 watts to cover a wide angle with even, bright light. Baselighting helps to create the kind of shadowless neutrality we have become accustomed to seeing in television game, talk or news shows.

Color Temperature

Another crucial aspect of lighting is its color temperature. This is an international standard that describes the "color" of the radiation emitted by a standard "black body" at a given temperature, measured on the Kelvin scale. In this scale, degrees are in Centigrade (Celsius), and 0° Kelvin equals –273.1° Centigrade. At 0°K, the standard black body has a temperature of 0°. But as it heats, its color temperature changes, becoming first red, then yellow, then gradually becoming a bluish white as it reaches the color temperature of bright, unfiltered sunlight, at about 6500°K.

As discussed in the Technical Appendix, all television color is designed around this daylight norm. However, in the studio, the yellowish light of tungsten at 3200°K is the lighting standard, which is compensated for in the camera by means of filters and white-balance adjustments.

Nevertheless, if all the lights are not at the same color temperature, the apparent color of the subject and the set will change as the camera moves from area to area. It is therefore important that a constant color temperature be established and maintained throughout a shot.

Inverse Square Law

Understanding the inverse square law is particularly critical for lighting, because it seems to contradict common sense. It seems logical, for example, that if a light is 4 feet from an object and we move it to 8 feet away, then we will only have half the light, because the amount of light will decrease proportionally. In actuality, however, we only have one quarter of the illumination on our object that we had at the outset. The inverse square law says, in effect, that the amount of light reaching a surface from a source decreases with the *square* of the distance from the source. It does not decrease proportionately. Thus, if we double (x2) the distance, we must multiply the light remaining not by 1 over 2, but by $1/2^2$, or 1/4th. In practical terms, this means that at eight feet from the object you now need *four* lights to do the job of *one* at four feet. Conversely, if we take a light that is 8 feet away and move it to within 4 feet, the amount of light on the object will not double, it will *quadruple*. Clearly, the inverse square law cannot be broken with impunity on a television set.

Measuring Television Lighting

To measure the amount of light available, nothing beats the final user: the camera. (While light meters can be checked, they really relate far better to film, where there is a far larger gray scale [range of grays between white and black] to play with and no other way to judge the light.) First of all, the way the image looks on the (preadjusted) studio monitor will indicate if the lighting is generally correct. This monitor will show if there are gross imbalances: color temperature differences, hot spots and shadows, as well as over- and underlit areas.

Another important indicator is the waveform monitor, which will identify overlit areas and hot spots as excessive video level. But the test equipment should not have the last word on lighting. A final check of the program monitor will not only tell if the lighting is technically correct, but whether it looks right to the final judges—the director and producer. Yet, even if the overall setup looks good, the perfect balance achieved in a medium shot may, on a closeup, break out into white blotches from overlighting. Before the first take, every camera move in a scene should be checked to avoid mid-scene disasters.

Set-to-background Distance

In the studio, the talent and the props must be away from the back of the set or the drop. This is necessary to minimize shadows on the background and to minimize the amount of light needed to wash out shadows. Ideally, the studio will be large enough so that the distance to the background will be great enough so that all the shadows can fall into the gap. Since this is not always the case, the producer often has to be content to keep the action as far from the background as possible.

Lighting Balance

Unless uneven lighting serves a dramatic purpose, equal parts of the set should be equally well lit. Similarly, if more than one person is on cam-

era, as in a dramatic presentation or a talk show, it is important that each person be lit equally in both intensity and color temperature. If one person (or area) is lit correctly and another is underlit, either the latter person (or area) should be given more light or, in some cases, the light on the first person (or area) should be brought down, and the camera opened up. There are no hard-and-fast rules, but it is important to know that "more light" is not always the right call.

Basic Lighting Setups

There are a number of basic lighting patterns used throughout the industry. Some are so simple a producer can use them without the aid of a lighting designer.

Figure 4.2: Lighting setup with softlights and backlights for flat keyless lighting.

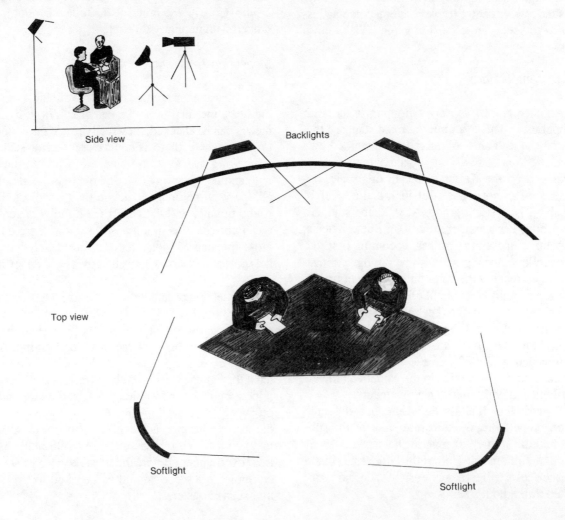

Figure 4.3: Basic three-point lighting.

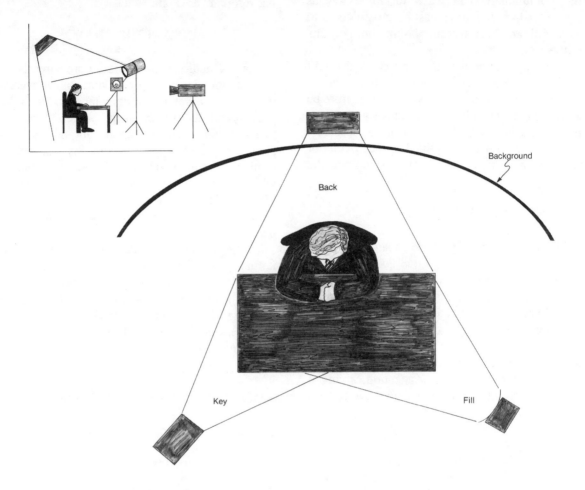

Flat Lighting

Figure 4.2 illustrates how a small set can be evenly illuminated with two softlights and two backlights. The lighting is unexciting and without character, but flat lighting serves many purposes and is often used. Unless the set is particularly dark or reflective, this kind of lighting will minimize shadows and hot spots.

Three-Point Lighting

Another basic pattern uses a "three-point" lighting configuration (shown in Figure 4.3) that consists of a *key light* (the apparent light source); a *fill light* (to soften shadows, especially those cast by the key); and a *back light* (which lights people and objects around the edges to pull them visually out of the background).

The angle at which the key light is placed in relation to the subject can vary. Low and covered with a warm pink gel, it can be the rosy light of dawn coming through the window; high, harsh and white, it can be the bare bulb on the ceiling of a jail cell. The closer the angle of the light is to the angle of the camera viewpoint, the flatter the light (as in our preceding setup with the softlights). As the angle moves away from the camera position, features and shadows become more defined. A spotlight with a fresnel lens is often used for a key light, because the light can be focused or diffused. To simulate a streetlight, for example, it can be focused; to simulate office ceiling lighting, it can be diffused. Colored gels can be clipped to this or any light for visual effect.

Fill light is provided by means of a moderately diffuse light that reduces shadows without washing out detail. It is directed from the side of the camera opposite to that of the key light. A wide range of luminaries can be used for fills, as long as they are adjustable, or at least have barn doors to trim spill, and keep it from washing out portions of the scene.

Back light is one-half to three-fourths as bright as the key light. It is generally positioned about 45° off the camera line of sight, and it may be above or below that line. If its angle is greater and it is above the subject, it will generate shadows that will then have to be filled. Either floods or spots can be used for back light, depending on the situation.

Adding Spots and Set Lights

Three-point lighting can be expanded by adding spots and set or background lights and additional fills as needed (see Figure 4.4).

Spots are focused lights that illuminate a small area. In television, they can be used much like theatrical spots to bathe a performer in a pool of light, or their effect can be much more subtle. Spots can, for example, illuminate an object on the set, and attract the viewer's attention, giving it dramatic impact without changing the camera angle.

Spots can also be used to lighten small, dark areas. They are often used to light the faces of dark-skinned people on a set where light-skinned people are also present. To do justice to both shades, one approach is to light the light-skinned people first and then spotlight the dark-skinned people, working to achieve balanced illumination on both.

Background or set light illuminates the objects and scenery behind the talent and is set up only after the rest of the scene and the talent have been lit. The light on the background can be adjusted in relation to the other lights until the correct balance is achieved. Almost any type of light can "wash" the back of a set.

Lighting for Cameos and Limbo

Limbo and cameo sets (discussed earlier in this chapter), often used for talk shows, require special lighting. As shown in Figure 4.5, both the key and back lights are directed onto the set and the talent, while the background remains entirely unlit. This gives the impression that the set is in an area with undefinable space. Whether the effect is one of

limbo or of a cameo depends on the tone of the background (see Figure 4.1).

AUDIO IN THE STUDIO

For the audio recordist, there are three basic types of sound sources: environmental, conversational and musical. Environmental sound includes background audio from such sources as streets, factories and audiences. Conversational sound includes people talking one at a time, as in speeches, seminars and dramatic dialogue. Music is music, whether it is a full orchestra or one person with a bird-whistle. Beyond these sounds there is synthesized sound, a specialized area we will not cover here.

In this section, we will discuss sound that is normally encountered in the studio: voice, music and effects (simulated ambient sounds). In the chapter on location shooting, we will deal with handling environmental sound. Although environmental sound may be used to create background audio in studio-recorded programs, this is added in post-production and is discussed in Chapter 7.

Basic Sound Recording Considerations

Before mapping out some basic sound recording techniques for the studio, it will help to note some general rules for recording sound for video.

Recording with Sync Sound

Video should never be recorded without sync (ambient) sound, because this is the reference audio. Even when double system recording is being used, or post-production dubbing is planned, one track of the videotape recording should carry the sync sound.

In most studio situations, the sync sound is intended for the final recording, and the action is carefully miked to that end, so that this issue does not arise. But in those situations where later dubbing or mixing is planned, and in almost all location shoots, recording the live audio created in the course of the action is important.

This audio can prove useful. It can serve as ambience; even if dubbing is done. The little sounds of life—the scrape of a chair, the tinkle of ice in a glass, the rub of clothing—give the sound a lifelike quality too often missing when a pure dub is made. The sync sound should also be recorded for

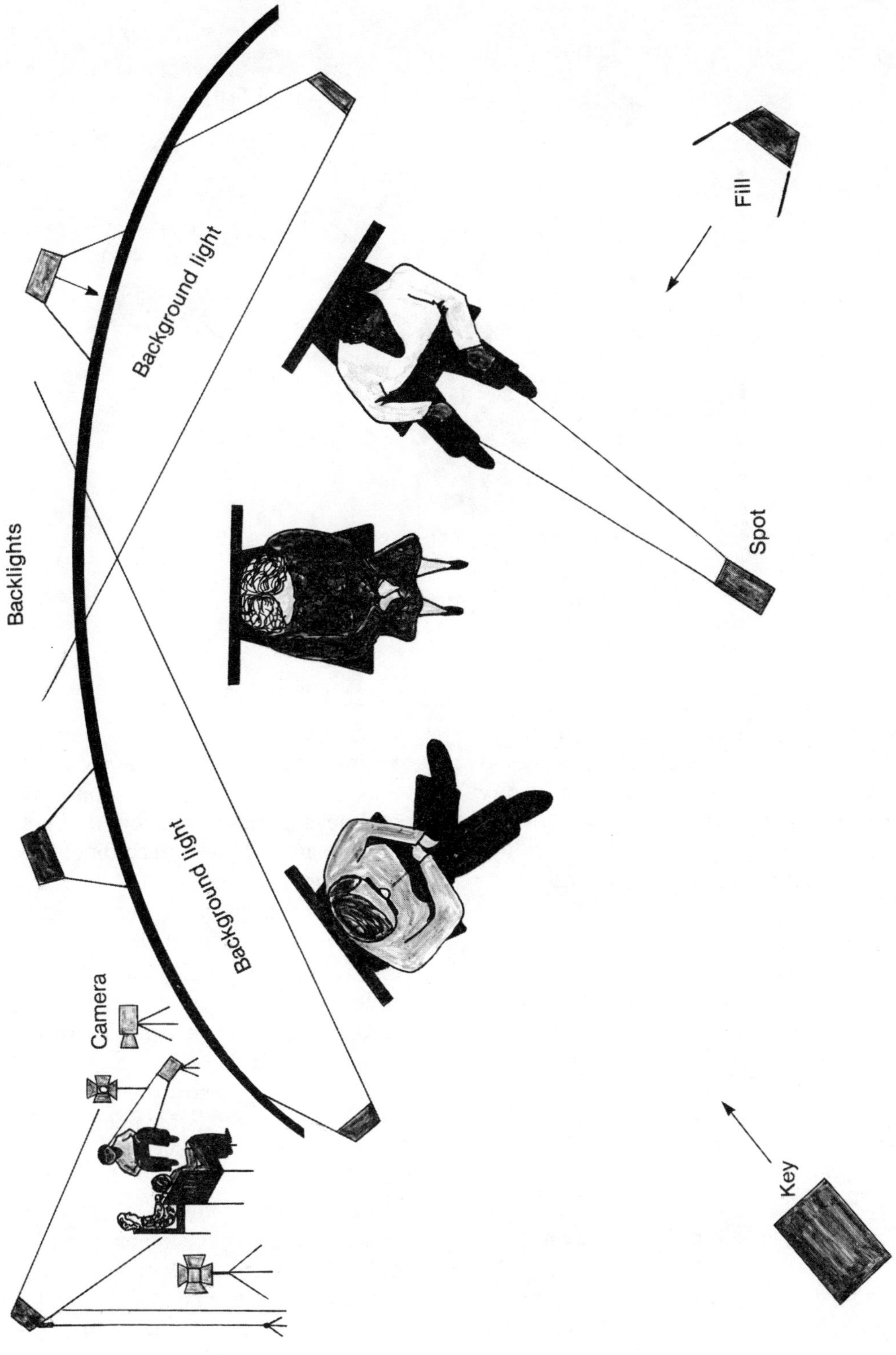

Figure 4.4: Basic lighting with wider background and spot lighting.

Figure 4.5: Lighting setup for limbo and cameos.

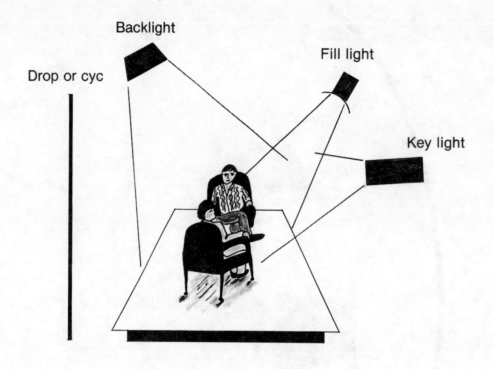

safety. Sometimes the sound planned simply does not work out, and only the original sound can save the day. It does not cost anything to record sync sound, so if it is not used, nothing is lost.

Recording Double System Sync Sound

As was noted in Chapter 3, when sync sound for video is recorded on audiotape, the audiotape recorder must either have crystal-controlled sync, or it must be able to record the time code used for the video on a separate track. If this is not done, the only way to resync the audio with the video is manually, at great trouble and expense.

Care in Time Code Recording

If time code is recorded on its own address track, this is not pertinent to audio recording. However, if time code is to be recorded on the second audio track, it can severely affect the audio recording. The problem is that since the time code must be recorded at a high level, it can "bleed" over to the program audio on the other track, especially in th ¾-inch and ½-inch video formats where the guard band between the two audio tracks is very narrow. As a result, the program audio will be permanently mixed with the time code signal and will not be usable. This bleed is not necessarily audible at the time of recording, because the recordist is listening E-to-E—to what is being recorded, rather than to what is on the tape.

Therefore, time code should never be recorded on an audio track at the same time that the original sound is being recorded. Rather, it should be stripped in later, as a separate operation. Since it requires only a single pass, this can be done when a workprint or window dub is made. In this case, the program audio is recorded on channel 2 and the time code is dubbed onto channel 1 to avoid problems with equipment that has only single-channel dub capability. On the other hand, if simultaneous time code dubbing on an adjacent audio channel cannot be avoided, then it should not be recorded at the maximum level, but at a lower level—at between –1db to –3db on the VU meter. However, it will have to be amplified for use in editing or making window dubs. Although "bleeding" across tracks does not often occur, it is not worth taking a chance.

Recording Speech in the Studio

Recording Talent in Place

In the studio, interviews and panel discussions are the norm, while the single speaker is a special case.

What characterizes this setup in audio terms is that everyone stays put. It is easy, therefore, to mic everyone with a lavalier, bring the lines directly into the mixer and set levels for each speaker involved (see Chapter 3 for more on microphones). Lavaliers are designed just for this kind of recording as they are very small, easy to hide on clothing, relatively insensitive to background noise and give excellent voice reproduction. Nevertheless, it is useful to have a single cardioid mic that is hung above the set to record whatever happens as reference sound. If one of the speaker's mics goes down, for example, there will still be a recording. It is, of course, necessary to get the best possible match between the cardiod and the lavaliers. This is not easy to do, but should be attempted at the time the mics are bought or rented. Another alternative is to give each speaker a pair of lavaliers.

Recording Talent in Motion

In dramatic productions, and in other programs where a fair amount of movement is involved, other miking approaches have to be used.

To mic for movement, it is necessary to use cardioid mics hung on booms, fishpoles or on hangers from the lighting grid. If the number of speakers is small, and they will not move far apart during a scene, it is often possible to use a single mic on a boom, because it can be kept within a consistent audio distance from the group by a boom operator. If, however, the program deals with widespread movement on a set, where several people are speaking from several locations, then it is necessary to use several mics hung at different locations from the lighting grid above the set and operated from the mixer.

A setup for the dramatic script segment used in Chapter 1 is shown in Figure 4.6. As can be seen, two mics have been set up, one for Jack at the door, and one in the middle of the set for Anne. As the scene opens, we pan and pull back on the set. The only sound is that of Anne's footsteps, off-camera, picked up by Mic 2, Mic 1 is off. When the camera is wide enough to show Jack standing

at the door, we close Mic 2 and open Mic 1 to get his line. Then we switch cameras (see marked script in the next chapter) to pick up Anne and open Mic 2 as she enters and crosses toward this mic, leaving Mic 1 open. (The computer beeps and the audio for the man on the screen comes into the mixer on a line input.) For the rest of the scene, both mics are open, picking up Jack at the door, while mic 2 picks up Anne over the small area in which she moves. (See the Floor Plan in Chapter 5, Figure 5.1.)

Television has to meet our expectations of reality in terms of audio as well as video. Therefore, when the viewer's relationship to a sound source changes, its level should change too, maintaining "sound perspective." For example, if a rider is first seen in a very long shot and rides toward the viewer's point of view, we expect that the sound of the horse's hooves striking the ground will get louder as he approaches. Similarly, if the camera holds on the point of view of speaker A, while speaker B, who is talking, walks out of the room, then we expect that the voice of speaker B will drop in level as he moves away (a boom mic should follow him).

However, it should be noted that sound, like light, obeys the inverse square law explained earlier in this chapter. If a mic is moved from 2 feet from the subject to 4 feet from the subject, the amount of sound picked up will not be halved, it will be cut by three-fourths. Accordingly, to compensate for this, the mic in the example above should not stay with Speaker A, but move part of the way with Speaker B as he walks so that his voice does not fall off too rapidly. For the same reasons, boom mics that are pulled out of the way when a camera pulls back must be moved slowly, because any change in the distance from source to mic is greatly exaggerated by the inverse square law and is very noticeable on the recording.

Recording Music in the Studio

Sound studios, unlike television studios, are basically designed for people who work in front of a mic, and their surfaces are designed to provide the proper amount of sound reflection without creating echoes, or otherwise sounding "boomy." TV studios are designed primarily for movement in front of cameras. They tend to be so well baffled (sound absorbent) that they have no audio reflectivity at all, or they have pockets where un-

Figure 4.6: Mic setup for dramatic scene.

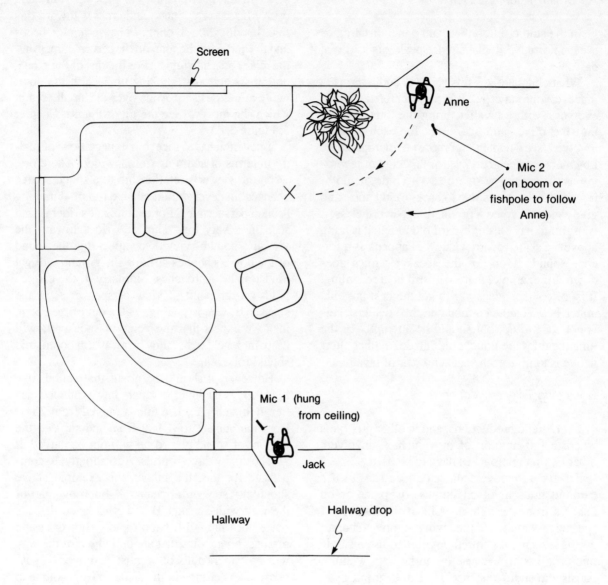

Figure 4.7: Mic set for recording a small group of musicians.

wanted reflections create excessive boom and reverb. If the studio is too "dead," this can be countered by putting some hard flats behind the musicians to give the sound a live, natural quality. On the other hand, if the studio is not baffled enough, it will be necessary to hang curtains or put up sound absorbent material to deaden the excessive audio reflection.

One of the factors that makes music particularly hard to record well is the need to record all the sound that is being created, including the over- and undertones. When we record human speech, we are less interested in the ambient aural nuances, because we are primarily interested in what the people are saying—in meaning—and in the emotional tone in which it is being said. That is why we use mics such as lavaliers, which pick up the voice and its tone even through a couple of layers of clothing, though they dampen much of the ambient sound quality in the process.

This is not so with music. With singing, the words are secondary to the sheer sound of the voice that is singing them. The sound of instruments is pure sound, and we want to hear it to the last reverberation. This means that music must be recorded with mics of great sensitivity and brilliance. But such mics also pick up every breath, the rub of fabrics, the squeak of a camera dolly wheel. Microphones designed for music recording have a flat response over as much of the audio range as possible—from 30 to 20,000Hz. These microphones can be rented at relatively low cost.

A setup for recording a small group with a vocalist in a studio is shown in Figure 4.7. When music is recorded in the studio, the mics can be hung above the musicians, above the range of the highest camera. This will be especially effective for the brass and percussion instruments, which produce audio at a high level. On the other hand, if the group uses strings and woodwinds, it may be necessary to hide mics in the music stands to pick up these instruments at a level at which they can be balanced with the brass and percussion instruments. For the vocalist, a mic on a stand, or a handheld mic is visually acceptable. Vocalists' mics are of a special design. Like a lavalier, the transducers of these mics are suspended within their case so that they do not produce noise with normal handling. These mics also incorporate a "pop" filter. This is a device that dampens response to the small puffs of air that vocalists constantly generate when they "mug" the mic.

Most videotaping of musical performances is, in any case, done on location. The problems and possibilities of recording music video out of the studio are covered more fully in Chapter 7.

THE "LIVE" EVENT

Business Television (BTV) is the one of the newest uses of live broadcasting and is considered a type of teleconferencing. BTV is one-way television broadcast via satellite to multiple locations, often with two-way audio communication. BTV is used by corporations and agencies to inform, educate and train their work forces.

This form of teleconferencing is a challenge to the video producer because it represents a return to "live" television production techniques. Most crews, directors and producers have grown accustomed to working with multiple takes and to working out problems during the post-production stage. However, BTV stresses the importance of having a studio crew that can work well under the constraints of producing programs that are transmitted live.

BTV program development uses the same techniques and follows the same steps as other video programs. In addition, BTV programs often incorporate pre-produced segments of videotape. Therefore, they may call for a mixture of live production and what is now considered traditional producing procedures. Live television production entails developing and coordinating the many elements of the video program from the start of transmission through the running of the final credits.

CONCLUSION

Whether producing a "live" event or taping for future post-production, shooting in the studio places great emphasis on knowing the facility, the crew and on having clearly defined program objectives. The producer must know what he will need to make his program effective, and must ensure that those needs are met.

5 Shooting in the Studio: Staff and Crew

A lot of people are needed to make a television program, and the jobs are generally divided into two categories: staff and crew. Staff includes the traditionally nontechnical types (such as producers, production managers, coordinators and casting directors), while the crew consists of those who operate the video equipment and get the program on tape.

The following is a rundown of the various job titles one is likely to encounter in the television industry. Of course, not every production will require all of the people listed here.

STAFF AND CREW

A great deal of industry budget talk deals with "above-the-line" and "below-the-line" personnel charges and status. The terms refer to a standard division between personnel on salary (those who work for a set annual amount, regardless of how much time they put in), and those on wages (those who are paid by the day or hour and are paid for overtime). Salaried personnel are above-the-line, and those paid on a time unit basis are below-the-line. Contract personnel (people hired for a specific project on a fee basis) are also above-the-line. In production, contract personnel often includes the talent and consultants, such as casting directors, special effects creators, scenic designers and the like. Producers and directors also work for

set fees if they are not on salary, so they, too, are above-the-line.

These are the primary distinctions between the two categories, but there are a lot of gray areas. Every large organization will have its own system for the fine points. If the production is sufficiently large, the producer will be assisted by a production manager and accountants, who will be conversant with the industry's standard budget and allocation procedures. For most small and independent productions, these distinctions are less useful than the three categories of staff, crew and talent.

The Staff

The executive producer (EP) holds the highest rank on a production roster, as he or she is the person who puts the project together. The project is often his idea, but most important, he raises the money for it (or convinces those in charge that it should be spent). The executive producer handles all contract negotiations and hires the top people, starting with the producer and director. His degree of involvement beyond this point is a matter of personal style; some EPs are rarely seen on the set, while others appear almost daily. Sometimes the EP only intervenes out of necessity: if the producer and director are having daily shootouts, it is the EP (or "exec") who must resolve the problem.

The producer is the glue that holds everything together, and the oil that makes the production flow smoothly. Since the division of labor between the executive producer and the producer varies, the producer may be responsible for most of the hiring of personnel, including the talent. Even where he is not responsible for hiring, he is usually consulted.

The producer is also ultimately responsible for the day-to-day production operations: schedules, budgets, procurement, payroll and the mitigation of hurt feelings. Some producers may have a great deal of input into the content and aesthetics of a production. Above all, the producer is an administrator, and his staff (if he has any) may include any or all of the following.

The production manager is a producer's first line of defense (or offense, as it is sometimes perceived). The production manager usually handles the administrative aspects of a production, including budgets, schedules and the procurement of facilities, equipment, props, materials and what-have-you, including the commissary. If a "sky hook" (something to hang the sky on—an old backstage joke) is needed, it is the production manager who will get it. In short, this person keeps the production on schedule and on budget.

The production coordinator may be just another title for the production manager, but if it is a separate job, this person is primarily concerned with seeing that schedules are met. The production manager may find and order the sky hook, but the coordinator sees that it gets to the right place at the right time and is returned in good order to its supplier. He schedules the cast and may be responsible for the "call." The call may literally be that: a morning call to ensure that everyone arrives on time for the first run-through, for makeup or for whatever their first step will be.

The line producer is a master technician who is responsible for all below-the-line operations, which may or may not involve facility procurement and staffing. He is the person responsible for getting the action on tape. Accordingly, he is in charge of all the equipment used and all the personnel that operate it. He is in charge of getting the equipment and personnel to the shooting site, and seeing that everything works. He is also in charge of the crew.

The associate producer plays the same role as any assistant producer, but is one notch higher. If the production is so large that several producers

are needed to act at a fairly high level, the producer may have one or more associates who can act on his behalf, and one or more assistants who report to the associates. Giving someone with a loosely defined role the title of assistant producer is also a way of rewarding someone for his or her contribution to a production, and of fitting in someone essential, who may not have a defined role.

The production assistant is lowest in the general pecking order—up only one notch from an untitled "go-fer" (someone who "goes for" things and fetches them), but it is nevertheless an excellent job for someone just getting started in the industry. It is important to a production to have one or more intelligent and generally capable people who can be asked to do anything, from fetching a prop to holding a scrim or logging the takes for the day. The production assistant can learn a great deal about many aspects of television production in a very short time.

The casting director is a person whose sole business is to know professional actors, so that he will have a large stable of types and talented individuals for the producer to consider. His fee is geared to the talent budget, and a good casting director can save a producer more than he costs.

The script supervisor keeps track of what has been shot and what has not, checking for continuity, if a continuity person is not part of the staff. A script supervisor (or someone who acts in that capacity) is essential if the script is shot film style: single-camera and out of sequence.

The director and the entire artistic staff are covered in a separate section later in this chapter.

The Technical Crew

The production organization may be perfect and the artistic staff may be great, but it is the technical crew that is responsible for the quality of the video that gets on the tape. Shaky zooms, late cuts and overly long dissolves, nose shadows on chins and boom-mic shadows on the wall, flutter on the bottom audio—these are the kinds of things a poor crew can be responsible for without even trying. The wise producer will choose his crew as carefully as his talent and keep them happy.

The technical director (TD) not only knows how-everything in the studio works, but he can set up and execute every shot or effect and any number of sequential transitions the director has called for. Before the production, the TD balances the cameras and checks the quality of the video recording. When the production starts, he sits at the switcher and creates the sequence of shots that the director's script calls for. To do this, he works closely with the director in advance, to make sure that what the latter had in mind will work as he had envisioned.

The camera operator and his importance to a production has traditionally been recognized by directors, but by very few others. In the hands of a skilled camera operator, the image on the screen seems to be the natural field of the eye. The camera's movements seem as simple and unconscious as those of the eye itself, although they may be quite complex. A camera person may also be a "lighting/camera," and in that case he will also be able to set the lights for the shoot.

The audio person is in control of the sound. He mics the performers and monitors their recording throughout the production. In the studio, he can make a good audio situation better and the sound more "alive." In the field, he can make good sound out of an impossible audio recording situation. The audio person has his own copy of the script, which he annotates to tell him which sound source to use at each point in the program, as shown in the sample script (Figure 5.1) that follows. The notations describe the operations discussed for this script under "Recording Speech in the Studio" in Chapter 4.

The boom operator works under the direction of the audio person to keep a boom mic properly positioned for a good audio level, while making sure that the mic and its shadow are out of the visual field.

The gaffer (or lighting technician) may operate at several levels. If there is a lighting designer, the gaffer sets up the lights according to the light plot that the designer has prepared. If the camera person is doing the lighting, the gaffer will do the same for him. However, if the gaffer also acts as the lighting designer (as happens in many small productions), he not only sets up and runs the lights, he works out the light plot.

The VTR operator turns the videotape machine on and off and puts it in pause, but that hardly conveys the importance of what he does. Any producer who has ever finished his best take to find that the tape deck has been in PAUSE all along, knows the importance of the VTR operator. From the director's first "roll tape" to the last "stop tape," it is the VTR person who either has gotten the show or has lost it. During the shooting, it is he who is watching the video and audio record levels on the VTR. On small productions, the VTR operator may also be watching the waveform monitor and vectorscope to verify that the video quality has not deteriorated.

The VTR operator may also be logging the shots and takes for use in cataloging and editing, as shown in Form 5.1, a form for the VTR TAKE log. The log is a very simple record of each shot. Each shot has been numbered on the shooting script by the Director, and each take made of that shot will be numbered in order. For reference, the script page on which that shot starts is also noted. Also for quick reference, the content of the shot is tagged—for example, "Man on screen" would be enough for this shot. The "start" and "end points" are, of course, the counter, control track or time code numbers (whichever is being used) of the recorded material. The condition of the shot can simply be identified as "good," "no good" or "possible." Or, it could be more detailed, such as "good except for Camera 3 jiggle." With a well-kept take log, a great deal of time can be cut from the cataloging process, discussed in Chapter 9.

Other crew members include operators of specific pieces of equipment (such as teleprompters, character generators and digital video equipment), various assistants to the other crew members and "go-fers."

THE DIRECTOR AND HIS STAFF

Until the day of production, the producers are in charge. But once production begins, the director is king—or queen. Whether the director has input from "day one," or whether he is hired after the talent and staff have been assembled, he remains primarily responsible for the way the show turns out. It is the director who must make everyone's contributions to a show flow toward one goal.

The television director also has a technical role, because it is he who literally calls the shots. Even on news programs, where the director may have little to say about the presentation of the material, he still affects the look and pace of the program by his selection of the shots that are transmitted. However, before those shots are called, he goes through several stages that vary somewhat with the type of show he is doing.

Form 5.1:   VTR Take log.

Shot no.	Take no.	Script page no.	Shot description	Start point	End point	Condition of shot

The Director's Job

Reading the Script

The director's job begins when he gets the script. He reads it to decide how to direct it in terms of pace and tone, and in terms of what he thinks the material should "say" to its viewers. Accurately conveying the script's intention—selling a product, communicating a point of view, enlarging a viewer's experience or providing straight information—is the director's number one priority. (Directing is a craft and an art and is discussed in sources listed in the Bibliography.)

Having read the script and come out with his point of view clearly in mind, the director communicates with his staff on several issues.

First, the director deals with changes that are necessary in the language, the sequence or even the content. This is a touchy area, because the writer and others will have an emotional investment in the script. Presumably, the director's changes move the program toward consistency rather than toward the director's desire to participate in authorship. Sometimes, others can be brought to see a problem and fix it. Sometimes, the director just has to jump in with both feet, demand changes and take his lumps. In some cases, he may have to direct his way around problem phrasing, illogical action, deadly dialogue or meaningless transitions.

The director also deals with special production requirements. For example, the director may wish to have a segment take place in a rainstorm. Or, if he has to intercut an interview in the studio with film footage shot earlier at the interviewee's ranch, he must decide whether to have a remote control on the film chain or an experienced film-chain operator, transfer the remote material to tape and have an extra deck during production, or preproduce the interview and cut in the rest of the material later.

Of course, the director will also have general discussions with the artistic staff, as well as the producer and his staff, so that everyone can get on with their jobs. These discussions merely communicate the director's point of view about the story and the characters, so the sets, costumes, lighting and other elements will be consistent with it.

Working Out the Shots

Working out the shots is the television director's main job. He does this directly on the script. (See the next section on directions and cues.) Most directors work in pencil, so that they can make changes and additions. The director also sets up the relative movement of every camera on the set, making sure that there is plenty of time and space for each planned camera move. For example, he must make certain that Camera 1 will have enough room to move to its next shot without entering the

Figure 5.1: Script marked for audio operator.

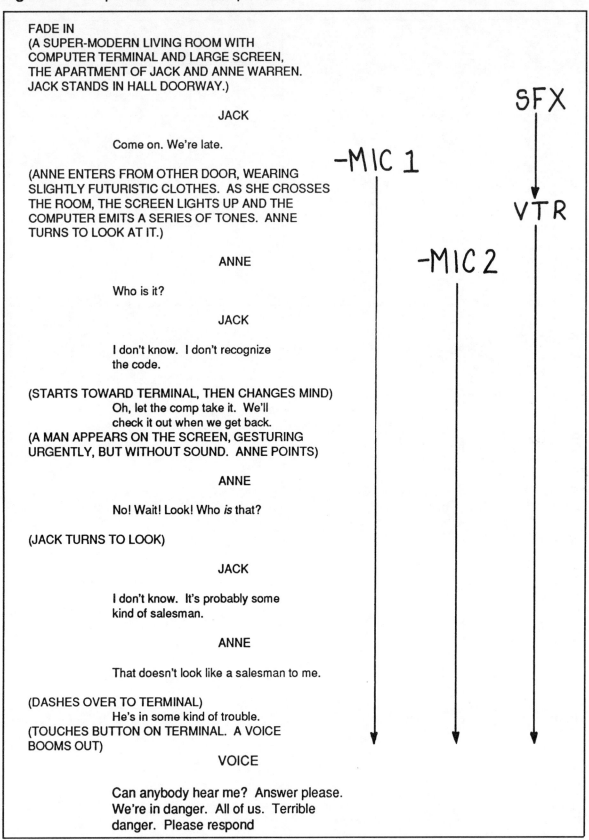

FADE IN
(A SUPER-MODERN LIVING ROOM WITH
COMPUTER TERMINAL AND LARGE SCREEN,
THE APARTMENT OF JACK AND ANNE WARREN.
JACK STANDS IN HALL DOORWAY.)

SFX

JACK

Come on. We're late.

-MIC 1

(ANNE ENTERS FROM OTHER DOOR, WEARING
SLIGHTLY FUTURISTIC CLOTHES. AS SHE CROSSES
THE ROOM, THE SCREEN LIGHTS UP AND THE
COMPUTER EMITS A SERIES OF TONES. ANNE
TURNS TO LOOK AT IT.)

VTR

ANNE

-MIC 2

Who is it?

JACK

I don't know. I don't recognize
the code.

(STARTS TOWARD TERMINAL, THEN CHANGES MIND)
Oh, let the comp take it. We'll
check it out when we get back.
(A MAN APPEARS ON THE SCREEN, GESTURING
URGENTLY, BUT WITHOUT SOUND. ANNE POINTS)

ANNE

No! Wait! Look! Who *is* that?

(JACK TURNS TO LOOK)

JACK

I don't know. It's probably some
kind of salesman.

ANNE

That doesn't look like a salesman to me.

(DASHES OVER TO TERMINAL)
He's in some kind of trouble.
(TOUCHES BUTTON ON TERMINAL. A VOICE
BOOMS OUT)

VOICE

Can anybody hear me? Answer please.
We're in danger. All of us. Terrible
danger. Please respond

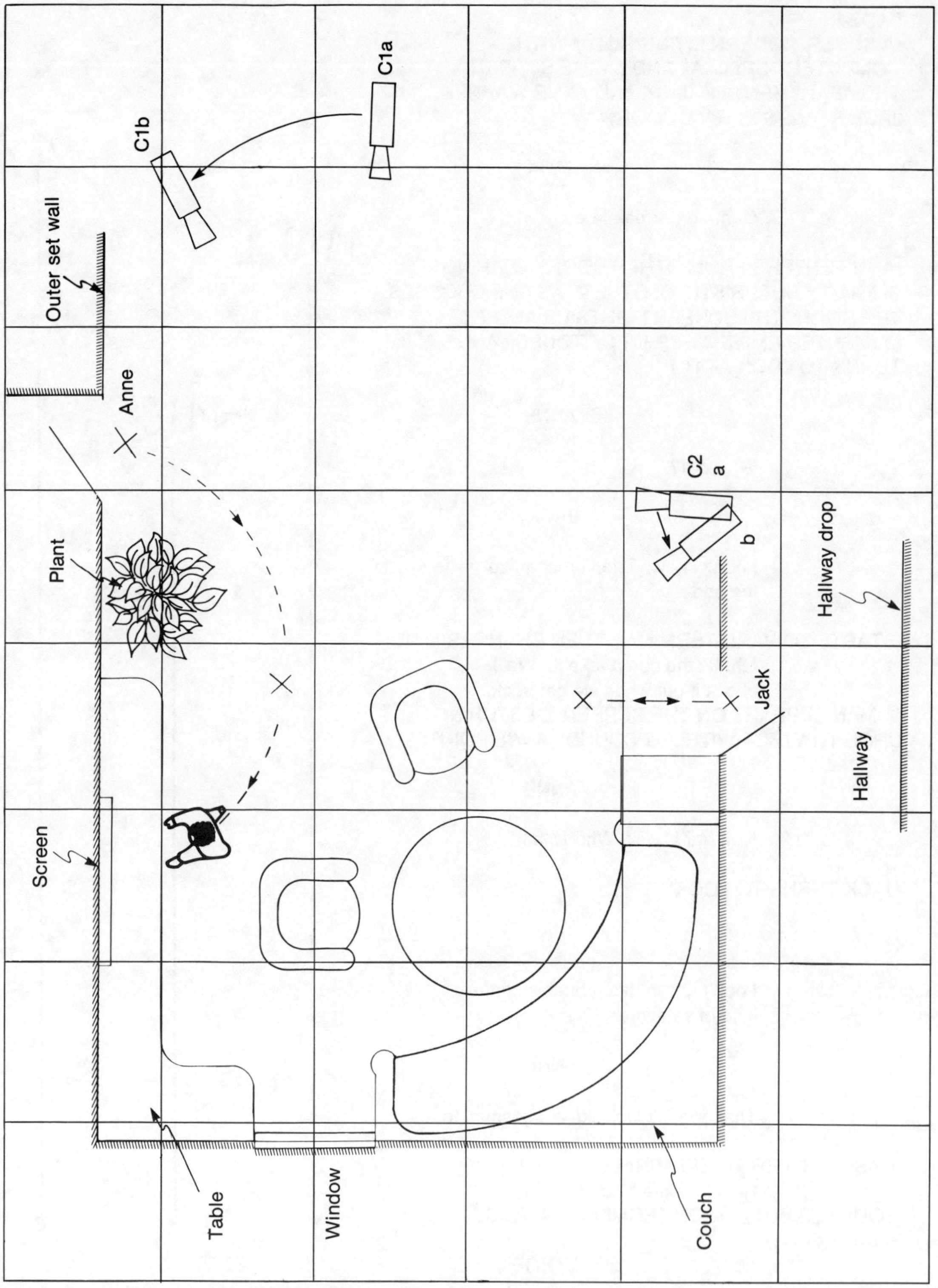

Figure 5.2: Studio floor plan showing set, talent and camera moves.

field covered by Camera 2. The camera moves are also charted on the studio floor plan, shown in Figure 5.2.

Conducting Rehearsals

Unless the studio to be used is freely available, the first rehearsals are held elsewhere. This is the time that the director can devote himself solely to the talent, concentrating on their needs and on his dramatic intentions. This is also the time he will finish "blocking" the show. Blocking involves determining the movement of the talent and the position of props on the set. This is necessary not only to establish the flow of action, but also to enable him to set up the shots during a sequence.

The run-through in the studio is usually the first time the director sees how the action and his plans for camera shots work together. If the show is scripted, the talent should have a good hold on their parts by this time, even if they are not "off the book" (have the script memorized). The run-through is, of course, a walk-through in which the talent carefully goes through all the motions but none of the emotions. The show—or as much of it as possible—is timed, and final corrections are made and incorporated into everyone's scripts. At this point, the director is working very closely with his TD, who will be becoming familiar with each call, and (hopefully) making suggestions based on his extensive knowledge of the switching and effects system available in the studio. The director is also working with the camera operators, the audio person and the floor manager.

Even partially scripted programs like interview and game shows, where the intros and questions are scripted, but the answers normally are not, may still be run through in their entirety. On the other hand, if the staff, crew and talent are very familiar with each other, a few blocking notes and timing checks may be enough. This last situation is generally true of news shows, even though everything is precisely timed and organized. In any case, most programs will not be broadcast live, but will be recorded in the studio on tape in segments one to several minutes long.

Dress rehearsals are rarely used for television shows, except for some complex performances requiring complex takes. For most shows, by the time things are ready for a dress rehearsal, it is time to start shooting. In any case, tape is cheap, and it may as well be rolling if everyone is ready

to go. The first performance may be the best overall performance the director will get; he can always retake a scene or do a cutaway for the shots that didn't work.

Directions and Cues Used in Production

There is no great mystery about the language of directing. It is true that different directors, different stations and different parts of the industry use slightly different terms. But basically, a take is a cut, and all other effects are called by their common names. Cameras may be addressed as Camera (number), or as a number only. But when there is more than one VTR, the different VTRs are addressed as VTR 1, VTR 2, etc. The main thing is that every source and effect has a clear identification on which everyone has agreed. There should be no confusion, for example, between a graphic that is being picked up from a graphics camera and the graphic that is being generated electronically.

During the actual production, the pace is set by the talent, and everyone must move with the synchronecity of a dance company in performance. To keep everyone on cue and moving within the television time frame, the director maintains the pace with terse and precise commands that can be quickly and easily followed. Working from his marked script (Figure 5.3) in the control room, he communicates primarily through the intercom with the technical director, the camera operators, the floor manager and the audio person.

While most television directors operate from the control room during production, some still prefer to work film style and stay with the talent on the floor. In this case, of course, it is necessary that he have an assistant director who can carry out his function in the control room, or a technical director who can work entirely from the director's written calls. Working on the floor sustains the director's contact with the talent and therefore extends his control over the content of the production. However, even when he has defined all the takes, it still reduces his control over the form, which is set in great part by the timing. Since a studio production is normally a multi-camera operation in which the program is being live-cut— that is, edited in process—the director who chooses the floor over the control room has to balance his concern with the talent against his intentions for the final shape of his program.

Figure 5.3: A director's marked script.

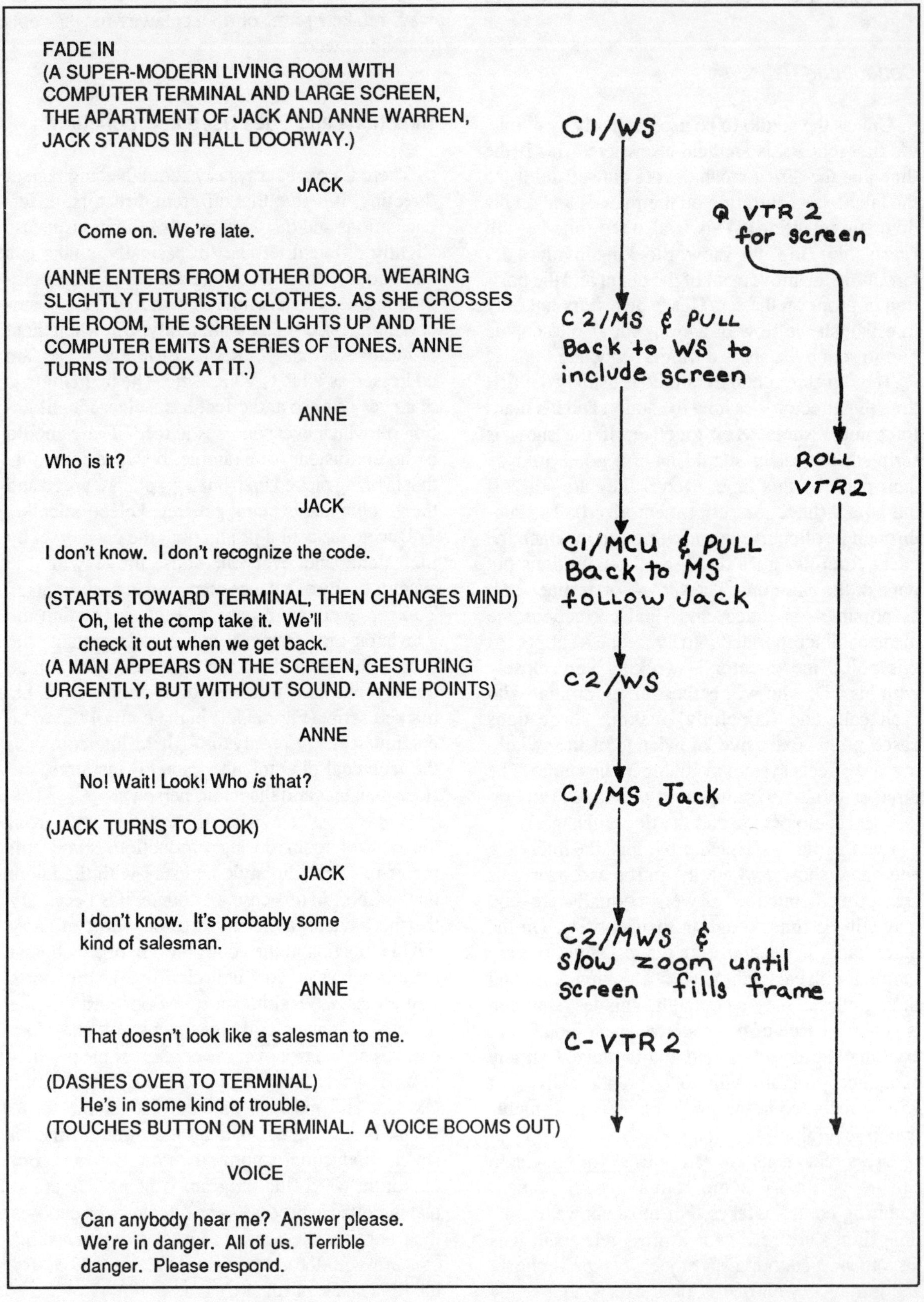

FADE IN
(A SUPER-MODERN LIVING ROOM WITH
COMPUTER TERMINAL AND LARGE SCREEN,
THE APARTMENT OF JACK AND ANNE WARREN,
JACK STANDS IN HALL DOORWAY.)

C1/WS

                    JACK

    Come on. We're late.

(ANNE ENTERS FROM OTHER DOOR. WEARING
SLIGHTLY FUTURISTIC CLOTHES. AS SHE CROSSES
THE ROOM, THE SCREEN LIGHTS UP AND THE
COMPUTER EMITS A SERIES OF TONES. ANNE
TURNS TO LOOK AT IT.)

Q VTR 2
for screen

C2/MS & PULL
Back to WS to
include screen

                    ANNE

Who is it?

ROLL
VTR2

                    JACK

I don't know. I don't recognize the code.

C1/MCU & PULL
Back to MS
follow Jack

(STARTS TOWARD TERMINAL, THEN CHANGES MIND)
    Oh, let the comp take it. We'll
    check it out when we get back.
(A MAN APPEARS ON THE SCREEN, GESTURING
URGENTLY, BUT WITHOUT SOUND. ANNE POINTS)

C2/WS

                    ANNE

    No! Wait! Look! Who *is* that?

C1/MS Jack

(JACK TURNS TO LOOK)

                    JACK

    I don't know. It's probably some
    kind of salesman.

C2/MWS &
slow zoom until
screen fills frame

                    ANNE

That doesn't look like a salesman to me.

C-VTR 2

(DASHES OVER TO TERMINAL)
    He's in some kind of trouble.
(TOUCHES BUTTON ON TERMINAL. A VOICE BOOMS OUT)

                    VOICE

Can anybody hear me? Answer please.
We're in danger. All of us. Terrible
danger. Please respond.

Before we get to the calls, we should also note that there are—especially at the networks—directors who almost never speak, but only snap their fingers to call shots. These directors supply their TDs with precisely marked scripts, their camera people with camera shot lists and everyone else with their cues. When they snap their fingers, the camera is ready and the TD merely executes the next take, which he has prepared. However, this kind of operation only works well when everyone involved is very experienced and has worked with the director. For most directors, it is best to stick with the standard calls.

• *Ready:* Every direction to the TD, cameras and audio requires prior notice that a direction is coming. The direction, "Take 3," meaning, "Cut to Camera 3," must be preceded by the instruction, "Ready Camera 3." Well before this, Camera 3 has been instructed as to what the shot is, so before the direction is given, it will be in place. However, the brief "Ready Camera 3" followed by a moment's pause and then the direction to cut, "Take 3," gives the TD enough notice to hit the switcher button at the right moment. It is also the final notification to the camera person that he is going online, and that it is too late to scratch his ear or do anything else but concentrate on the shot.

There are also some preparatory cues for which there is no precise code. In setting up a shot, the director often talks to the camera operator in plain English: "Three, check your focus"; "One, tighten up" (leave less space around the talent or object). The director will also give the TD fine corrections on his previews of effects. In addition, he will give those who need the time numerous reminders, such as "Cue tape," or "Ready phone" (so it will ring on time). The director may also give a number of in-process corrections, such as directing the floor manager to "Tell her to slow down."

• *Camera directions* are simply instructions to get the shot: a medium shot or a closeup, a two-shot or a single-shot, a pan, a tilt, a dolly, a zoom—all the camera moves and their combinations. If the show is completely scripted, the camera operator has practiced every shot and will know them as well as the director. In many cases, he will have his own "shot sheet," on which each shot is numbered and described. For example:

No. 14: WIDE SHOT of set from Jack to screen. On CUE, "Oh no!" PAN LEFT WITH ZOOM to MCU of Jack.

When shot sheets are used, all calls for camera setups are by shot number.

If the show is not scripted, or is partially scripted, the cameras are directed as the action requires, but each camera can be given a specific task. For example, Camera 2 may be responsible for staying wide on the action. Camera 1 stays tight on the host, and Camera 3 gets in tight on the different guests when they speak. Yet, although camera operators have more responsibility in unscripted shows, they will still follow the director's call as he gives it.

In any case, once a shot is set up, the camera calls run: "Standby Camera 2" (a warning that two is next), then, "Ready dissolve on 2 . . . dissolve 2."

• *Directions to the TD* determine what goes on tape. The TD needs to know two things: the sources (cameras, VTRs, film, slides, graphics or character generators, etc.) to be switched and the process (cut, dissolve, wipe, fade, key, super, etc.) to be used to make a transition from one shot to the next. There are often several sources and several processes used in quick succession. The intro, for example (if it has not been prerecorded), may involve the talent on the set, a graphic and a tape-recorded segment. The call might then be:

"Standby 1 on the host. Standby VTR. Roll VTR. Standby graphic. Fade in VTR. Key in graphic and zoom in on graphic. Ready dissolve to 1. Dissolve effect to 1."

• *The audio cues* are given in the same way as the visual cues. Persons creating "live" sound effects are cued and put on standby, as are persons starting audiotape machines. However, unless the audio is also being handled through the SEG (a capability of very few SEGs), the actual audio to go online is recorded by the audio person operating the audio mixer. He sets up and directs all the audio inputs, including effects and prerecorded material, as well as mixing the mix inputs.

• *Talent cues* are entirely communicated during taping by the floor manager, who is on the

Figure 5.4: Talent cues from the floor manager.

Standby
(hand up, facing talent)

Start action
(bring hand forward to point at
talent)

Slower
(taffy-pulling motion)

Faster
(move pointed finger in circle)

Face *this* camera

Louder
(lifting motion)

Softer
(patting motion)

Wrap it up
(both hands circle)

Cut/stop
(flat hand across neck)

floor of the set. He is tied by the intercom system to the director and uses hand cues (shown in Figure 5.4) to communicate with the talent on the set. Through the floor manager, the director tells the talent when to get ready, when they are on camera and when they should speed up, talk louder, wrap it up or end it.

The Director's Staff and Artistic Associates

The assistant director (AD) takes certain burdens from the director's shoulders. How much he does, however, is partly a function of how much the director will let him do. ADs get to make very few decisions. Usually, their main job is take the director's shot plot and work it out with the TD and camera people, so that the director is free to prepare the talent. Other jobs ADs perform include timing the show and cueing camera and other operators to set up shots. In some broadcast situations, especially when all the major segments of a show have been live-cut in the studio, ADs also supervise the post-production. As this involves primarily linking the segments together and setting in some cover shots, it does not usually involve major input.

However, the AD also has the considerable but unofficial responsibility of keeping the talent happy. This usually involves combining the roles of confidante, den mother and diplomatic liaison. However, he should never lose sight of the fact that his first responsibility is to the program and the director and, even if the director is difficult, it is his job to support him.

The art director works closely with the director, and is in charge of the "look" of the show, which may include sets, makeup, costumes, props and even lighting. Depending on his ability and prestige, he may even affect the way the director presents the production. A good art director can give a program an enormous amount of style and production value.

The set designer creates all the sets that are used, preparing drawings of each set, selecting the materials and supervising construction. He also selects all the props and is responsible for obtaining them or having them made. If there is an art director, the set designer works for him. If not, he works closely with the director.

The lighting designer, as was noted earlier, must be capable of bringing a great deal of scope and variety to the lighting used in a show, especially in the studio. Like the set designer, this person may report to the art director or, if there is none, to the director.

The director of photography is a title more prevalent in filmmaking, but it is becoming more common in television production. In television, the title is DPE (E for electronics) to differentiate it from the DP of film. The DPE will supervise the lighting and determine the camera shots, leaving the director to deal with the talent and the overall production. Often, especially on location, the function of DPE is filled by a particularly skilled camera person who contributes to the director's design of the shots. Because of his knowledge of camera and lighting techniques, a good DPE is often able to suggest original and effective approaches to shots.

This covers the production process in a studio, but television is a medium that works just as well on location—out in the real world.

CONCLUSION

This chapter deals in detail with the individual jobs performed by the members of the production crew. Perhaps what is lost in focusing on specific tasks is how essential it is for the crew to interact as a *team*. Teamwork increases program quality and individual productivity.

The producer can contribute greatly to the team building process. Each producer has standards and expectations that he must communicate clearly to each crew member. He must anticipate what is expected of each of them and set up rules they can reasonably follow to meet those expectations. At the same time, the producer must be willing to change rules when necessary, and convey this to his crew.

Critical to team building is forming lasting team bonds. One skill used to accomplish this is "listening." Although most of us "hear", few actually "listen". Listening to the crew members and then communicating that they have been heard is a difficult and time-consuming task. However, the rewards can be improved two-way communication and understanding. Team bonds form the glue that will serve to hold the crew together through the adversities of production.

6 Shooting in the Field: Equipment

ENG AND EFP

One of the great benefits of video production systems is that instant feedback is possible. That is undoubtedly why videotape is the preferred medium for shooting in the field—i.e., any location outside of a television studio. On-location shoots are also called "remotes." Over 75% of the videotape shot for nonbroadcast program production is shot on location. Because this production mode is so important, manufacturers have put a lot of effort into creating new ENG (electronic news gathering) and EFP (electronic field production) equipment.

Electronic news gathering was the first commercial application of portable video cameras in the mid-1970s. More recently this term has come to stand for a style of equipment and techniques that emphasizes mobility and ruggedness. In ENG production, both the camera and deck operate on a battery out of necessity and convenience, although AC lines may be used when available. The immediacy of the situation, the inaccessibility of the site, or the mobility and flexibility of the equipment are paramount. An ascent of Mt. Everest, man-in-the-workplace interviews, scene-of-the-crime coverage and shots of the CEO on the steps of new corporate headquarters are all shot ENG.

Electronic field production describes production situations that take place in the field and are normally highly orchestrated. Sports, concerts, conventions and major public events are all produced EFP. Although EFP usually involves portable video cameras, its similarity to ENG ends there. In an EFP shoot, multiple cameras are connected to a switcher and digital effects (page turns, Mosaic, etc.) may be added on site. Separate recording are often made of each camera as well as the switched program feed, all using studio decks. A makeshift control room may be set up in a room close to the location or a fully equipped van may provide this capability.

There is no hard-and-fast line that separates ENG from EFP. However, ENG shades into EFP when the camera is operated from a camera control unit (CCU) on an "umbilical cord," leaving the operator free to move while the recording and camera control are done from an AC-powered location. Although the terms ENG and EFP refer to two very different remote situations, the information that follows will be useful for both.

PORTABLE CAMERAS

Functionally, there is relatively little difference between studio and portable cameras, but in terms of physical design, they are worlds apart in ergonomics and packaging. Where studio cameras are unbound by considerations of size, weight, power use and setup time, field cameras must be on the short side of all four parameters (see Figure 6.1). Portable professional cameras are designed for on-the-shoulder operation, or for mounting on a medium-weight tripod. To make setup and image adjustment possible under field conditions, most of the controls that are located in a studio camera's remote control unit are located directly at the portable camera head. (See Figure 6.2, and refer to the Technical Appendix and the Glossary for explanations of terms.) The following pertains to cameras designed for use in the field.

The Lens

Portable cameras must be prepared to operate at greater camera-to-object distances than studio cameras. Therefore, they are equipped with zoom lenses with a fairly high wide-angle to telephoto ratio. A 14:1 ratio is fairly common, although an 18:1 ratio or greater lens may be needed (and can be rented) for special situations. With the increased use of the CCD camera it is important to note that the quality of the lenses is very important. Because CCD cameras do not face the same limitations of having the pick-up device "tuned" to the optics, faults in the lenses' optics are more pronounced. Lenses for CCD cameras are easily changed to suit the application, a real advantage over the past.

A further concern in selecting a lens should be its aperture, or f-stop: the ratio of its focal length to the lens diameter with an open iris. The lower the ratio, the more light the camera can "see" and the lower the illumination required to get an acceptable image. The optimum is a f1.4 lens, although an f1.7 lens is common.

Overall, lens quality is a direct function of price. However, for most applications, a lens costing less than $1000 will provide adequate quality. The type of lens used sets the limits on the size and quality of the image. As with all the equipment discussed, the best way to evaluate a lens is to use it in a familiar shooting environment.

The Auto Iris

Unlike studio shoots, where the lighting is reset and controlled, field operation involves wide ranges of lighting conditions that can vary from dark shade to brilliant sunlight within a single panning shot. To contend with this, portable cameras have auto-irises that automatically open in the shade and close down in the sunlight, maintaining an even video level as the lighting conditions change. In better cameras, the auto-iris closes completely when the camera is shut off or is in the standby, color bar or "auto-black" mode. This prevents accidental exposure of the imaging device to bright light sources.

The Viewfinder

Portable camera viewfinders use a black and white 1½-inch screen that displays a number of camera status indicators. These indicators may appear as status lights or alpha numeric readouts. The viewfinder also serves to check return video for the VCR when a monitor is not available.

The status readouts include those for video level, light levels, white balance, black balance and gain settings. Status is checked by pressing a status button. Additional status readouts indicate operational modes, VTR status (operate or pause) and tally for EFP applications. Because of the complexity of today's ENG cameras the viewfinder becomes a important monitoring tool during production.

Color Temperature Filters

Portable cameras have a wheel of color filters that rotate into the light path to compensate for the different color temperatures encountered in the field. Multiple filters are not needed in the studio because the lighting there is always based on 3200°K tungsten illumination. On portable cameras, the following filters are normally supplied: a 3200°K filter for tungsten illumination; a 5600°K filter for daylight illumination; and a 5600°K + ND filter for reduced daylight illumination. The standard neutral density filter used is a 25% ND filter, although 12.5% and 50% filters are supplied on some cameras. As with film cameras, ND filters can always be fitted to the front of the lens.

Other Image Quality Controls at the Camera Head

White balance

Because the color filters provide only gross correction of the balance of hues reaching the imaging device, fine correction is needed. This is done by using a plain white surface that fills the

Figure 6.1: Betacam camcorder

Figure 6.2: An EFP configuration

Courtesy of Ikegami Electronics.

camera's visual field (a large white card, for instance) and adjusting the white balance control. This causes the adjustment (manual or automatic) of the proportions of red and blue light (relative to a constant of green) composing the image.

Black level

In the field, where waveform monitors may be scarce, many portable cameras have a built-in black level control or automatic adjustment that sets the black set-up parameter at its correct value for the existing lighting conditions. The automatic adjustment may also be referred to as auto black balance.

Other Adjustments at the Camera Head

Color bar generator:

All professional portable cameras provide a set of full- or split-field color bars that can be displayed on a field monitor as a camera output. These should be recorded as a reference at the beginning of a tape and used to set the monitor for a visual check of the image.

Gamma and shading correction

Better portables provide a control for the adjustment of the linearity of the tube's response to different light levels between the extremes of the white and black levels of the camera. They also may provide a horizontal and vertical sawtooth (test signal) and a parabolic signal adjustment to control shading. These are manual adjustments that need some expertise to use correctly.

Blanking adjustments

Both horizontal and vertical blanking can be adjusted at the camera head and CCU, usually by a selector switch. This feature is essential when operating multiple cameras so that timing can be matched between cameras and the switcher.

Gain switches

To permit operation under low light conditions, portable cameras permit you to temporarily increase the beam current by specific, switchable amounts. Typical gain adjustments are 3, 6, 9, 12

and even 18 dB. Usually no more than two or three of these dB increments are present in any one camera. Here the difference between lower- and higher-end cameras is particularly evident. Lesser cameras generate increasingly noisy images under higher gain conditions, while the better cameras provide low-light images that are comparable to adequately lit scenes.

Structural Design

Portable cameras are housed in rugged but lightweight alloy housings. Metal (often laced with copper stripping) is used rather than plastic, because it reduces RF (radio frequency) interference. The optical prism and the imaging units are rigidly mounted on the frame to ensure that the registration remains constant (subject only to the fine adjustments previously described). This assembly sits behind the lens and constitutes the camera's "front end." The rest of the camera body contains circuit boards for the electronics.

Battery Power and Standby Provisions

Most cameras and associated equipment require a 12-volt DC power supply, typically a battery. Normal field use requires a large supply of batteries to conduct an ENG shoot. To conserve battery usage, ENG cameras provide a standby mode in which the camera is in pause, ready to go, but drawing a minimum of power.

CAMCORDERS

ENG camera/portable VCR combinations traditionally consisted of two-piece systems. The portable camera was connected to the VCR by means of a multi-pin cable. This cable provided connections for power to the camera, control of the VCR functions from the camera, and sent audio and video signals to the VCR for recording. These two- piece systems were often heavy and difficult to move around during shooting.

In the past several years, with the advent of CCD and component technologies, the dockable and one-piece camera-VCR system (camcorder) has been made possible (see Figure 6.3). These lightweight combinations have provided the ENG producer with shoulderable systems which maintain the quality of "larger" format systems. How-

Figure 6.3: Camcorder with S/VHS Recorder.

Courtesy of Ikegami Electronics

Figure 6.4: Portable ¾-inch VCR.

Courtesy of Sony Corp.

ever, the following discussion on portable video-cassette recorders holds true whether applied to standalone VCRs or those used in camcorders.

PORTABLE VIDEOCASSETTE RECORDERS

Aside from being smaller, lighter, more rugged and limited in recording time, portable videotape recorders have only a few features that differentiate them from studio units (see Figure 6.4).

Portable decks which offer multi-power source capability are usually able to use both a 12-volt DC battery supply and a standard 120-volt AC supply. With an appropriate cable adaptor, a 12-volt DC car or marine battery can also be used. Battery voltage is normally metered, and most decks have a "low battery" warning indicator.

When recording from a camera, most portable decks will backspace automatically from the last frame recorded at shutoff to the last technically coherent frame. The deck will then automatically start the next shot as a clean assembly edit, right on the vertical frame interval. This is known as auto backspace.

All portable decks are built to operate in various vertical, as well as horizontal, positions. Better portable decks offer gyroscopic error suppression. They are designed to read the motion errors that are created when the deck is moved or swung while the tape is moving. These errors are particularly manifested when the deck moves in the same or opposite direction as the tape, creating acceleration or deceleration of the tape respectively. These error readings are then used to adjust the tape speed to compensate for the errors so that each track is laid down exactly where it is supposed to be.

PORTABLE SWITCHERS

Most studio special effects generators are hooked into their video systems by a dense network of wires and connectors. However, many of the smaller production switchers have fewer inputs, allowing for easy hookup and disconnect. This makes them popular for field use. Portable switchers are designed especially for remote use and operate from 12-volt power supplies. These units are basically standard production switchers adapted for remote operation.

A switcher suitable for field operation will incorporate the following features:

• Phase-adjusted sync, black burst and subcarrier. All three outputs are required to operate and align two or more cameras with each other. The phase adjustment must be provided independently for each output.

• Color bar generator and blanking adjustments. These are required to guarantee flexibility when timing the system. They provide a means by which all cameras can be adjusted to the same operating standards.

• Intercom and tally. While intercom and tally systems designed especially for remote operation are available, it is convenient to be able to access these capabilities through the switcher. Many of the smaller switchers come equipped with these features.

• Return video. Return video from each camera should be available through the camera-to-

CCU umbilical cable. This will reduce the number of interconnections required.

• DC power capability. This feature is only significant if the remote shoot must be done on battery or other 12-volt DC power.

AUDIO EQUIPMENT IN THE FIELD

The general requirements for audio equipment in the field are similar to the general requirements for cameras and switchers. The units must be portable, capable of operation on DC power, rugged and easy to use. When we speak of field audio, we speak solely of mics, mic mixers and tape recorders. Other audio equipment, such as that used for audio "sweetening," is part of the post-production process.

Microphones

The microphone designed especially for field use is the "shotgun" (Figure 6.5). The shotgun microphone is highly directional, it damps out sound from all but a narrow forward angle. Only sounds coming from some distance directly in front of the mic are thus received with a high degree of sensitivity. As a result, a good shotgun mic can pick up a conversation on a busy city street or in a factory without picking up more than reference background (ambient) noise. Because shotguns are designed for operation in the field, they are also less sensitive than studio mics to shock and wind noise.

Other types of microphones can also be used in the field. For considerations involved in their use, see "Sound Recording in the Field" in Chapter 7.

Audio Mixers

Battery-operated mixers (Figure 6.6), capable of handling several channels of source audio and featuring switchable inputs/outputs (line or microphone), are available for field use. They are lightweight and easy to set up and provide clean mixing of location sound. Because the inputs and outputs are switchable they offer flexibility for equipment hook up. Desired features for the portable mixer include a reference oscillator, built-in slate mic, switchable pass filters, phantom powering and an accurate headphone monitoring system.

Figure 6.5: Condenser Shotgun Microphone.

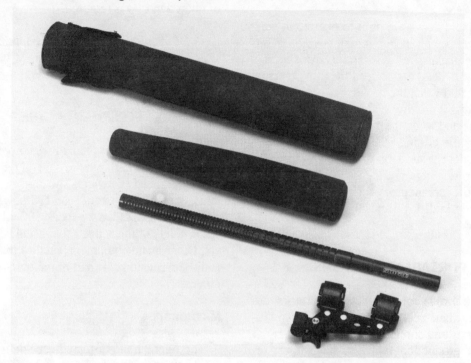

Courtesy of Shure

Figure 6.6: Field Mixer.

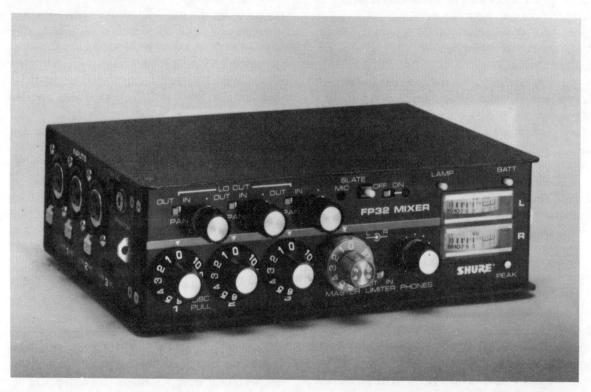

Courtesy of Shure

Audio Recordings

The requirements for dual-system audio recording in the field are almost identical to those for field VTRs: small size, lightweight, rugged, multipower source recording capability and gyroscopic error suppression. In other respects, including the capability for providing a crystal sync, they must meet the same quality requirements as studio audio recorders.

Top quality reel-to-reel field ATRs, like the NAGRA, are extremely expensive for the nonbroadcast producer, about the same price as a good portable ¾-inch VCR. However, for wild track (nonsychronized) recordings in the field, a top-quality portable stereo cassette recorder can be used. It should be understood that this method provides double system audio capabilities but does not offer the synchronizing capabilities the NAGRA recorders do. The stereo cassette recorders are very well-designed, provide excellent recording quality, and are rugged, inexpensive and easy to use under field conditions.

LIGHTING EQUIPMENT FOR THE FIELD

In the field, a variety of lights, filters and lighting accessories may be required.

Lights

All but the heaviest lights used in the studio are suitable for use in the field, assuming that there is AC power to operate them. For small remote shoots, a standard light kit provides an ideal lighting system. This consists of a set of two, three or four adjustable 650- or 1000-watt lights with stands, shown in Figure 6.7. These kits are made by several lighting manufacturers and come with fitted carrying cases. They are also available from equipment rental houses for a nominal fee.

The only battery-operated lights are sun guns, small floods that are designed to be hand-held or mounted on top of the camera. These use a substantial amount of battery power and are therefore suitable only for ENG situations where there is no other ready source of illumination.

Filters

Lighting filters are used in the studio only for special effects, but they are a lighting staple in the field. There are three basic lighting filters in use. These are:

Sun 85

This is an optical gel that converts 5600 K daylight to 3200 K tungsten. In large sheets this material can be used to cover windows, matching the incoming daylight to the color of other lights in use at a location.

Blue 50

This is an optical gel that converts 3200 K tungsten lighting to 5600 K. Although it is available in large sheets, it is usually used in foot-square gels to cover tungsten lights and match them to daylight in the field. For example, a Blue 50 filter may be used when a tungsten light is used as a fill in an outdoor situation.

Fluorescent light filters

There are four types of filters commonly used to correct white fluorescent lights. One type is used over the camera lens to match daylight to fluorescent light. A second type converts tungsten lighting to match fluorescent light and is also used with a correction filter over the lens. A third removes the greenish cast from fluorescent lights and matches their light to daylight 5600 K. The fourth corrects fluorescent lights to 3200 K. The last two correction filters are usually placed directly on the fluorescent tubes.

Remote Lighting Accessories

In the field, especially outdoors, some of the most important lighting devices are such items as black cloths to reduce or block excessive light, black tape to cover light flares, aluminum foil and white cards to bounce and direct light, scrims and barndoor extensions to screen harsh light, and clothespins and gaffer tape to hold these items in place.

POWER AND ACCESSORIES IN THE FIELD

The most common sources of power in the field are rechargable nickel-cadminum batteries, "nicads," which come in a great variety of shapes. Most nicads are fitted to a compartment within a

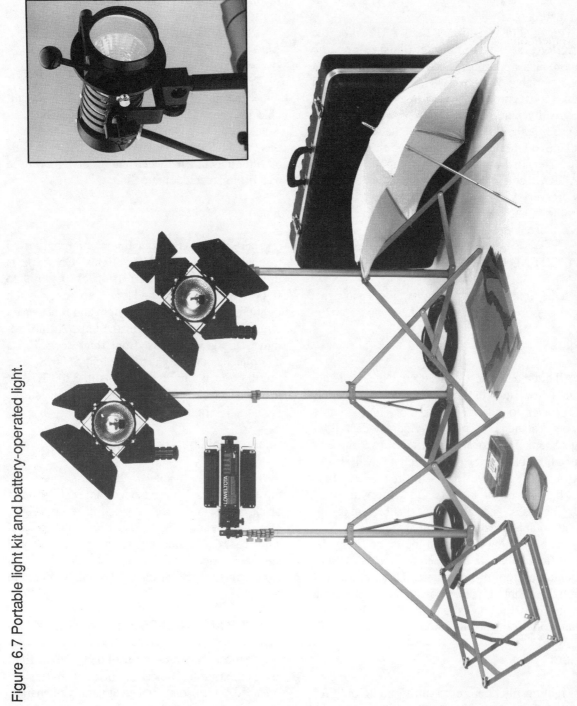

Figure 6.7 Portable light kit and battery-operated light.

Lowel Tota/Omni Light Kit courtesy of Lowel Light-Manufacturing, and Frezzi Mini-fill courtesy of Frezzolini Electronics Inc.

specific piece of equipment. Others are available in special formats, such as the "cine-belt" of eight 1.5-volt nicads that can be worn around the waist and plugged into the recorder or camera.

Another power source is marine batteries. They offer larger amp hour ratings, thus allowing several hours of use before recharging. Because of their increased weight and size over "common" ENG batteries, they are best suited for applications that use carts and require limited equipment movement on location. A small gasoline powered 12-volt generator that outputs 12-volt DC power can be used, but care must be taken to compensate for the noise the generator makes.

There are two different methods of charging batteries, a slow charge (overnight) and a quick charge (couple of hours). The length of time that a charge lasts depends on the amount of wattage being drawn and the condition of the battery. To ensure healthy batteries follow these general rules: one, use batteries in cycles; two, do not recharge hot or cold batteries; and three, know your power requirements and power units individually.

Accessories for a portable shoot are too numerous to list fully. Items of note include:

- Tripods: the type of tripod required for a shoot is determined by the weight of the camera system (i.e., camcorder, Teleprompter) to be used. A fluid head is the most desirable, because it offers the smoothness of movement essential for "good" camera work. A full tripod outfit should include a leg spreader and portable dolly. The spreader serves to keep the legs firmly apart and stable, while the dolly offers the ability to roll the camera system over smooth surfaces. Special dollies can be rented to address the problems of rough surface often found on location. They offer larger wheels and often use a track system. (Because of their cost these special application dollies are better rented than owned.)

- Cables: more shoots have been aborted because of missing and defective cables than because of equipment failure. Therefore, checklists should be developed to ensure that commonly used cables are packed and that power cables are long and heavy enough to reach power sources. Some tips for avoiding cable problems include: label all cables, handle them by their connectors, check out cables after each shoot for operational condition, and pack cables by function.

- Cases and carts: to transport equipment safety to and from remote shoots, it must be packed securely. While ENG cameras are sold in rigid, cushioned cases, most equipment is not. Each major unit (i.e., VCR, lights, etc.) should have its own case. These cases may be hard construction (plywood, metal or plastic) or soft construction (canvas and other heavy-duty fabric materials). Packing your ENG/EFP package by function (camera, audio, lights, etc.) can be a real time saver. Carts designed to carry entire ENG/EFP rigs are useful for remote shoots. They provide the ability to move the entire system without the necessity of disconnecting. This is especially helpful where the crew must remain mobile and help is limited.

CONCLUSION

Shooting in the field places great importance on having a developed and proven equipment package that meets your needs. While dry runs and rehearsals are expensive, they prove beneficial when they point out equipment package inadequacies. Testing your ENG/EFP system under stress—similar to actual conditions—is the only method to validate that your equipment choices will allow the flexibility required for field production. Rehearsals also provide an opportunity for fine-tuning.

7 Shooting in the Field: Production

Although careful planning is essential for any successful shoot, the remote shoot is the most demanding. That is because if you don't have an item with you, it won't be there, and if you don't anticipate a problem, it becomes a disaster. Accordingly, planning a remote production begins the moment the project is decided on. A place to start is scouting the location.

SCOUTING THE LOCATION

Few things can defeat the location producer as easily as a two-pronged outlet when he has no "cube taps" to adapt his three-prong plugs. Yet this is only one of the many things that can foil the best-laid production plans. That is why it is necessary to check potential locations carefully, and in person, whenever possible. Even the cost of a day's time and a plane fare is a well-spent addition to the budget, because it can save so much over the cost of arriving unprepared. Often, the locations are within a 50-mile radius and can be checked in a morning or afternoon.

To keep track of the information that will be needed, Form 7.1 covers the site of each shoot, while Form 7.2 provides information about such local conveniences as parking and caterers. The "site" checklist (Form 7.1) covers a specific place, such as a church or temple for a wedding; a hotel

banquet room for a seminar; or an apartment for a dramatic show. Looking at the list, the first item is a simple description of the site, such as "A small, white country church," "A mid-sized banquet room" or "A lavish seven-room apartment."

The second item—the size of the interiors—is important, if only because it is one indication of the amount of lighting that will be required. There may be several interiors. For example, for the wedding, there may be the church proper, and there may be a chapel where the bride waits. There may be more than one exterior. On all points, the list provides for the location scout's comments.

Knowing the availability of the space is also critical. If it is a city street, a permit and a certificate of insurance are often necessary. If it is a hotel banquet room, it may be occupied just before the seminar, because no one has provided for setup time. In that case, it is essential that alternatives be worked out with the client.

The importance of knowing the nature and wattage of the lights at the location and the number and wattage of the outlets is evident. The fifth item on the list—"Facilities available"—may specify a place where the talent can prepare, or simply indicate whether a bathroom is handy.

While the "site" checklist can be used for every remote production, the "area" checklist of Form 7.2 is especially important when shooting out of town. The "catering" item can account for a pro-

101

Form 7.1: Site checklist for remote shoots.

LOCATION CHECKLIST: SITE _____ (TITLE)		
Item	Description	Comments

SITE
1. General
    & special
      features		

2. Interiors(size)
   Main area _____
   (1) _____
   (2) _____
   (3) _____
   (4) _____
	____ x ____ x ____ ft
	____ x ____ x ____ ft
	____ x ____ x ____ ft
	____ x ____ x ____ ft
	____ x ____ x ____ ft
		_____
		_____
		_____
		_____
		_____

3. Exteriors
   (1) _____
   (2) _____
	_____
	_____
		_____
		_____

3. Availability
   Times avail.
 	
   Permissions
   & permits
	_____
	
	_____
		_____
		
		_____

4. Illumination	Type	No. of lights	Watts/ light	Total watts
Main area _____	_____	____	____	____
Other _____	_____	____	____	____
	_____	____	____	____
	_____	____	____	____
	_____	____	____	____

4. Power	No. of outlets	Watts/ outlet	Total watts	Feet to outlet
Main area _____	____	____	____	_____
Other _____	____	____	____	_____
	____	____	____	_____
	____	____	____	_____
	____	____	____	_____

5. Facilities		
a. Dressing	_____	_____
b. Bathrooms	_____	_____
c. Kitchen	_____	_____
d. Other _____	_____	_____
	_____	_____

Form 7.2: Area checklist for remote shoots.

Item	Description	Comments
Lodging, Food, Travel		
1. Lodging	Type Rate single Rate double	
(1) _____	____ ____ ____	_____
(2) _____	____ ____ ____	_____
(3) _____	____ ____ ____	_____
2. Catering	Type Cost/person	Cost/day Total cost
(1) _____	____ ____	____ ____
(2) _____	____ ____	____ ____
(3) _____	____ ____	____ ____
3. Travel Car rental		
(1) _____	_____	_____
(2) _____	_____	_____
Taxis		
(1) _____	_____	_____
(2) _____	_____	_____
Local equipment, Crew & supplies		
1. Equipment suppliers		
(1) _____	_____	_____
(2) _____	_____	_____
(3) _____	_____	_____
2. Local crew		
(1) _____	_____	_____
(2) _____	_____	_____
(3) _____	_____	_____
(4) _____	_____	_____
3. Props		
(1) _____	_____	_____
(2) _____	_____	_____
Other _____	_____	_____
_____	_____	_____
_____	_____	_____
_____	_____	_____

LOCATION EVALUATION CHECKLIST: AREA _____ (TITLE)

fessional caterer, or just using a local restaurant or coffee shop to supply meals on order.

The second part of the "area" checklist—"local equipment and crews"—can mean anything from an entire remote shooting rig and crew, to a place from which to get an extra cable or hire a production assistant. A place to rent a stuffed elephant, for example, can be valuable if the production requires it and the only alternative is to send it air freight.

If only a single location is involved, one copy of this form would suffice. If there were two locations at one city, then each site would have its own site page, but only one sheet of local information would be necessary. If location shoots in more than one area were planned, then each area would have to be covered by its own complete site and local checklist. In any case, the location scout has his work cut out for him.

REMOTE PRODUCTION CHECKLIST

The production is planned; the personnel are hired; the location has been secured. All is ready, and the day (or days) of production is approaching. What did you forget? To reduce the chances that something important has indeed been overlooked, there is nothing as handy as a production checklist.

Form 7.3 is especially designed for small and mid-sized remote productions. With it, all the objects and papers needed to make a shoot go smoothly can be checked in at the staging point. Subsequently, their packing can be verified, their repacking noted and their return recorded. As can be seen, the list is far more detailed than the budget in respect to the items used. The latter deals with categories in terms of their cost; the checklist deals with specific items in countable quantities that need to be verified. It is also useful as a planning tool when determining what must be rented, bought or otherwise obtained.

The list calls for the number of packages required for the shoot to be accounted for. This is the number of bags, boxes, cases and crates that all the needed items have been packed in. If the production has left for the location with nine packages and the producer takes a quick count at each transfer, he is far less likely to leave one in the back of a taxi or in a hotel closet. The last item in the checklist is the script—with all final corrections and notes—in as many copies as will be needed.

The script is, of course, the director's concern, but it does not hurt to have it there and to check with him about it.

The checklist does not concern itself with personnel, because it assumes that there are not so many that they cannot be kept track of. Needless to say, everyone must be clearly informed—preferably in writing—of the schedule, the itinerary and what is expected of them. As remotes often involve long extra hours and require that everyone pitch in to do more or less menial tasks, it is important to be clear about expectations. It is annoying to work with a prima donna (or primo don) who "never works after seven o'clock" or "can't lift more than five pounds."

THE REMOTE PRODUCTION BUDGET

A remote budget is very like the budget for a studio production, but there are important differences, itemized in Form 7.4. Again, it should be noted that this is a form for a small- to mid-sized production—anything budgeted at from $5000 to not much over $100,000. If a remote is costing upwards of $100,000, excluding pre- and post-production, it needs a production manager and one of the standard television production management forms.

The budget begins with the cost connected with the remote location. This may be a street corner or the home of a friend, but it is also likely to be a rented space. That cost is entered under item 1 on the budget form. Even the street corner may involve some expense. In most larger cities, insurance and permits are required, and even fees for police assistance are charged. Provision for these expenses is made in item 10.

The section on equipment is fairly straightforward. To those who have not done a lot of remote production, an SEG might seem out of place in the field, but in fact, many shoots—such as those of large business conferences—are shot multicam and cut live on the scene. Obviously, then, an intercom system will be needed, and—because a fair amount of money is involved—the equipment would probably include a waveform monitor, if not a vectorscope. (Remember to account for the technical director who will be reading the waveforms.) Other equipment might include a separate audiotape recorder, a character generator and, in some cases, a teleprompter.

"Supplies" covers not only the obvious item, videotape, but all the gels, bulbs, cables, gaffer's tape and miscellaneous items that the production might require. The "etceteras" can add up to a tidier sum than the contingency fund will recoup, and (within reason) should be accounted for at the outset.

While not many remote productions use constructed sets, and while most graphics are prepared in post-production, many remote shoots require some props and sufficient attention to wardrobe to require the rental or purchase of some items. Some relatively modest productions also require the assistance of a makeup specialist— who may be deemed "staff" or "crew," as the producer sees it. The "staff," "talent" and "crew" sections are the same as in studio budgets, explained in Chapter 4.

The "travel" and "food and lodging" sections represent substantial costs for productions that take place at a distance from a producer's home base. But even when a production is local, it is usually necessary to hire a van to transport equipment and personnel to the site and to use cars and taxis to fetch people, objects and food (if a caterer is not used).

If full production insurance (which is expensive, but covers everything from bad weather to bad equipment and the lead's bad back) is not carried, then the producer will only deal with insurance for the equipment and some form of accident insurance. A lot can go wrong on location, and the wise producer will carry some form of insurance to protect himself if someone's life, limb or property is damaged. A personal or general liability policy can cover such unfortunate contingencies at reasonable cost.

The section labeled "other" can be used to specify such expenses as telephone, shipping and legal fees, should these apply. Then, a contingency fee of 5% to 10% of the total should be added to cover the unforeseen.

Accounting for the time, facilities and effort that go into planning this production and preparing this budget presents a difficult problem for most small and independent producers. If an accountant has not determined a suitable overhead figure to use, one way of dealing with this is to charge pre-production time as additional staff days in item 5, and include such expenses as pre-production travel and telephone in the production budget. While this does not cover the fixed costs of the roof overhead, the producer can take comfort in the fact that if the roof were a substantial business expense, he would have an accountant who would have put a value on it.

While this budget can account for a certain amount of pre-production effort and for some overhead expense, it is not designed to handle such extensive pre-production work as script development and preparation, extensive research or rehearsals in rental halls, and it does not deal with the area of post-production at all. Post-production is covered in Chapters 8-11; budgeting the entire program, from concept to delivery, is presented in Chapter 12.

LIGHTING IN THE FIELD

Almost everything that was said in Chapter 4 about lighting a studio set can be used to light an interior shot or a scene in the field—if there is no other ambient illumination to contend with. In fact, there will be many situations in which the location scene will have to be lit from scratch. But in many, if not most, remote production situations, there is existing illumination that must be dealt with: the fluorescents in offices and factories; the incandescent lamps in stores, homes and offices; and daylight—from the true blue (yes, blue) sheen of high noon to the warm orange of a sunset to the purple shades of evening. Each situation requires different lighting tools and techniques, which are discussed in the following sections.

Lighting Interiors on Location

When shooting indoors, ambient light from incandescent and fluorescent sources or daylight entering through windows can be encountered. Each of these light sources is a different color temperature from the 3200°K source that is the camera's basic reference. Ordinary incandescent lamps—the light bulbs we normally use in our reading and work lights—read in the range of 2700°K to 2800°K, yielding a warm, golden light. Fluorescent lamps—the ordinary "white" untinted kind—read at about 4300°K. And daylight, as we noted earlier, averages around 5600°K, although its range is broad—from under 5000°K to as hot as 6500°K.

When working under these conditions, adjusting the filter wheel, or placing the proper filter over the lens, and shooting with available light

Form 7.3: Remote production checklist.

REMOTE PRODUCTION CHECKLIST						(Page 1 of 2)
Item	Source or type	Qty	Recvd	Packd	Repac	Ret'd
<u>EQUIPMENT</u>	Total # of packages on shoot					
Camera: w/CCU__ a						
w/CCU__ b						
w/CCU__ c						
VTR's a b c						
Lights: Kit						
Other						
Mics: Lavaliers						
Other						
Mic Mixer						
Monitors: Port						
Waveform____						
Vectorscope						
Other						
SEG						
Intercom: Master						
Remotes____						
Headsets ____						
Other ____						

Auxiliary Equipment & Accessories						
Tripods: a____						
b____						
c____						
Light stands: a						
b						
Battery: Belts						
Other						
Generator						

Form 7.3: Remote production checklist (cont'd).

REMOTE CHECKLIST						(Page 2 OF 2)
Item	Source or type	Qty	Recvd	Packd	Repac	Ret'd
ACCESSORIES & SUPPLIES						
Bulbs: ____ W						
____ W						
____						
Cables:						
Cam/CCU ____						
Cam/VTR ____						
Mon ____						
Audio ____						
A-C ____						
Other ____						
____						
Gels & ____						
filters ____						
Scrims & ____						
reflect						
Took kit						
Videotape: a ____						
b ____						
____						
Miscell ____						
Supply ____						
____						
____						
On-camera materials						
Graphics ____						
Props (Ref prop list) ____						
Makeup ____						
Costumes (Ref wardrobe list) ____						
PAPERS						
Insurance ____						
Permits: Street ____						
Other ____						
____						
Reservations:						
Travel ____						
Hotel ____						
Car Rental ____						
Script	# copies					

Form 7.4: Remote production budget.

BASIC REMOTE PRODUCTION BUDGET, Page 1 of 2					
Title _____					
Item	Qty	Item per day	No. days	Item total	Total
1. Location Rental					
Loc. a _____					xxxxxxx
Loc. b _____					xxxxxxx
Location subtotal	xxxx	xxxxxxxx	xxxx	xxxxxxxx	$
2. Equipment					
Cameras _____					xxxxxxx
VTRs _____					xxxxxxx
Lighting _____					xxxxxxx
Mics & mixer _____					xxxxxxx
Monitors _____					xxxxxxx
S&G _____					xxxxxxx
Intercom system _____					xxxxxxx
Test equipment _____					xxxxxxx
Tripod & lt. stands _____					xxxxxxx
Other _____					xxxxxxx
_____					xxxxxxx
_____					xxxxxxx
Equip. subtotal	xxxx		xxxx	xxxxxxxx	$
3. Supplies					
Videotape _____					xxxxxxx
Other _____					xxxxxxx
_____					xxxxxxx
Supplies subtotal	xxxx	xxxxxxxx	xxxx	xxxxxxxx	$
4. Props, graphics, etc.					
Props _____					xxxxxxx
Graphics _____					xxxxxxx
Costume _____					xxxxxxx
Makeup _____					xxxxxxx
Sets _____					xxxxxxx
S&G _____					xxxxxxx
Subtotal	xxxx	xxxxxxxx	xxxx	xxxxxxxx	$
5. Staff					
Producer _____					xxxxxxx
Director _____					xxxxxxx
_____					xxxxxxx
_____					xxxxxxx
Staff subtotal	xxxx	xxxxxxxx	xxxx	xxxxxxxx	$
6. Talent					
_____					xxxxxxx
_____					xxxxxxx
_____					xxxxxxx
_____					xxxxxxx
_____					xxxxxxx
Talent subtotal				xxxxxxxx	$
Page subtotal xxxxxxxxxxxxxxxxxxxxxxxxxxxxxxxxxxxxxxxxxxxxxxxxxxxxxxxxxxxxxxxxx					$

Form 7.4: Remote production budget (cont'd).

REMOTE BUDGET, Page 2 of 2					
Title					
Item	Qty	Item per day	No. days	Item total	Total
Balance carried forward	xxxxxxxxxxxxxxxxxxxxxxxxxxxxxxxxxxxxxxxxxxxx				$
7. Crew					
Tech. director					xxxxxxxx
Camera					xxxxxxxx
Lighting					xxxxxxxx
Audio					xxxxxxxx
VTR					xxxxxxxx
					xxxxxxxx
					xxxxxxxx
					xxxxxxxx
Crew subtotal			xxxx	xxxxxxxx	$
8. Travel					
Air fares					xxxxxxxx
Car rental					xxxxxxxx
Local					xxxxxxxx
Other					xxxxxxxx
Travel subtotal	xxxx	xxxxxxxx	xxxx	xxxxxxxx	$
9. Food & lodging					
Meals	xxxx				xxxxxxxx
Catering	xxxx				xxxxxxxx
Lodging	xxxx				xxxxxxxx
Subtotal	xxxx	xxxxxxxx	xxxx	xxxxxxxx	$
10. Insurance, permits					
Production Ins.	xxxx				xxxxxxxx
Travel Ins.	xxxx				xxxxxxxx
Permits	xxxx				xxxxxxxx
Other	xxxx				xxxxxxxx
Subtotal	xxxx				$
11. Other					
					xxxxxxxx
					xxxxxxxx
					xxxxxxxx
					xxxxxxxx
Subtotal					$
Budget subtotal	xxxx	xxxxxxxx	xxxx	xxxxxxxx	$
Contingency (%)	xxxx	xxxxxxxx	xxxx	xxxxxxxx	$
Total remote budget	xxxx	xxxxxxxx	xxxx	xxxxxxxx	$

will rarely give correct color. Ambient light, especially indoors, is rarely bright enough to produce a professional quality image. Even when it does, in such situations as a sunny outdoors, this only provides key light; it is still necessary to fill. Where the light is bright enough—especially outdoors—reflectors can sometimes be used, but often, fill lights are required. Choosing the best way to deal with these problems is the subject of this section.

Outdoors, of course, the sun makes all the choices—although we can control its effects to some extent. But outdoors, the lighting person can choose to "beat 'em or join 'em"—obliterating and filtering out the existing light, or matching the lights to the existing illumination.

Dealing with Fluorescent Lighting

We can "join 'em" when confronted with ambient fluorescent or daylight, which are "hotter" than the required level. Take, for example, the shoot at the Good Health Foods plant that was used in our example of a documentary script (Chapter 1). Here, almost all of the illumination would come from fluorescents, giving faces and objects a cold, greenish cast. Yet undesirable as these lights might be, they are very much a part of the environment at this location, and (presumably) the producer does not have the budget to re-light the factory for a one- or two-day shoot. There are nevertheless several lighting options.

Light for Close Shots

One way of dealing with fluorescents is to tread a narrow line between obliterating them from the shot and lighting entirely at their color temperature. One way to do this is to work mainly in close and medium-close shots and light them entirely with 3200°K lights (presumably from the light kit). The result will be an island of relatively warm light with a cold blue-green background. Because the viewer's eye is likely to be concentrated on the subject, this discrepancy will either not be noticed or will be accepted as a correct "reading" of the situation.

Light to Match

If wide shots are also taken where the fluorescent illumination predominates (and there is no plan to separate these shots from the 3200°K shots on the final edit with related takes from other locations or with pertinent graphics), then it is time to use the "join-em" strategy. To do this, cover the 3200°K lights with a gel that is especially designed to raise their color temperature to match that of the fluorescents (see Chapter 4)[1]. Then, use a camera filter that will correct tungsten for fluorescent lighting. The result will still appear slightly cooler than pure tungsten lighting, because most fluorescents have other color temperature components that appear to be on the "cool" side.

However, because fluorescents from different manufacturers are not standardized for the spectrum of light they emit, this cool tone is extremely difficult to correct fully. Some additional correction can be obtained by using multiple gels that will move the color temperature more toward blue. It is important to remember that while the gels correct color temperature, they reduce light output.

It is also important to remember that as color temperature gets hotter, the visible color of the light gets cooler, changing from red to yellow to green to blue to violet as it goes from under 2000°K to 6500°K.

Matching Daylight to Fluorescents

Correcting for fluorescent lighting is a tricky business, though it can be done. Let's assume an executive is in his office and we need to show or use the daylight coming in through a window, possibly because we don't want to draw the drapes (if there are any) and imply that it is nighttime. However, the fluorescent ceiling lighting cannot be turned off (perhaps because they are under a master control for a larger area). Where only a couple of lights are involved and the ceiling is low, the fluorescents can be removed. Where removal is not possible, the window can be covered with a gel especially designed to cool the color

---

[1]This gel and other temperature compensating materials are available from a number of video supply houses. Although they are carried by very few equipment dealers, a professional video dealer should know where they can be obtained, or can get them on special order.

temperature of daylight to that of white fluorescents. If the day is bright enough, the window light will still make an excellent key light, and the shadows created by the ceiling fluorescents and the daylight can be reduced or removed by one or more lights covered with the appropriate gels (see Figure 7.1).

Matching Fluorescents to Daylight

A better choice in the aforementioned situation may be to cover the fluorescents with a gel that will match their color temperature to that of daylight. If that is done, the lighting setup will be the same as in Figure 7.1, but the gels covering the tungsten lights will change their color temperature

to that of daylight, rather than to that of fluorescents.

Matching Fluorescents to 3200°K Tungsten

If daylight is not the issue, and only a few accessible fluorescents are involved, the best solution may be to adjust the fluorescent illumination to 3200°K by covering the lights with the appropriate gels. In that case, however, it is necessary to decide whether the ceiling illumination will be used as part of the baselight, with a tungsten key light or front light, or whether tungsten illumination from above the set will be used to make the ceiling illumination provide the key light. In any case, whatever lighting setup is used, the tungsten

Figure 7.1: Interior location lighting for daylight matching.

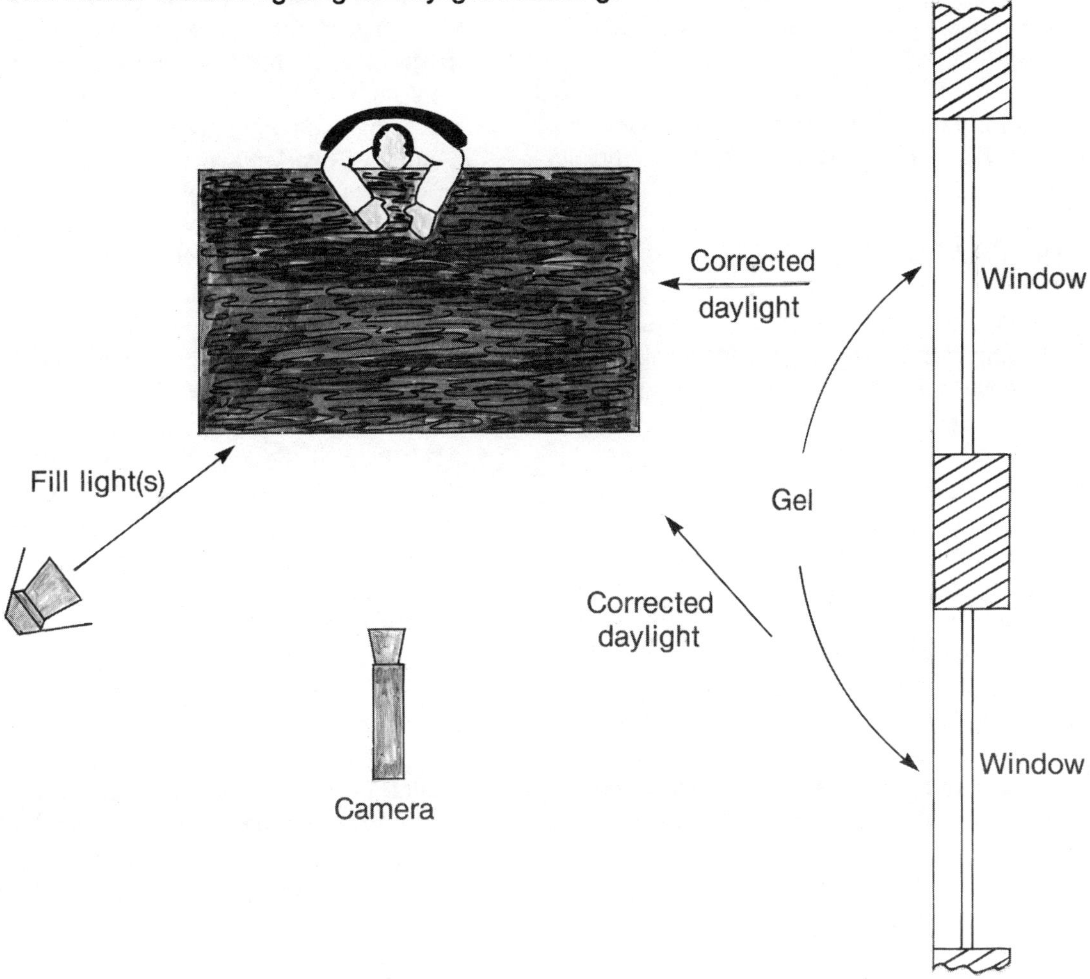

lights are used without gels once the fluorescents are covered.

Dealing with Ordinary Incandescents

Ordinary incandescent bulbs of the kind used in 40- to 100-watt sizes in ordinary lamps cast a warm, golden glow—as seen by the television camera. In most cases, presuming these lamps are on at all, the wattage of these lights is small (relative to the wattage used for optimum lighting), and therefore does not have to be dealt with separately. However, for a shot in which the warmth of such incandescent illumination is desired—as, for example, when the talent is sitting and reading peacefully by lamp light—the wattage of the bulb in the lamp can be substantially increased to, say, 250 watts. This will also increase its color temperature, but not so much that the warmth of the lamp will be lost. By lighting so that this bulb remains the apparent key light, the desired effect will be obtained.

To use a table lamp on a set without getting a low color temperature effect, one can use one of the 3200°K screw-in bulbs available for this purpose in various wattages.

Dealing with Daylight in Interiors

The various approaches that can be used when producing television programs in locations with fluorescent light (discussed above), also apply to interiors exposed to daylight.

Matching the Tungsten

One approach is to cover the windows with an amber gel that cools daylight to 3200°K and then light the scene normally, taking the corrected "daylight" as the key light. However, as this and all such gels are expensive in quantity, it can become costly and clumsy if large expanses of window must be covered. Nevertheless, by this means we can take advantage of a great supply of existing illumination while using our full lighting complement.

Matching the Daylight

Still, it is often better to correct the tungsten lights to match the daylight. This approach requires far less gel, since it is only necessary to clip sheets of a standard blue No. 50 filter/gel over the lights to change their color temperature to 5600°K. While reflectors can also be used, they are always a little tricky to use in confined spaces because they may cast unwanted reflections—which are difficult to wash out—on the walls. Nevertheless, this system also gives the advantage of plentiful illumination with a strong sense of realism.

Following the Sun

When dealing with daylight interiors, however, there is one drawback: the key light (the sun) is always changing. How this can be dealt with depends on the situation. If the subject is "A Day in the Life of," the shifting key would reinforce the theme, so it is possible to take advantage of it. However, if the action to be depicted is not related to time in a meaningful way, then it is better to work in an apparently static lighting condition.

Fortunately, the average viewer will accept quite a large shift in lighting if it happens slowly enough and if he is sufficiently immersed in the material. Accordingly, daylight productions should be shot in either of two kinds of intervals. One is where the sun has passed out of the visual field of the window—for example, where it has risen high enough to be shining down from above, so that it is illuminating the outside but is no longer a visible light source. Except in winter, in most temperate latitudes this means that the window light can be expected to stay roughly the same intensity and color temperature for several hours.

However, if the window faces south, the producer has to reconcile himself to the fact that the sun will be with him most of the day, especially in the winter half of the year when it is lower on the horizon. In that case, it is probably best to start work early and break for a one-hour lunch around noon. Arrange the set, if possible, so that it faces the window, as shown in Figure 7.2. In the morning, use the sun as the key light, and fill from a complementary angle from the west, changing the fill angle to keep your shadows constant from shot to shot. In the afternoon, use a tungsten key light in the east, and fill with the sun from the west.

This technique is given here not because it is an orthodox approach to lighting, but because it illustrates the fact that there is endless room for ingenuity in lighting—as in other facets of production. There is more than one way to tackle a problem. In the south-facing window situation, for example,

Figure 7.2: Using the sun to keylight and fill an interior.

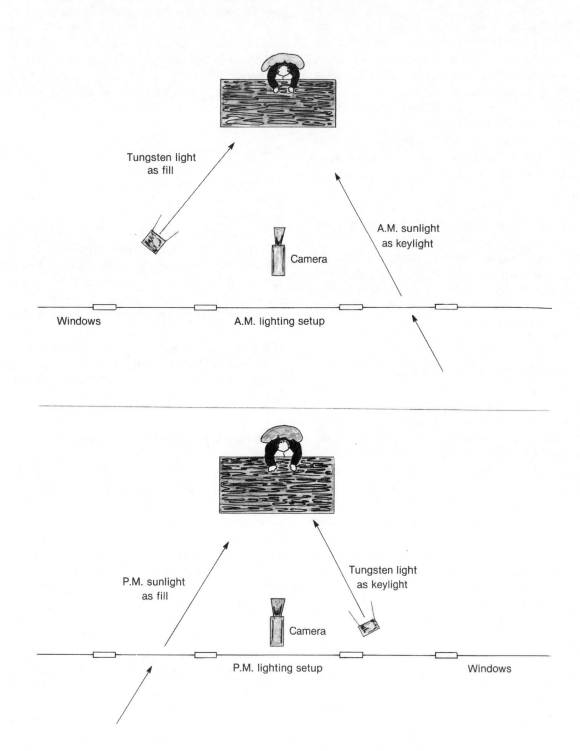

the producer could pull the drapes. If there are no drapes, he can always use his gobo.

Using Your Gobo

The lighting term "gobo" is used somewhat differently in different parts of the country, but in all cases the term deals with a device that reduces the amount of light—especially reflected light—reaching the camera. The various "flags," "dots" and "targets" (small, black nonreflective metal sheets) used to block spill and remove lighting hot spots are gobos. Barn doors are really gobos, as are larger screen or sheets of black cloth (at least 9' x 12') that should be part of every remote lighting kit.

Some of the lighting situations previously described could be simplified by blocking off the undesired light source with a sheet of black cloth. This would have worked in the last instance, where the set faced the windows so that they were not in the image. In any case, blocking light is as important as generating it, especially when the shoot takes place outdoors.

Lighting Exteriors on Location

Lighting the outdoors sounds pointless, akin to "wetting the sea." In fact, however, lighting exteriors often requires a great deal of work, know-how and ingenuity, even when the sun is shining brightly. For example, everyone has seen photographs in which the subject appeared deformed by an acute squint, a nose shadow across the chin and skin like parchment. Although the camera was closed down enough so the exposure was correct, the picture hardly communicated anything about the subjects but their determination to smile through it all. While the exigencies of newsgathering often demand that television news crews shoot public persons at less than their cosmetic best, the wise producer knows he must try to do better.

Reducing the Light

Step one is to reduce the amount of light falling on the subject. One way is to place a piece of scrim—a stretched piece of bobbinet or metal screening, on a pole, if necessary—between the source of excessive light and the subject. On the other hand, the excess illumination may be the result of light reflected from a light-colored or shiny surface, like the wall of a white building. In that case, the amount of light can be reduced either by moving the subject away from the wall, or by covering the wall with a gobo, assuming that the wall is not in the shot. If the white wall is in the shot, the excess illumination will close the camera's iris down so that the subject's face will appear to be dark. The techniques needed to correct this problem are the same as those used to reduce shadows.

Filling the Shadows

Shadows are, of course, reduced by adding fill. Sometimes adequate fill light can be provided by reflectors—in the form of umbrellas or other surfaces that are designed to reflect light in a diffuse pattern without generating new highlights. But in many cases, lights have to be used to fill. In that case, of course, the lights—which are 3200°K tungsten—have to be covered with a gel that will bring them up to proper color temperature. Because daylight is seldom at 5600°K, it is useful to have a kit of tungsten-to-daylight conversion gels that cover a range of daylight color temperatures. (Again, it is necessary to remember that gels reduce light output.)

Shooting in Twilight, Overcast and Shade

Sometimes scenes must be shot in the shadows of trees, buildings and natural objects. While the objects differ, the shadows are always bluer than sunlight and therefore of a higher color temperature. It is seldom suitable or even desirable to correct the color of the entire scene, because the television viewer will accept a certain blue cast in a shadowed area. It is usually necessary, however, to warm up the skin tones; tungsten lights with daylight gels will usually do the job. One should remember, though, that the lighting needs to be kept down to the level where the sense of being in shade is not disturbed. Dealing with lighting in overcast or twilight conditions requires similar strategy.

Lighting exteriors at night involves creating locally lit areas that appear to have ambient lighting or "day-for-night." (Day-for-night is the term for shooting night scenes in daylight with a stopped-down lens.) Both are best left to a first-class lighting designer. While it is not too difficult to produce a sinister effect in the dark, it is very difficult to create a sense of normalcy and still get an image of good technical quality without expert help.

RECORDING AUDIO IN THE FIELD

It takes good technique to record good sound in a television studio, but it takes a lot more than mere follow-the-rules to get good sound in the field. Everything is against the producer—there is a great deal of ambient sound which can bury and distort the audio; there are unexpected sound reflections that create echoes and similar distortions; and there is RF interference that may put the local radio station on the audio track. While the goal of sound recording on location has nothing to do with the pristine audio recorded in the studio, the audio should nevertheless be clear and reinforce the viewer's perception of the video.

Working under the pressure of location shooting, it is tempting to consider the "out" of redubbing the audio later. But even when it is appropriate, dubbing and mixing in the background audio takes skill, time and a great deal of money. In many instances, of course, dubbing is not practical, because the people or situation that created the need for field production will simply not be available for a post-production dub. And in fact, when the production involves the recording of real, fast-moving events, getting the shot and the sync sound is more important than audio finesse. But even when the shots are planned, it is much better to get a good recording in the first place than to patch it up later. While nothing beats experience and ingenuity, the following material will be of value. (See Chapter 3 for more on microphones.)

Recording Background Audio

Recording background audio (or bee gee, as it is sometimes called in the industry) usually involves little more than recording a normal level of sync sound on one of the audio tracks. However, it should be pointed out that this means a *separate* recording on a separate track. This might be needed, for example, if it is later decided that a segment will have narration over it. In that case, the best quality will be achieved if that narration goes over a subdued level of sync sound.

However, if there is only an original voice track that was picked up with a shotgun or a parabolic mic, it might not be possible to get a good background affect. This might happen, for example, if the subject is a crowd being addressed by various speakers. If the speakers are picked up on a highly directional mic, that recording will, in fact, contain some background audio. However, if narration is laid down over that, the viewer will unconsciously try to pick out the speakers' words—and lose the narration. But, if the speakers have been recorded on one track and the background audio has been recorded on the other with an omnidirectional mic, all the possibilities have been covered.

A very different situation exists, however, when the actual background sound is the primary audio. This might happen when we are shooting a scene in a field, and all the sounds of that field—crickets, birds, the wind in the trees and the movements of the talent—are to be dominate the scene. To record such complex sounds and get them to sound right requires dual-system recording—on a separate audiocassette or tape recorder (with sync). As always, when dual-system recording is done, a slate and clapstick should be used to facilitate synchronizing the sound and video later. Of course, it is also possible to use recorded ambience, but that is a matter of aesthetics and funds. Usually, the real thing costs more.

Recording Primary Audio

Recording Audio for ENG

In virtually all ENG situations, the primary audio is recorded with a single microphone—usually a shotgun, certainly a cardioid. If an additional mic is used, it is an omni for recording background audio. The main goal here is to get the sound, because it will not happen again.

Recording with a single mic in an ENG situation is not difficult, but it requires careful concentration in the midst of what is usually some sort of chaos. The sound has to be monitored—ideally on a VU meter, but always on earphones. Otherwise, the producer may find, when he returns from the shoot, that the earnest speaker is merely producing a series of truck roars and car horn noises. The earphones assure the recordist that he is recording comprehensible speech; the VU meter tells him that the level is correct. However, it is important not to rely on the VU meter alone. It may be moving in time to the speech, but the level may be

90% ambient noise that will make the speech virtually unintelligible.

Typical ENG situations include the range of news event coverage, such as press conferences and corporate announcements; man-in-the-street type of interviews, which include any spontaneous one-on-one type of recording; and other situations which are best covered by a single portable unit. In all, the sound must be recorded with a highly directional mic, pointed at the primary source of audio. Because the mic is very directional, it is sometimes possible to improve the recording by changing the angle to the source. For example, if there is a great deal of noise behind a speaker, the recordist can kneel down and point the mic up at the speaker's mouth. When the situation permits, the speaker can talk directly into the mic. In all cases, the mic should be as close to the speaker as possible.

A familiar example of a situation that can be recorded as an ENG production is a wedding. Using a portable camera and a single cardioid mic—preferably a shotgun—the mic would be pointed at the guests (or congregation) from the front, while the bride walks down the aisle. Then from a position at the front, the recordist could point the mic from the person performing the ceremony to the piano or other instrument providing music, to the choir when it is singing, and back to the bride and groom, when they are speaking.

Recording Audio on EFP

Remote recording is not confined to ENG situations. In many cases, we are dealing with EFP—Electronic Field Production—where the "PV" (the "production value," the visible evidence of money or effort spent on production) is often a criterion that the producer must meet. Certainly, he cannot offend the audience's ears with the poor quality of the sound he records, even though he may be under considerable budgetary constraints.

Fortunately, recording good audio is not one of the most expensive things a television producer has to do, even when it involves contending with troublesome audio conditions. Sometimes, when the subjects are indoors and are not going to be moving around, the audio recording can be obtained simply by wiring them up with one or more unobtrusive lavaliers. But in most cases, especially if more than one person or source is being recorded, it is necessary to use several mics and a

mic mixer. Of course, if we are talking about recording a major public event or a symphony orchestra, then professional sound recordists and special audio equipment should be used. The following is written for the producer who must do his own sound recording, with a professional, but minimal crew.

An EFP Wedding

The same wedding we recorded ENG-style can also be recorded as an EFP production, as shown in Figure 7.3. Whether one camera is used or several, the sound can be gathered with several mics set up before the ceremony and routed to a mixer. Mics No. 1, 2 and 3 are cardioids. No. 1 records whatever passes among the bride, groom and the person performing the ceremony; No. 2 records the piano or other musical instrument used to provide the music. (If an electronic organ is used, this might be available as a line output. If not, the mic has to be pointed at the organ pipes, not the organ.) The musical instrument is recorded on its own line during its solos only. Mic No. 3 records the choir, and the accompanying musical instrument is mixed in at that time. (If a powerful organ is used, the organ audio recorded on the choir's mic will probably be sufficient.)

The output of these three mics (or two mics and a line) is controlled at the mixer and recorded as a mix on VTR channel 1. The fourth mic is an omni which is recording the whole event from all sides. Its output goes directly on VTR audio channel 2 at a fixed level. It is the background and reference sound, which can be mixed in later, or discarded, as the final edit requires.

Other Small EFP Setups

The pattern set by the wedding, with variations, will be useful for many ceremonial occasions: award ceremonies, presentations and even concerts. Groups of up to four musicians can be recorded by miking each one individually and providing an omni for the audience. If the group is using amplified instruments, they might have lines-out on their amplifiers. If not, the mics should be placed as close to the source of the sound as possible: in the piano, in front of the amp, looking right into the alto sax and right over the drums. Special singers' mics (discussed in Chapter 3) should be used for vocalists and percussion. The audience can be recorded on the second track of the VTR and the band, mixed live, is recorded on channel 1. having gone to all this trouble, it may be worthwhile to record the mix simultaneously on a separate audio recorder with sync.

If nothing else is possible, and the producer has to record a music performance with nothing more than two decent mics and his VTR, there is no need for despair. Especially when recording for documentary purposes, it is possible to get an acceptable stereo recording with a very old-fashioned stereo technique. Simply place one mic at each side of the group to the front and set matched levels for both mics with the band flat out on a chorus on the VU meters. Put one mic in each audio channel. As always, record the audio on manual and ride the channel control knobs. If there is no manual audio control, just hope that the system's automatic level control will take care of the peaks without killing the highs.

A last, fairly typical EFP situation is the seminar, or any production where both speakers and members of the audience must be recorded. As shown in Figure 7.4, a cardioid mic is mounted at a rostrum if the speakers will change throughout the program, and individual mics are used if the same speakers are to remain on stage all the time (lavaliers are best if the speakers are seated). The speakers from the audience are then picked up with a very directional mic on a boom, or with a shotgun. The speakers' mics and the boom mic are controlled at the mixer. An omni may be used for ambience. Again, the mix goes into one audio channel on the videotape, the ambience into the other.

Figure 7.3: Mic placement at a church wedding shot EFP.

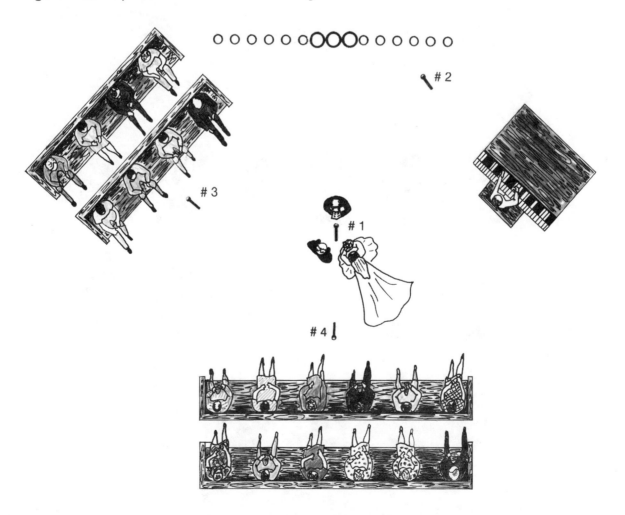

Figure 7.4: Miking speakers and audience at a seminar.

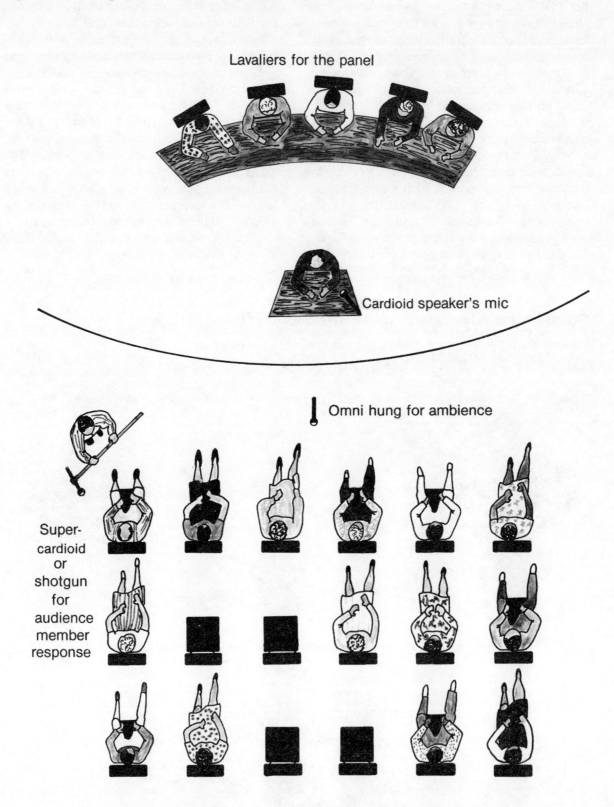

STAFF AND CREW IN THE FIELD

Working on location, the roles of the staff and crew of a video production remain about the same as they were in the studio (see Chapter 5). The role of the producer, especially, is still that of the person who is ultimately responsible for everything— for securing the location, getting everyone to it and getting things done. The similarity to a studio production is closer if the shoot is a multi-camera EFP operation, because this requires essentially a studio without walls. In this case, the producer and technical director (TD) will obtain and supervise the equipment, and the shoot will be conducted very much like a studio operation. When working EFP, the director's role is identical to the one he performs in the television studio. He prepares the talent, blocks the actors and cameras and calls the shots.

But when we are dealing with a single-camera operation, as probably 80% of location shoots tend to be, the roles of the staff and crew are less rigidly defined. For one thing, the number of personnel tends to be smaller on a single-camera remote than it is in the studio. As a result, people work more closely and roles tend to overlap somewhat. At the crew level, it is common for members to be hired with their personal equipment, so that these people tend to have more technical responsibility than they would in the studio.

The Director on Location

On all shoots, the object is to get information that will fit into a scheme—usually the sequence of events and ideas that has been embodied in a script. Keeping this scheme clearly in mind, the director either plans each shot so that it conforms to the script or selects, during an ongoing event, the shots that will further the program he is working on. That does not mean, of course, that every shoot must have a person bearing the title of director.

For news programs, for example, the function of the director is filled by the reporter who accompanies the ENG crew and decides what shots will be taken. Often the writer or producer on a shoot will perform the directional function. On industrial productions, a public relations person or the designer of a product will often decide how it should be presented. All of these people perform the essential function of choosing shots, angles and actions that are intended to further the objectives of the production.

But working out the shots is the major job of the professional television director, whether he is working in the studio or in the field. Accordingly, he familiarizes himself with the script, works with the producer to determine the best location for each segment and prepares the talent for the production. If there are to be several cameras, he decides where they will be placed and what they will cover. In these respects his role is still very much the same as when he works in a studio.

But what does the director do when there is no SEG, no TD to obey his commands and the talent are trained actors? the answer is: plenty.

Directing for Documentaries

When the subject is an event—a concert, a wedding or a missile launch—that will proceed independently of the production, the script outlines the expected sequence of actions that will occur. Nevertheless, because the director plans the shots, it is he or she who creates the view of the event that the completed television program (or segment) will convey.

For example, if the event was the nuclear accident at Three-Mile Island that occurred in 1979, different program objectives would radically change the shots planned. If (as discussed in Chapter 1 on "script preparation") the objective was to present the impact of this accident on energy-source development, then the script would call for shots of the site and interviews with various experts and persons in authority at the site. The interviews would be planned and blocked in the script. The director, however, working within the constraints of the site, might determine whether the interviewees would be sitting, standing or walking about, and what the camera angles would be. When things on a location shoot don't go as planned, it is the director who decides how the shots should be changed to reflect the changed situation.

Directing Dramatic Shows on Location

When he directs shows that include professional talent on location, and he works with a single camera, the role of the director is exactly the same as that of a director working in film. He is concerned with the actors, with the way each shot is lit and taken, and with continuity—the way each shot relates to the next. Like a film director, he is much closer to his camera person, and to his crew generally. His responsibilities, of course, remain the same.

The Crew on Location

Shooting on location creates special demands on the crew members. Every on-location shoot is new and full of unexpected events and situations. There are, inevitably, numerous technical problems that call on the crew's ingenuity and experience. Personnel for remote crews reflect the producer's mode of working and may change to fit the individual production. The following describes one possible remote crew: camera person, audio engineer and production assistant.

The camera person (videographer) works closely with the director to meet the image requirements through variation of camera angles, focal length, selective focus or camera movement. Because of the trend toward "camcorder" systems, the camera person is often called upon to operate the VCR. On many single camera productions, the videographer frequently does the lighting and blocking of the location site. Skilled camera persons with the ability to light, shoot and set up the equipment are always in demand and are valuable members of the production crew.

The skills of the audio engineer on a remote shoot are always taxed by the problems created by ambient sound, mic selection, mic placement and the mixing of audio sources. A competent field audio engineer can anticipate the sound requirements and select the necessary items to accommodate them.

The production assistant (PA) is often an apprentice and has a basic knowledge of production equipment (entry level experience). The PA assists in the production by serving as grip, gaffer (lighting technician), gopher and keeping an accurate "take" log. The PA is a significant part of the crew, often filling in as needed. Therefore, the selection of a good PA is an important choice.

The PA can also be assigned to make sure that each tape is numbered and that each tape is correctly labeled to reflect the actual footage shot when it is taken out of the deck. Labels should include: Project name and number, producer, program title, length of footage and date recorded. The label may also include notes on the tape's content, including shots or scenes recorded, to correlate this data with the take log. In any case, every tape should be clearly labeled with its content in accordance with a consistent system that has been set up beforehand."

CONCLUSION

"Adaptability" best describes the basic requirement for shooting in the field. From choosing equipment to crew selection, the ability to perform several functions or duties on location is essential. Careful planning is needed to make the right choices. Location scouting, checklists and careful selection of crew require valuable time, energy and money. The payoff is the control gained by being fully prepared. When shooting in the field, control and being ready for the unexpected is essential for success.

Whether a program is recorded in the studio or on location, the footage is compiled in post-production. Therefore, the following three chapters are devoted to the editing process.

8 Editing: Concepts, Equipment and Basic Operations

Once the footage has been recorded, the process of building the program begins. Considering how hard producers work to plan and produce the footage, it seems contradictory to say that the editing process is a beginning rather than an end. However, because most projects cannot be "started" until all the materials have been gathered, editing is begun only after all footage has been collected.

For most video programs, editing is a two stage process. The first stage is the preparation of a rough-cut program that approximates the completed product. The second stage is the editing of a fine-cut to create the final program.

The rough-cut program is usually a "cuts only" version without effects, titles and graphics. Its production begins with the cataloging of window dubs: duplicates of the camera master footage that have "burned-in" time code. From this catalog, the shots are organized into an editing script that is based on the original script. The editing script also takes into account any changes that were made during the shooting process. Most important, the rough-cut process provides an edit decision list (EDL) which can take the form of a handwritten list or a computer-generated listing. Even when the rough-cut stage is bypassed, as it is in most news programs, an editing script listing and timing all parts of the show is normally followed.

The fine-cut program is created by editing the master footage according to the EDL created earlier. During this stage the full capabilities of computerized editing systems are applied and special effects are introduced. Titling, graphics and the final audio mix are usually reserved for the fine-cut stage. Figure 8.1 shows an editing session in progress.

BASIC CONCEPTS

It will be useful to look at some basic concepts that are not encountered in the production process. These include the definitions of offline and online editing, time code, black bursting, and assembly and insert editing modes.

• *Offline* and *online* editing refer to the editing stage the program is in rather then to equipment, although specific equipment is generally associated with each stage. These terms have held several different meanings in the past, from a description of the type of equipment used, to where in the transmission chain the process occurred. Currently, offline editing refers to the compiling of the rough-cut program. An online session is the compiling of the fine-cut or finished program.

• *Time code* is digital information used to assign each frame on a videotape a permanent identification number. A frame is identified by its position in hours, minutes, seconds and number of

Figure 8.1: An editing system at work.

frames from the tape head. The hour designation may serve to note reel numbers. For example, the first tape produced is reel number one, the second is reel number two, and so on. However, this cannot be done if tapes longer than one hour are used. A complete time code readout in the format specified by SMPTE (the Society of Motion Picture and Television Engineers) is 03 44 56 23. This would identify the 23rd frame, in the 56th second of the 44th minute of the third tape (or hour) of footage.

Time code can be recorded on an audio track, on a special address track, or during the vertical blanking interval. The first two methods of recording time code are referred to as "longitudinal" time code (LTC), while the third is called "vertical interval" time code (VITC). A significant difference between time code placed on an audio channel and time code recorded on address track or VITC is the ability to add time code after the first recording. Post striping can only be performed on an audio channel. Address track and VITC require the time code to be recorded with the video. If VITC or address track capabilities are not available during the original recording, a duplicate tape must be made to add time code.

• *Black bursting* is the process of recording a steady "black" signal (also termed "basic" or "black burst") that includes horizontal and vertical sync, color burst and control track. Black bursting establishes a stable control track pulse over the duration of the tape readying the tape for electronic editing.

• *Insert mode* provides the ability to insert images and sound over prerecorded material using the existing control track as a timing reference. The preferred prerecorded material is black burst. Because the signal appears black on the screen, cuts to black are possible and if spacing occurs between edits it is not as noticeable. In this mode it is possible to insert video only, audio channels only or video with any combination of audio channels. This flexibility makes it the primary mode for editing.

• *Assembly mode* provides the ability to lay down video, audio and control track on a blank tape. However, unlike insert mode which allows images and sound to be placed anywhere at any time, assembly mode editing must be done se-

quentially. In other words, the edit sequence proceeds in order, i.e., A,B,C,D. The assemble mode actually functions as a duplicate of the source material, transferring sync, video and audio. Assembly editing is often used for "quick-and-dirty" rough-cuts, where the operator does not need to go back and forth on the edit master.

EDITING EQUIPMENT

In the following sections, "cuts only" editing equipment and its operation will be discussed.

Editing Controllers

Video editing systems are designed around a controller that enables the images and sound available at a source deck to be transferred onto a master tape. The controller is in part a remote control, and in part a "dedicated computer," entirely devoted to the performance of editing operations. In the latter respect, the functions of the controller are very similar to those of an electronic alarm clock, that counts timing pulses and delivers a signal to an actuating circuit at a specified, memorized moment. However, unlike the alarm clock, the controller can count backwards and forwards and remember more than one item at a time. Figure 8.2 illustrates some of the basic functions of a controller in an editing system. Its operation is discussed later in this chapter.

The controller illustrated can read either control track or time code, in order to control speed and to determine an edit point. When the operator marks an IN point for the source and editing decks, the controller stores that information in digital form. From then on, any change in the tape position, forward or reverse, is automatically added or subtracted by counting control track pulsed in the appropriate direction. On PREROLL (described later in this chapter), the controller counts back from the IN point for each deck until both counts are equal, and then starts both decks simultaneously. By comparing the timing of the source and record decks, the controller can measure the difference in timing between the decks and generate a differential signal. Once this difference is known, the editing VTR is slowed down or sped up until the vertical intervals of the two decks are perfectly matched. When the now aligned IN point for each deck is reached, the controller directs the editing deck to take the action that has been set

Figure 8.2: Functional diagram of a basic editing system.

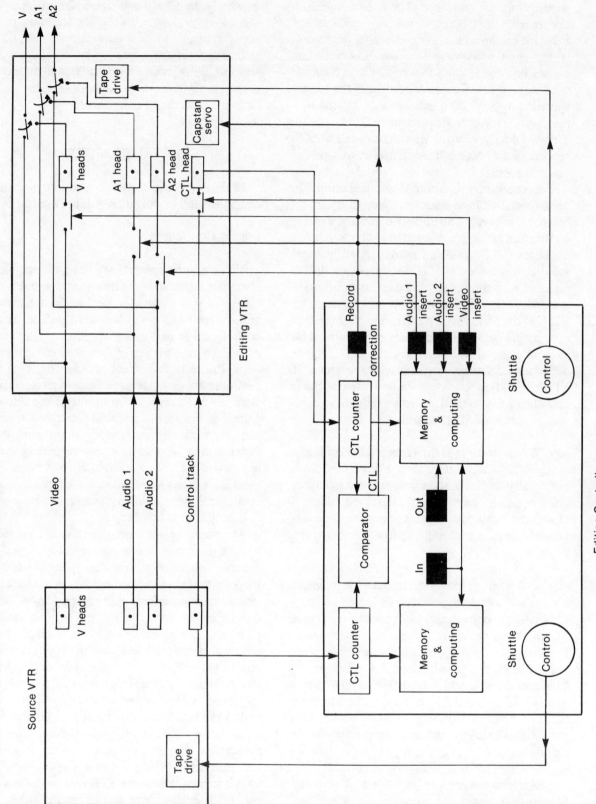

up by the editor, such as "inset video and/or audio" or "assemble."

The actuating function is accomplished when the controller generates an electronic signal that initiates the recording process on the record deck. Normally, all source deck output signals are present at the recording VTR. In fact, they are used to present the source deck's video and audio information to the edit deck monitor in the "E-to-E" mode when the edit deck is not in operation. When the editing deck is in operation, these outputs are overridden (symbolized by the switches at the top of the edit deck diagram in Figure 8.3) and the editing VTR output is displayed on its monitor.

When an INSERT VIDEO instruction is given with the AUDIO INSERT lines in the off position, only the video recording system operates. The new video information is timed by the control track information already on the master tape. This action, which is really performed electronically, is symbolized in the illustration by the closing of a contact switch in the video line. The same occurs when any of the audio channels, with or without video, are used.

When an ASSEMBLE instruction is given, all the heads in the editing deck operate in the RECORD mode. All existing video and audio are erased, as new video, audio and control track are laid down.

Edit control is possible from most edit-capable VCRs. Edit features are provided at the VCR's front panel, including insert, assemble, setting of in/out points and preroll. However the control capabilities of the front panel are limited. They can only control the VCR's recording functions, while the source must be manually activated. This method of having control of the record deck only is referred to as "editing on the fly."

Editing VCRs

Common to all VCRs capable of performing edits is the ability to reference the recorder playback signal to the incoming signal from the source player. This requires a separate capstan servo control system which regulates tape speed. This system includes a separate motor for the capstan, thus allowing for more accurate control of tape speed. Direct-drive technology has replaced older belt-dependent systems, greatly reducing problems associated with wear and aging. Tape shuttling also benefits from direct drive. Tape transports have

been upgraded to handle the hours of wear and tear as the tapes shuttle back and forth during the edit session.

Another important feature that editing decks provide is a DUB mode. This makes it possible to copy a tape with virtually no signal degradation. The need for such a mode arises from the fact that small-format systems handle chrominance information on a "low-band" mode. Instead of its normal (subcarrier) frequency of 3.58 MHz, the chroma information within the deck is taken down (heterodyned) to the KHz frequency range and then beefed back up to 3.58 MHz on playback. The result of this step-down and step-up is a substantial increase in chroma signal-to-noise level with each generation. However, with dub-capable editing decks, both the chroma and the luminance are sent from the source to the recording heads in the record deck directly and arrive in the same shape in which they were sent.

Routine Maintenance

To ensure long-term durability and accuracy from VCRs, a documented and periodic maintenance program is essential. Maintenance includes cleaning, calibration and measurements performed pursuant to the manufacturer's suggested maintenance schedule.

The simple use of dust covers when the equipment is not in use and the maintenance of a smoke-free atmosphere can lengthen the editing deck's life considerably. Another simple method is to keep a videotape of the color bars recorded on the editing decks when they were new. These bars when played should have sharp demarcations between colors and steady, straight sync on the cross-pulse monitor. When instabilities start to appear as this tape is played, it is time to have the deck adjusted. This simple test ensures mechanical and electronic accuracy. However, no matter what method is employed there must be a procedure to check edit performance routinely.

EDITING OPERATIONS

At a casual glance, most editing controllers appear to be a maze of buttons that is difficult to master. While selecting and juxtapositioning material does require both expertise and talent, the actual manipulation of a basic small-format editing system is relatively easy. To help the producer who has access to a "cuts only" editing system, the following information is provided.

Basic Operations

The object of a simple "cuts only" edit is to place each new segment on the edit master so that the first frame of the new material will start at precisely the point at which the last desired frame of the previous segment on the master ends. The first step is to position the videotape on each deck at the "edit point." The record deck will be paused on the point at which the previous edit should end. The source deck (or player) will be paused at the point where the new piece of material should begin.

To perform this edit on the simplest type of editor, all that is necessary is to press the EDIT button together with the INSERT or the AS-SEMBLE button, depending on the mode in use. The controller then rolls the tape in both decks back an equal number of seconds from the edit points, puts both decks in the FORWARD mode and, when the edit point is reached, puts the record deck in RECORD to lay in the new material. This is illustrated in Figure 8.3.

In order to accurately record or duplicate video information with the same precision with which it is laid down, the videotape must be moving at precisely the same speed at all times. However, due to inertia, it is not possible for the tape speed to stabilize instantly out of a dead start. Accordingly, the tape is rolled back for several seconds (depending on the VTR's requirements), exactly the same amount on both decks, prior to an edit. This is PREROLL. Therefore, when the decks roll forward to the edit point, both tapes are moving at the same speed. This ensures that the first field of the next edit is placed correctly.

Because the counting is done using control track, at least 10 seconds of prerecorded video are needed before the first edit can be performed. The color bar test signal may be substituted for black for these seconds. The color bars are also used to adjust the video screen for monitoring the program.

Performing an Insert Edit

While the full capabilities of a computer-assisted editing system can only be realized in the hands of a experienced editor, the basic editing operations needed to create programs can be out-lined here. Using the controller illustrated in Figure 8.4, we can perform a practice edit. For this edit, we assume that the master tape has an unbroken control track.

Setting Up the Source VTR

The editor begins by setting the source deck to the first frame of the material to be put on the master tape. This is done by using the remote controls for the player on the left side of the controller as follows:

1. Run the tape to within a minute of the desired edit point by starting the tape from its head and using FAST FORWARD (FF).

2. As the tape nears the edit point, shift the deck to PLAY.

3. When the start of the edit appears on the monitor, press the STILL button (always working on the left side of the controller.)

4. Press the SHUTTLE/JOG DIAL. The JOG mode is activated by pressing down on the knob, while SHUTTLE is the normal position.

5. In JOG mode, rotate the DIAL until the player monitor displays a still frame at the edit point.

6. Note (in writing, on the edit decision list or on the editing script) the minute and frame number of the edit point as it appears in the window dub or on the left-hand LED readout.

7. Now move slightly to the right of the editing buttons labeled PLAYER IN/OUT and press the button marked IN and then the button marked ENTRY. This will record the edit IN point for the player. (We will, for this edit, omit the OUT, or EXIT point, which is dealt with at the end of this chapter.)

Setting up the Recorder

This process is identical to the set-up procedure for the player, except that the controls for FF, PLAY, PAUSE and SEARCH, as well as the recorder's own SHUTTLE/JOG DIAL, are at the right side of the controller. The recorder control code is read out on the LED at the right, and the

Figure 8.3: Edit point layouts on tape.

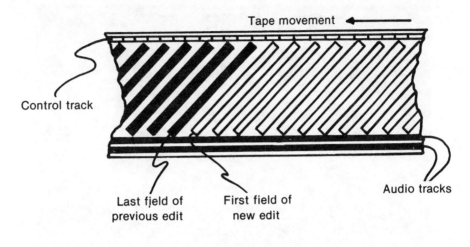

a. The edit point

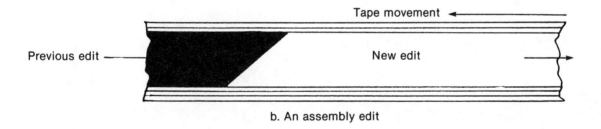

b. An assembly edit

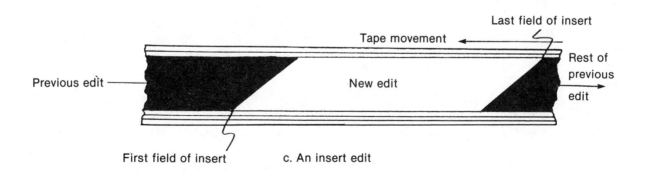

c. An insert edit

Figure 8.4: Editing controller.

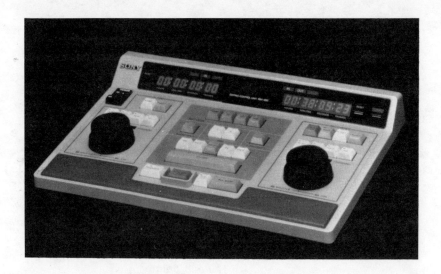

Courtesy of Sony Corp.

ENTRY button under the RECORDER ENTRY section is pressed.

Preparing the Edit

For this practice edit both audio tracks, CH1 and CH2, and the video signal will be transferred. To do this, depress the three EDIT MODE buttons at the top of the controller: VIDEO, AUDIO CH1 and AUDIO CH2.

Pre-Checking the Edit

The PREVIEW function provides an opportunity for the editor to see a finished edit without actually committing it to tape. This involves the following steps:

1. Press the PREVIEW button. Both decks will automatically preroll and then run forward to perform the edit.

2. With most controllers, the decks go five to ten seconds into the new edit and then stop. Some controllers then automatically return the decks to their initial entry points. With other controllers, including the one illustrated, the editor must instruct the controller to return, by using the ALL STOP button.

3. The TRIM buttons are used for refining the in and out points of the edit. The TRIM+ and PLAYER IN buttons are depressed to add frames to the edit. This backs up the tape on the player one frame each time it is pressed, and simultaneously shifts the recorded IN point for the player. Where we stop is now automatically the new IN point for the new material. To subtract frames, the TRIM− button is used. To TRIM the edit point on the record deck, the same procedure is followed, except the TRIM button is now used with the IN/OUT for the RECORDER.

4. Preview the edit again.

Performing the Edit

With all preparations completed, all that is necessary is to press the red AUTO EDIT/END button. The controller prerolls the decks, puts them into play and performs the edit automatically.

However, because no OUT (or EXIT) point has been specified, the system will continue to record the material from the player onto the master tape until the operator manually interrupts the process. To do this press the AUTO EDIT/END button. However, it should be noted that every edit needs a few extra frames at the end to provide a "pad" for the next edit. If the next edit should come in even one frame late, the pad from the old edit then provides an extra frame to avoid a gap.

Reviewing the Edit

Once the edit is performed, it must be checked, and this is the purpose of the REVIEW button. When review is depressed, the controller backs the record deck up to its preroll position and runs the last edit sequence.

The review process is important because it can help expose small instabilities that often occur at an edit point as the deck shifts from PLAYBACK to RECORD. Often these instabilities do not show up when an edit is first made. They can constitute a potential problem "hook" on which no experienced editor will hang a new edit. (This is not a problem on high-format machines.)

Performing an Assembly Edit

Like so many terms found in video production and post-production, "assembly edit" can describe two entirely different methods, depending on the context in which the term is used. Strictly speaking, the assembly edit as it applies to the mode represented on most "cuts only" edit systems refers to the method explained in the basic concepts section. However, when an auto-assembly feature is offered on a sophisticated computerized editing system, this feature makes it possible to assemble the finished program using an EDL. It is performed on a blacked tape in the insert mode.

The procedure for setting up an assembly edit is similar to that used for insert editing. However, there are two important differences:

One is the loss of control track at the out point. This requires the editor to go past his OUT point, providing enough control track to lock up the next IN point. Without this "pad" or overrun there may not be enough control track for the new IN point. The other important difference is that all channels of audio and the video are transferred. There is no opportunity during the assembly edit mode to choose a different combination of video and audio channels.

Loss of Control Track

It is sometimes necessary to revert to assembly editing from the INSERT mode when a fault in the control track is encountered. This may happen because of equipment faults that went unnoticed when the control track was laid down or because an assemble edit is accidentally performed by the editor. It is essential to understand that once the control track is broken, coherent insert editing is not possible. The resulting master will always be defective and roll or tear at the points where the control track is broken.

However, as long as the loss of control track is not due to a physical defect in the videotape, the tape may still serve as the edit master. All that is necessary is that new black burst be laid on the master tape. This may be done with an assemble edit that starts a couple of seconds before the point at which the control track was lost. When the new control track is laid over the rest of the tape, a continuous control track is reestablished and insert editing can safely proceed as before.

Other Editing Operations

In addition to the procedures outlined above, there are a few more functions that can be used. These include OUT and GO TO operations.

Using OUT, or EXIT, Points

It is often useful to specify an OUT point, rather than end the edit manually, particularly in the insert mode. When the controller has an OUT point entry button, it is only necessary to position the player or recorder deck at the place on the tape where the OUT point should occur and then press the OUT (or EXIT) button for that deck.

The OUT point is normally specified for the source deck when the edits are first being performed. Because the OUT point on the master is black and unmarked, there is no point in using it. On the other hand, by specifying an OUT point on the source material that is a few seconds after the actual planned end of the edit, the controller will automatically provide a pad.

Conversely, if a true INSERT edit is performed on a edit master it is essential that the record deck's OUT point be used. Thus, the new material will not impinge on the existing material that follows the edit.

Using GO TO Points

Many controllers provide functions labeled TAG, AUTOTAG, or GO TO, all of which provide a means of returning the record deck automatically to the last specified IN or OUT point. The controller shown in Figure 8.4 features a GO TO button. Some controllers perform this operation automatically.

There are a number of other functions that are available on sophisticated editors, but these will be touched on when we discuss the online session in Chapter 10. The next chapter deals with preparing and budgeting for post-production.

DESKTOP VIDEO

Desktop video is commonly referred to as a compact video production system based on personal computer technology. The system may be used to provide character generation, video painting, low-end graphics, sound/voice synthesis and video editing. It is the video counterpart of desktop publishing.

Desktop video system capabilities may include word processing, job management, library control, color animation, color graphics, character generation, digital effects, audio control, video editing control and teleprompting. These capabilities are achieved through the mixing of different combinations of hardware and specialized software.

The PC platform used for desktop video must be able to produce color images and output them to NTSC video for recording by a VCR. In addition it must be capable of performing "multi-tasking." Multi-tasking allows the user to run more than one software program at a time. It allows switching between software programs without interrupting any of the programs running. Multi-tasking is not available on all PCs; for example, the IBM PC EXT does not offer multi-tasking.

Desktop video is evolving as new PC platforms are refined and capabilities are increased. Although there is much confusion about desktop video, what is important to the video producer is its ability provide pre-production, offline and graphic tools at his or her desk. In these times of working smarter as well as harder, desktop video can give a producer added control over the producing process, always a real plus. It is too soon to speculate as to its final place in the video production process.

CONCLUSION

Building a quality program requires close attention to detail, organization and planning, especially during the editing process. This is why the post-production map or EDL is essential.

But it should not be forgotten the process of editing is not only a matter of equipment. Editing equipment only serves as a tool, putting images and sound together in such a way that the essential ideas conveyed by the subject are communicated to the viewer.

9 Editing: Preparation and Budgets

Most production planning does not place enough emphasis on the editing process as if post-production were some sort of "wrap-up" operation. However, editing needs to be an implicit part of the production process, considered even before shooting begins.

In a multi-camera production, the editing usually consists of inserting a few cover or reaction shots into the finished sequences and assembling these sequences into a finished program. Of course, multi-cam production makes planning especially important. If it well done, the payoff in efficiency is enormous; when the shoot is finished, the program is virtually complete. Since the cost of a multi-camera production setup may be less than the cost of the editing sessions needed to produce a program of equivalent quality, multicam production is often worthwhile.

In the single-camera shoot, the purpose is "footage gathering." The final choice of the precise points at which transitions are made lies with the editor. However, while the script can be far less specific about the timing of a shot and its details, the transitions that will be used between shots must be carefully noted. One aspect of this is implicit in the function of the continuty person, part of whose job is to make sure that the blue-shirted actor knocking on the door in the exterior location shot does not enter the studio's interior set in a red vest. In effect, the single-camera shooting script also provides a great deal of information for the final edit.

However, even the best-planned production may not conform even to the most carefully written script. An actor comes up with a better way of doing a scene that changes the shot sequence, or the documentary situation turns out to be very different than the one on which the script was based. Therefore, in many cases, different editing tactics will be required.

No matter which type of production is chosen and whether or not the original plans are followed, several steps are required before editing can begin. These include preparing worktapes (copies), a catalog of shots, an edit decision list (EDL) and a rough-cut.

PREPARING WORKTAPES

The first step in preparing to edit is to confirm that each of the source tapes has been properly identified and labeled during the commotion of shooting. Labels should include project number, producer, program title, length of footage and date recorded. Although additional information may vary depending on the program type, every tape should be clearly marked with its content, using a system appropriate to the program.

The second step in preparing to edit is to make copies of the production footage. These worktapes are used to catalog the footage and make a rough cut without risking damage to the original videotape. In cataloging and rough editing, the tape is shuttled back and forth many times over the VTR heads, with possible wear on the oxide surface. Occasionally, physical damage is caused by a tape machine. A damaged worktape is annoying, but damaged original footage can spell disaster for a program.

The stock for the worktapes may be "used," but it cannot be damaged or exhibit significant dropout, because one of its functions is to enable the editor to evaluate the technical quality of each shot. Guessing whether video noise or other damage is on the transfer or on the original footage is a waste of time that can quickly add up to more than the price of adequate tape. Worktapes can be made on any format, but ¾-inch or ½-inch tapes are preferred. Small-format systems are more cost effective for rough edits than high-format systems and are perfectly adequate for this purpose.

Worktapes Without Time Code

If the final cut is performed using a control track editor and will not use time code, the worktapes should be the same length as the originals to make cataloging easier. That is, if the footage was shot on 20-minute tapes, the worktapes should each be the same length. It is especially important when using control track systems to slate the beginning of each cassette (reel). This slate provides a place to zero the machine and sets a reference mark. Several source reels may then be placed on a longer worktape. For example, a VHS T-60 tape can contain three source reels of 20-minute lengths, as shown in Figure 9.1. This conserves tape, but complicates the editing process because it will be necessary to zero the counter at the beginning of each source reel.

As long as time code is not used, it must be remembered that a segment on either the worktape or on the original footage can only be found by its number by starting each tape manually at its head. This is because the control track numbers are referenced to the beginning of each tape.

Time Code and Worktapes

If time code is used, so much the better. Time code is specific information that is recorded for each frame, as described in Chapter 8. The value of this is evident. If, for example, a tape has been run forward for three minutes and it is put into a deck without being rewound, the control track readout will start at zero and all subsequent read-

ings will be three minutes off. With time code, the location code for an image can be read out correctly from any tape, whether it is rewound or not.

Working without time code during editing can be tedious. Every time an original tape without time code is removed from the source deck, it must either be rewound back to its head, or its position must be recorded. Then, should the tape position be noted on the edit list with, say, the wrong reel number, it becomes necessary to search through the original catalog, with considerable loss of expensive time. With time code, the reel number (recorded as hours, with the segment position given in minutes, seconds and frame number) is on each frame, and the editor is never at a loss for this information.

Time code can be recorded on the original tape at the time of production, or when the material is being duplicated for worktapes. A time code generator can be hooked up to a VTR to record time code on the original tape. But whether time code is recorded on the original on an audio track, or on a time code address "track," it can be converted to a visible image on the worktape by means of a time code printer, as shown in Figure 9.2. This device transforms the time code into video and either superimposes it directly on the workprint image or drops it into a "window" or box. (Whether superimposition or a window is used, the process is often referred to as making "window dubs." An alternate term is time code "burn-in.") This time code is an integral part of the worktape image and cannot be removed. However, because the worktape is only a reference copy, this does not matter.

The windows are only for visual reference. For the machine, the worktape carries the time code in electronic form on its track, from which the editing controller reads it to establish edit position. With the more sophisticated editing controllers, it is also possible to use known time code numbers to locate segments. These controllers incorporate a numeric keypad, which enables the editor to insert a tape in a deck, "punch up" the time code for the start of the desired segment and let the controller run the tape automatically to that point.

CATALOGING

Novice editors often underestimate the importance of meticulous cataloging. It seems such a dull, unrewarding job compared to the glamorous, result-producing activity of editing a finished tape. Until they have paid in time and anxiety for an

Figure 9.1: Original-to-worktape relationships.

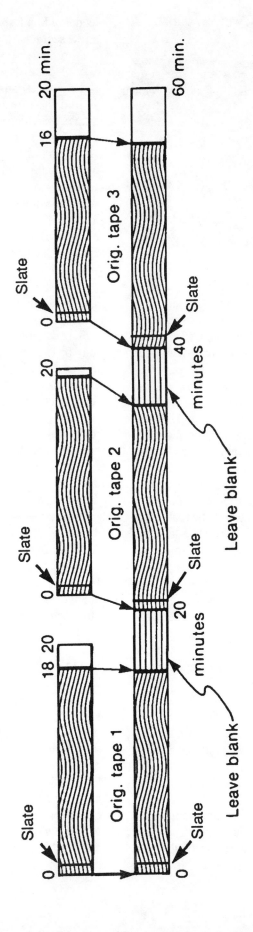

Figure 9.2: A time-coded "window dub."

inadequate catalog, they may think that, for example, it is enough to list that a certain shot is at position 11 26 12 (in minutes, seconds and frames) on reel 3. At the same time, they neglect to record that: the first 11 minutes of that reel have extra takes of the last shot on reel 2, each of which should be listed separately; minutes 14 to 17, although they are called for in the script, are virtually unusable because of bad lighting; and minutes 17 to 20 have some cover shots for the three previous scenes that will probably not be needed (but then again, who knows?).

Chances are 99 out of 100 that this approach will cost more in time than making a complete catalog in the first place. In the end, the realities of the visual material supersede written intentions. Even if the script was very good and complete, the rough-cut will reveal the need for a change here and there—a superfluous shot removed, a new transition selected, and at some point, an additional shot or even a whole sequence inserted to make a point clear. Minutes rush into hours of online time spent searching for shots that the editor knows are "somewhere near the beginning of the fourth—or is it the fifth—cassette." The answer is to catalog well and carefully on a catalog sheet, such as the one shown in Form 9.1. Each tape of footage should have a reel number, and if it does not, this is the time to assign it and mark it clearly on both the tape and its box. If eight-digit time code is used, then a different "hour" number should have been assigned to each reel to identify it. The "shot" location" is the starting point of the shot only, whether control track or time code is used. Its OUT point is the IN point of the next shot—because *everything* is recorded, including

leader or blank spaces and false starts of more than a few seconds.

Shot descriptions should be written out in enough detail to identify the shot in a script or, if it is documentary material, with enough information to find the shot on the basis of content. For example, the video section might say "MS of Rogers with 3 men, incl. Parsons and Diaz," while the audio section might say "Discussion of need for better quality control of capstan diameter." The condition of the shot is also important. In most cases, the entry may be no more than "Good," but it might be very specific, as for example: "Dropout at 41 16 25; soft focus 42 30 00 to 43 33 00; camera shake at 44 17 & 18."

The Editing Script List and the Rough-Cut

The catalogued material and the original script may be used together to prepare an editing script, or the producer may decide to go directly to an edit decision list (EDL). The editing script, using a form such as the one shown in Form 9.2, still permits the producer to think things through, to review his decisions on paper as well as on tape, because the editing script still contains short references to content. The EDL, which is discussed in detail in Chapter 10, is a computer oriented list of time code and transition codes and speaks only the language of the computerized editing system. Theoretically, it should be possible to produce a final editing script simply by "plugging in" the desired shots in the order called for by the script. However, the material that was actually shot may change the final form of the show. Even Alfred Hitchcock, who was famous for having "shooting scripts" that hardly varied in sequence from the final cuts, had to select the particular takes he would use and had to select the particular frames at which each cut would begin and end.

Except in such situations as broadcast news segments, where there is little time for deliberation, the editing script is both the design for and the result of the rough-cut. The rough-cut is an edited version of the finished program that will have all its segments in correct relationship to one another, but will not necessarily have any of the effects or titles planned for the final edit.

The value of the rough-cut is both economic and aesthetic. It is economic because an inexpensive, small-format (¾- or ½-inch) editing system

Form 9.1: Footage catalog sheet

FOOTAGE CATALOG SHEET					
Hz/ Reel no.	Shot Location	Shot Time	Shot Description		Condition of Shot
			Video	Audio	

Form 9.2: Edit decision list.

EDITING SCRIPT _____ (Title)								
Edit No.	Script Page No.	Edit Time	Total Time	Original Footage			Edit Description	
				Reel No.	In Point	Out Point	Video	Audio

can be used to perform rough edits, saving the cost of thinking an edit through on expensive fine-cut equipment. It improves program aesthetics because it allows the editor to try various approaches before selecting the takes and edit points that will make up the final program. This freedom to edit without the cost and pressure of working on an online system helps the editor to create a better product.

Anatomy of the Editing Script

Form 9.2, for an editing script, provides first for the number of the edit and the edit time (the duration of the edit in seconds, or in minutes and seconds). The next element is the page of the original script, which enables the editor to look back, if he needs to, and see what a particular shot was intended for. The total time is the program clock that starts at zero and tells the producer at any moment where he is in the program. With time constraints (especially if commercial breaks are needed), this is an essential element. Even if the program is being produced for closed-circuit presentation, the total time figure tells the editor how he is doing; if he is midway in program time, is he midway in the presentation of the material?

The information about the original footage (in the next column of the editing script) comes, of course, from the catalog sheet (Form 9.1), from which the shots to be used are selected for the edit. The IN point here—with room for minutes (M), seconds (S) and frames (Fr) in control track or time code—however, is not the same one that appears on the catalog sheet, because that is the frame at which the VTR started rolling. Even with the best equipment, it is wise to select an IN point that is *at least* five seconds after the start of a shot, to ensure that the material to be used was laid down after the deck that recorded it reached the correct speed. The selection of the OUT point is not as critical in terms of technical quality, because if the material is technically sound, it will be sound until the point at which the deck or camera was turned off.

At this stage of the editing process, the entry of the video and audio information need not be as specific as it did on the catalog, because it is not as critical. At this point, the control track or time code numbers identify a location precisely, and the editor no longer has to evaluate the content, because that has already been done prior to listing

the edit. A short note for the video and the first and last words (or phrase) of audio are enough. The numbers carry the story.

When VTR counter numbers are used to locate edits, a somewhat different editing script format can be used, as shown in Form 9.3. This format provides more space for the video and audio information and less for the IN and OUT points, because these are only three- or four-digit VTR counter numbers, rather than six digits of control track.

BUDGETING FOR POST-PRODUCTION

Now that the process of preparing for post-production has been examined in some detail, it will be easier to see the logic of a post-production budget. Form 9.4 can be used to determine the cost of post-production.

1. The *worktape* is a dub of all the footage collected. If no time code was recorded during production and time code will be used, the process of recording and burning it into the video on the worktape is budgeted here. The form allows for each of these processes to be entered separately, but usually, the "TC burn-in/transfer" entry will cover the whole process. If no time code burn-in is called for during the transfer to worktape, then a simple transfer can be entered here. In all cases, labor and equipment on a per-diem basis can be entered separately in the columns provided, or, where a single price may cover both labor and equipment, a single entry can be made for the whole item in the space provided. Similarly, materials like videotape can be entered on a cost-per-cassette (or reel) basis. By entering the quantity and multiplying, the cost of videotape for the worktape can be determined.

2. The *catalog* requires machine and personnel time to review all the tape used in production. If a separate cost for equipment is incurred, the labor and equipment can be entered separately. Otherwise, a single entry is made for the entire process, multiplied by the number of days anticipated.

3. The *EDL* may be estimated by taking into account personnel and material expenses. Materials required may include computer supplies and reproduction services.

4. *Graphics* introduced during editing may be of different kinds. The aspect that is dealt with in this part of the budget is the actual preparation

Form 9.3: Edit Decision List, Rough-Cut.

				\multicolumn{3}{c}{Original Footage}	\multicolumn{2}{c}{Edit Description}
Edit No.	Script Page No.	Edit Time	Total Time	Reel No.	VTR In Point	VTR Out Point	Video	Audio

EDL (VTR Nos) _____ (Title)

of the graphics before the edit. Board graphics are drawings or illustrations that require the use of a graphics camera during editing. Slide graphics may involve the use of a slide chain. However, all that is covered here is what needs to be done to get the graphics to the editor. The same is true for computer graphics. If they are generated as part of the editing process, then they should not be entered here. But if they are generated separately and brought to the edit as footage to be integrated into the program, this is where they belong. As before, if any one of these is provided as a service, a unit price and quantity give the "Item total." If they are provided in-house, a separate labor and materials or equipment charge can be entered.

5.   *Slide/film transfer* is covered here if it is done separately from the editing process, so that the transfer is brought to the editor as footage. The preparation of the slides is covered above, while the shooting of film is normally a separate production operation.

6.   *Audio materials* may be obtained as part of the production process, but more often they are taken care of during the post-production period.

Narration usually requires the cost of a sound booth, which may be available at the editing facility. Payment for music and sound effects is also provided for here.

7.   The *rough-cut* has been covered in considerable detail earlier in this chapter. Rough-cuts can be estimated on a per-day basis, or in terms of the labor and equipment time involved.

8.   The *online edit* is the big step toward which the post-production process is directed. It may involve not only an editing system but a number of auxiliary pieces of equipment: noise reducers, time base correctors, frame store and other graphics units, graphics cameras and almost always a character generator of some sort. There are usually additional charges for each item when the editing system is rented. On the other hand, if a completely equipped system with an editor is rented on a per-day basis, the first line and the videotape cost may be all that are needed.

9.   *The audio mix* may be part of the edit, but just as often it is a separate process. If it is, an audio for video facility may be involved, and it

Form 9.4: Post-production budget.

Item	Item Per day/each Labor	Equip.	No. days or qty.	Item total	Total
1. Workprints					
Time Code Record	xxx	xxxx			xxxxxxxxxxx
Labor					xxxxxxxxxxx
Equipmen	txxxxx				xxxxxxxxxxx
TC Burn-in/Transfer	xxx	xxxx			xxxxxxxxxxx
Labor		xxxx			xxxxxxxxxxx
Equipment	xxxxx				xxxxxxxxxxx
Videotape:	xxx	xxxx			xxxxxxxxxxx
Other					xxxxxxxxxxx
Workprint subtotal	xxxxx	xxxx	xxxxxx	xxxxxxxxxxxx	$
2. Catalog	xxx	xxxx			xxxxxxxxxxx
Labor		xxxx			xxxxxxxxxxx
Equipment	xxxxxx				xxxxxxxxxxx
Catalog subtotal	xxxxxx	xxxx	xxxxxx	xxxxxxxxxxxx	$
3. Edit Decision List (EDL)					
Labor		xxxx			xxxxxxxxxxx
Material					xxxxxxxxxxx
					xxxxxxxxxxx
EDL subtotal	xxxxxx	xxxxx	xxxxxx	xxxxxxxxxxxx	$
4. Graphics					
Board graphics	xxx	xxxxx	xxxxxx		xxxxxxxxxxx
Labor		xxxxx			xxxxxxxxxxx
Materials	xxxxxx	xxxxx			xxxxxxxxxxx
Slide graphics	xxx	xxxxx	xxxxxx		xxxxxxxxxxx
Labor		xxxxx			xxxxxxxxxxx
Materials	xxxxxx	xxxxx			xxxxxxxxxxx
Computer graphics	xxx	xxxxx	xxxxxx		xxxxxxxxxxx
Labor		xxxxx			xxxxxxxxxxx
Equipment	xxxxxx				xxxxxxxxxxx
Graphics subtotal	xxxxxx	xxxxx	xxxxxx	xxxxxxxxxxxx	$
5. Slide/Film Transfer	xxxxxx	xxxxx			xxxxxxxxxxx
Labor		xxxxx			xxxxxxxxxxx
Equipment	xxxxxx				xxxxxxxxxxx
Videotape	xxxxxx	xxxxx			xxxxxxxxxxx
Transfer subtotal	xxxxxx	xxxxx	xxxxxx	xxxxxxxxxxxx	$
6. Audio Materials					
Narration	xxx	xxxxx			xxxxxxxxxxx
Labor	xxxxxx				xxxxxxxxxxx
Equipment		xxxxx			xxxxxxxxxxx
Music/Effects					xxxxxxxxxxx
Audio material subtotal	xxxxxx	xxxxx	xxxxxx	xxxxxxxxxxxx	$
Page subtotal	xxxxxx	xxxxx	xxxxxx	xxxxxxxxxxxx	$

Form 9.4: Post-production budget (cont'd).

Item	Item Per day/each		No. days or qty.	Item total	Total
	Labor	Equip.			
Balance carried forward	xxxxxxxxxxxxxxxxxxxxxxxxxxxxxxxxxxxxxx				
7. Rough Cut _____	xxx_____xxxxx		_____	_____	xxxxxxxxxxxx
Labor _____	_____	xxxxxx	_____	_____	xxxxxxxxxxxx
Equipment _____	xxxxxx	_____	_____	_____	xxxxxxxxxxxx
Videotape: _____	xxxxxx	xxxxxx	_____	_____	xxxxxxxxxxxx
Other _____	_____	_____	_____	_____	xxxxxxxxxxxx
Rough-cut subtotal _____	xxxxxx	xxxxxx	xxxxxx	xxxxxxxxxxxxxx	$
8. Online Edit _____	xxx_____xxxxx		_____	_____	xxxxxxxxxxxx
Labor _____	_____	xxxxxx	_____	_____	xxxxxxxxxxxx
Equipment: standard _____	xxxxxx	_____	_____	_____	xxxxxxxxxxxx
Other _____	xxxxxx	_____	_____	_____	xxxxxxxxxxxx
_____	xxxxxx	_____	_____	_____	xxxxxxxxxxxx
_____	xxxxxx	_____	_____	_____	xxxxxxxxxxxx
_____	xxxxxx	_____	_____	_____	xxxxxxxxxxxx
Videotape	xxx_____xxxxx		_____	_____	xxxxxxxxxxxx
Edit subtotal	xxxxxx	xxxxxx	xxxxxx	xxxxxxxxxxxxxx	$
9. Audio Mix _____	xxx_____xxxxx				
Labor _____	_____	xxxxxx	_____	_____	xxxxxxxxxxxx
Equipment _____	xxxxxx	_____	_____	_____	xxxxxxxxxxxx
Audiotape _____	xxx_____xxxxx		_____	_____	xxxxxxxxxxxx
Other _____	_____	_____	_____	_____	xxxxxxxxxxxx
Audio Mix subtotal	xxxxxx	xxxxxx	xxxxxx	xxxxxxxxxxxxxx	$
10. Duplication					
Labor _____	_____	xxxxxx	_____	_____	xxxxxxxxxxxx
Equipment _____	xxxxxx	_____	_____	_____	xxxxxxxxxxxx
Videotape _____	xxx_____xxxxx		_____	_____	xxxxxxxxxxxx
1-in _____	xxx_____xxxxx		_____	_____	xxxxxxxxxxxx
3/4 in. _____	xxx_____xxxxx		_____	_____	xxxxxxxxxxxx
Other _____	xxx_____xxxxx		_____	_____	xxxxxxxxxxxx
_____	xxx_____xxxxx		_____	_____	xxxxxxxxxxxx
_____	xxx_____xxxxx		_____	_____	xxxxxxxxxxxx
Duplication subtotal	xxxxxx	xxxxxx	xxxxxx	xxxxxxxxxxxxxx	$
11. Other _____	_____	_____	_____	_____	xxxxxxxxxxxx
_____	_____	_____	_____	_____	xxxxxxxxxxxx
_____	_____	_____	_____	_____	xxxxxxxxxxxx
_____	_____	_____	_____	_____	xxxxxxxxxxxx
Other subtotal	xxxxxx	xxxxxx	xxxxxx	xxxxxxxxxxxxxx	$
Budget subtotal	xxxxxxxxxxxxxxxxxxxxxxxxxxxxxxxxxxxxxx				$
Contingency (%)	xxxxxxxxxxxxxxxxxxxxxxxxxxxxxxxxxxxxxx				$
Total post-production budget	xxxxxxxxxxxxxxxxxxxxxxxxxxxxxxxxxxxxxx				$

may be a substantial budget item, involving not only the cost of the mix but a good deal of preparation.

10.   *Duplication* is an item that can run-up costs much faster than is usually anticipated. The wise producer will want enough copies for himself, and his client will usually need more than he originally requested. Whether made in-house or bought, unbudgeted duplicates can eat up a lot of profit.

11.   *Other items* tend to crop up more often than not. Transportation and commissary are not as basic to post as they are to production, but these may be factors. Telephone and mailing costs may be added here, though they are usually not a direct cost item for this kind of budget.

The tallies at the bottom of the form are simple totals that may be used directly, or added to an overall production budget.

The discussion of editing continues in Chapter 10, which covers the fine-cut: the creation of the master tape.

CONCLUSION

The editing process creates the final product out of the raw materials of production. Preparing and budgeting for the final edit is an intermediate process that determines the quality and controls the cost of the finished program.

10 Editing: Elements of the Fine Cut

Everything that has been done up to this point is just preparation for the fine cut—the last stage in the editing process that creates the final program. When the producer reaches this stage in the program's development, all the aesthetic decisions regarding the shots and graphics to be used, as well as the sequence in which they will appear, should have been made. What remains is to instruct the editing system where to find the material and specify how each piece will be assembled. If an edit decision list has not already been prepared in the process of assembling the rough cut, this is the point at which it must be created, presumably from an editing script (discussed in Chapter 9).

However, before proceeding to discuss the EDL, it will be useful to look at some of the processes that the EDL is designed to use and control.

A/B ROLLS

A/B roll editing is the method most commonly used when working "on-line"— on the best equipment available to the producer.

If effects such as wipes and dissolves are used, then it is necessary to specify two points for the beginning of each segment that starts with an effect, and two points for the end of each segment that ends in an effect, so that there may be as many as four rather than two points listed for each segment. Two points for each are necessary, because an effect—unlike a hard-cut—has duration; it occupies a number of frames. A fade starts at a specific frame and continues through several frames—and perhaps lasts for seconds. A dissolve, where one image fades out at the same time that another fades in, requires that frames be specified for two source tapes.

This is necessary because new video cannot be recorded over old video without erasing the recorded material. This means that the fade-in over the fade-out in a dissolve cannot be done by merely fading out one edit, backing up the recording deck, and fading the next edit in over the previous segment (as you can, for example, with reversible consumer Super-8 cameras). Instead, we have to put the segments that will be mixed for the transition on two separate source decks—A and B. To perform the dissolve, we line up the edit that ends in a fade-out on source deck A and the edit that will fade in from source deck B. We then create the dissolve electronically, as the two images are recorded.

Using Three-Machine Editing Systems

To accomplish the edit just described, we use an editing system that is configured as shown in Figure 10.1. The two source decks, A and B, are operated by an editing controller. Both their outputs feed onto a special effects generator, which

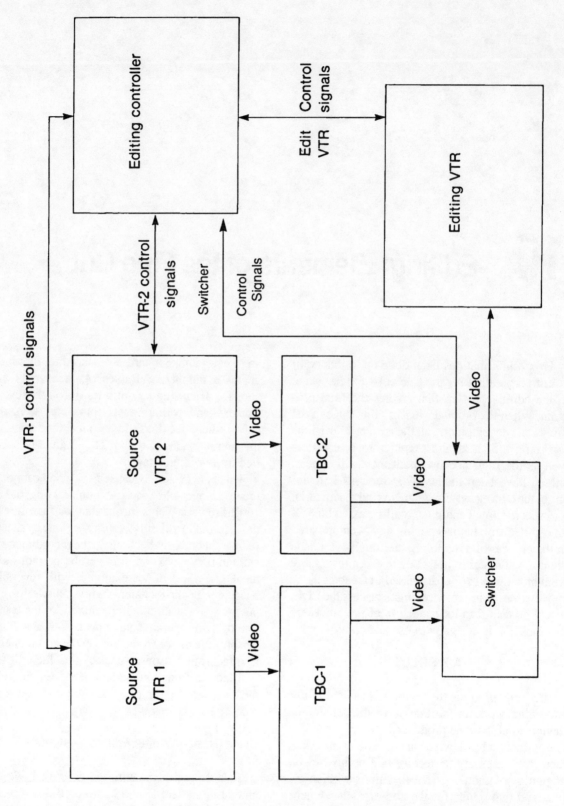

Figure 10.1: A three-machine system for A/B roll editing.

provides the output to the recorder. The controller still locates edit points, and positions, prerolls and rolls the tapes. However, it is the operation of the mix, or fader controls on the SEG, that actually determines the source that will be recorded on the master tape.

This mixing of sources is made possible by the two time base correctors (one for each source deck) that ensure that all the signals coming into the switcher are on the same time base. Just as in the studio, where all the cameras and other sources must be genlocked to a single sync source for mixing, the decks coming into the switcher have to operate synchronously. Possible inputs can also, of course, include the output of other sources such as cameras and graphics generators, and these will be discussed in more detail.

Setting Up the Numbers for Effects

Let us say we have recorded a previous edit on our master tape on the recording deck and have marked an OUT point for a simple cut edit. The next segment will start with a hard-cut, but will dissolve into the segment that follows it. Accordingly, we put the tape containing the first new segment on source deck A, and the tape containing the second segment on source deck B. We will assume, for the moment, that we have a sophisticated controller and switcher that can perform programmed effects automatically, so we time the entire edit (using a two-second dissolve) as follows:

A Roll: Edit start, 36 41 36
         Dissolve start, 37 15 03
         Dissolve end, 37 17 03

B Roll: Edit start, 12 01 23
         Dissolve start, 12 35 00
         Dissolve end, 12 37 00
         Edit end, 13 00 00

It should be noted that the "edit start" time on the B deck was "backed-timed" from the "dissolve start" time. That is, we knew when we wanted Roll B to dissolve in, but we had to start deck B well before that—at the same time we started the A deck. Accordingly, we determined the exact length of time that it took the segment on A deck to get from the start of its edit to the dissolve point (33 seconds, 7 frames) and subtracted that from

our dissolve-start point on deck B to get the B deck edit start point. The process and the dissolve are illustrated in Figure 10.2.

However, although we are starting both the A and B source decks—and, of course, the recording deck—at the same time (after preroll), the SEG is initially set to output only the material from A deck. Thus, initially, only the material from A deck is recorded. Then, at the programmed time, the switcher automatically dissolves from the A to the B bus and outputs the material from deck B. The controller then ends the edit at the specified OUT point.

If the system does not have automatic effects control capability, it is still possible to operate a three-machine system with effects by doing them manually. In this case, the controller programs both the A and B source decks to run for the entire length of both edits. The edit is then done entirely as if it were a hard-cut, but at the appropriate moment, the editor switches inputs as he manually performs the dissolve on the switcher. Although the timing of the dissolve may not be as precise, with an experienced editor, the effect will probably look just as good (as if the operation had been controlled electronically).

The Match-cut

In the edit just illustrated, the effect followed a hard-cut, which provided a precise point from which both the A and B rolls were timed. However, when two or more effects with durations follow each other, a "match-cut" has to be made between them. A match-cut is made by selecting an arbitrary point toward the end of the segment that was just inserted. The next edit then starts at this point. By reinserting the last few seconds with exactly the same material as was previously there, we match the first frame of the new edit to the last frame of the old, as if no transition at all had occurred. The "edit" thus created is not visible.

This is necessary, because after one transition is completed, the decks are not normally in the correct position (nor always on the correct reel of tape) to roll toward the next transition. If we were, for example, to go from a wipe from A to B, and then, a few seconds later—and without stopping—into a dissolve from B to A, there would be no time for Roll A to get into the correct edit position. Thus, the sole purpose of the match-cut is to give the editor a place from which to start.

Figure 10.2: Image transfer on videotape for A/B roll editing.

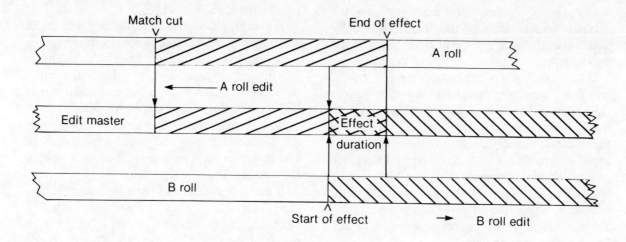

a. Relative positions of information on tape

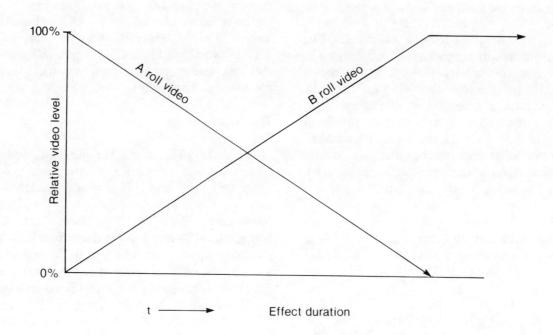

b. Relative A & B roll video levels in a dissolve

Because the search for the next edit takes real time, even the most sophisticated machines must use this method to get from one effect to the next. The only alternative that high-end equipment offers to this problem is the "auto match-cut," in which the machine selects and creates a match-cut automatically, so that the edit decision list need not specify tape numbers for it.

Separate A/B Rolls: Conforming

Because online editing suites are expensive, both to own or rent, any function that can be performed before the final editing session should be done separately. Creating A and B rolls on separate source tapes is one of these functions. *Conforming* is the process of performing a *super-*

vised dub of camera masters onto the A and B rolls to make sure no signal degradation is introduced. If necessary, color correction is done at this time, as well as any other signal processing such as time base correction.

The nature of conforming is schematically illustrated in Figure 10.3. Here, we can see that all the material that will be assembled on the master (the tape at the center) is already sorted out on the conformed tapes, roll A and roll B. Every segment on these rolls has been assembled in correct order, with extra seconds of image called "pads," at each end. These pads provide extra frames for effects transitions, for an occasional one-frame machine error at the end of an edit, or even extra material for extending an edit, should it become necessary. With conformed tapes, no tape changing at all is required. The source machines just roll back and forth to find each edit. Although it constitutes an extra expense, the hourly rate for a supervised dub is one-quarter to one-third the cost of editing time on the same equipment.

The benefits of this process can be substantial in terms of both cost and smooth operation of the edit. For example, say that there are 40 reels of original footage—not a particularly large number for a documentary. Yet the sequence of images in the program may require that the tape on the A and B decks be changed for almost every edit. This can add several hours to the cost of the fine-cut. Further, if color correction has to be done during the edit, it is charged at the higher rate for the same amount of time.

When a program has been properly conformed, the time required to perform a fine-cut can be halved. Including the cost of conforming, the overall cost of a fine-cut can be reduced by as much as one-third by using this process. (If conforming is used, the edit decision list is, of course, prepared for the conformed copies.) Nevertheless, judgment is necessary. If a program is in good order, the images are in good shape and only a few rolls of tape are involved, the cost of conforming may not be warranted.

THE EDIT DECISION LIST (EDL)

The edit decision list contains the producer's final decision in computer language. It may be compiled as a handwritten log sheet of the off-line-produced rough cut, or it may be generated on a floppy disk. The EDL that is stored on computer disk offers a big advantage in that it can be used to input the editing information directly into the on-line system. This means that it is not necessary to input the EDL manually, saving time and money as well as avoiding the introduction of input errors. As with any item used in a video system, the format used for the EDL stored on a disk must be of the same format as that used by the (on-line system.

Figure 10.3: Scenes conformed on A and B rolls.

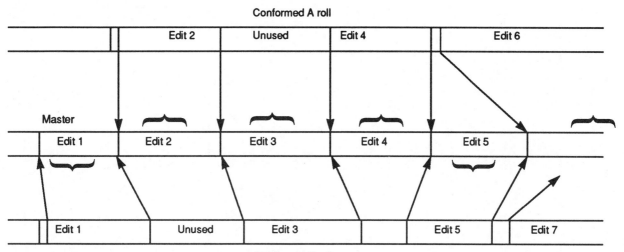

Form10.1: Edit decision list.

Edit No.	Type of Effect	Effect Time	A.B. Other Mach.	Edit IN Point	Effect IN Point	Effect OUT Point	Edit OUT Point

The edit decision list (EDL) provided in Form 10.1 will be suitable for most users. The form starts, naturally, with a edit number, because we still need a "name" for every event—something to call it by. The "Type of Effect" column describes the edit. It may be a simple cut, designated by a C; a dissolve, designated by a D; or any of a large number of complex wipes, keys or graphics transitions. Wipes or borders may be soft- or hard-edged, and they may have a variety of patterns. For example, we may have a soft circle wipe, which can be designated as CW.

With some systems, if we are dealing with a wipe or more complex effect, it may be necessary to specify a number or provide another type of effect identification. If the edit controller to be used for the fine-cut is known beforehand, it will be possible to specify the effect format in terms of its code number. For example, if a circle wipe (CW) can be called up as number 209 on the editor, then 209 is all that need be entered here. The type of edge—hard, soft or colored, for example—may also have to be specified, so that the full ID for a soft circle wipe might be CWS or 209S.

The next two columns in the form indicate the duration of the effect (Effect Time) and the identity of the machine to be used (A, B, or Other). A hard-cut has, of course, zero duration, and that is then indicated. A dissolve may be any duration longer than zero, but is usually measured in frames, rather than seconds, as are most effects. The identity of the machine being used as the source is also specified: R/recording deck, A, B or C/source deck or ATR/remote-controlled audiotape recorder, for example.

The rest of the form provides columns to record the precise frames with which each edit and effect starts and ends for each machine. There are four edit points for each deck (or roll), because each effect must start with a match- or hard-cut that starts each effect transition. From this point, the program segues into the next transition, and thus into the next edit.

One important element not listed here in a separate column is the total program time, the time from the start of the first fade-in to the current edit. How this information is built into the record deck time code is described in the next section.

ONLINE EDITING SYSTEMS

An on-line system should be able to meet the producer's requirements for technical quality as well as being capable of performing all the effects he has planned. Most on-line systems today use a sophisticated computer-based edit controller, dynamic tracking VCR's that can handle variable speed playback, a character generator, a digital effects unit and a switcher. Although most on-line systems also incorporate video signal processing units that constantly shape up the signal coming from each VCR, it is still important for the editor to monitor the various source signals with a vectorscope and waveform monitor (discussed in the Technical Appendix). In this way the producer can make certain that the apparently stable image on his monitor will retain its integrity through several stages of dubbing, and survive playback on less-than-ideal systems in other settings.

Setting the Master for Real Program Time

It is very valuable to know—at any moment during the edit—exactly how far into the program an edit falls. This is particularly important when programs are produced for broadcast, where they must be timed to the second. Starting to edit with the clock at 00 00 00 00 is not adequate, because the necessary time for bars and clocks may be as much as a minute.

To get a real program time on the time code, it is necessary to set the record deck for zero time at the start of the first program edit. To accomplish this, all prior material, like the color bars and the countdown (a 5-4-3-2 clock wipe that enables a VTR operator to cue up the tape for play) must be timed to occur *before* zero time. This is done by starting the time code clock at the end of the 23rd hour (see Figure 10.4). For example, if we start with 30 seconds of color bars, ten seconds of black and a ten-second countdown, the clock for the record deck would be started at 23 59 10 00. Fifty seconds later, when the first edit starts, it will be set at 00 00 00 00—the start of the 24th hour, or time zero. The time code at any point on the tape will now automatically read real program time.

NARRATION AND THE AUDIO MIX

Even when most of the sound in a program is sync sound recorded with the video, the show may also use narration, music or other background sound, and sound effects. In some cases, the narration may be laid down first and the video cut to fit. Broadcast news is often edited in this way.

Figure 10.4: Setting time code for real program time.

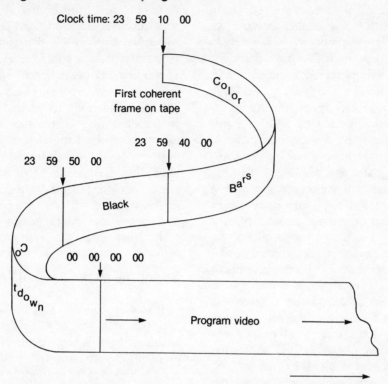

However, in most cases, the video is laid down first with whatever sync sound there is, for reference. Other audio is added later, transferred from audiotape and other sources during the video edit. More sophisticated video editing systems, in fact, are capable of taking synchronized inputs from audiotape recorders and using them as sources during an edit.

Some programs receive extensive "audio sweetening," where the processing and mixing of the separate voice, music, background and effects tracks is done separately, after the video edit is completed, as it is done in film production. The audio tracks for the final tape are "built" on a sophisticated audio system in an audio editing suite that has the flexibility to produce audio for computerized video systems. At this level of audio production, sweetening suites are manned by audio specialists, and it is prudent for the producer to include their input during pre-production. But whether the sound is treated separately or as part of the on-line edit session, the following will be useful.

Recording Narration

Narration should definitely be recorded in a soundproofed booth in a sound studio. The record-ing needs to be absolutely clean, without any hint of background. Like the narrator himself, his location should be indeterminate—an audio "space" in its own right. This way, if the producer decides to insert background audio under the narration, he is free to do so.

When recording each section, the director should give the narrator his cue for each segment. The narrator should then count out loud, "five, four, three" and continue, at the same pace, to count "two, one" silently. At "zero," the narrator should start reading the segment. The audible count is a cue to the operator to drop the background and raise the audio level of the narration. The "five, four, three" enable him to get ready, while the silent "two, one" interval gives him time to adjust the levels without the risk of recording the count.

In recording narration, it is customary to record more than one take of each segment. If these are later spliced, so that, say, the first sentence of one take is put together with the second sentence of another, the producer has to make certain that the word splices are not too close. It is important, for example, that natural pauses between phrases and sentences not be cut out and that adjacent parts of spliced takes are consistent in tone.

The Audio Mix

While it is possible to mix program sound as a part of the video edit, it is often desirable to do a separate audio mix. When there is not only sync sound and narration, but also music and sound effects, a professional sound-only mix at a sound shop may be the producer's best bet. For our purposes, this facility must have a multitrack audio system that can operate on time code and a video playback unit that can be synched to the audio. To keep the discussion within a manageable range, we will limit it to an eight-track edit.

Lining up the Audio Elements

The process starts when the video master is assembled with all sync sound in place on one audio track. Sync sound, as discussed here, in-

cludes all sound recorded with the video that will be used on the final program. This includes audio that was recorded on a separate audio deck but was intended for use as sync sound on the video-tape. It does not necessarily include ambient audio recorded on the videotape for reference only.

The video master is dubbed, together with its time code, to create an audio workprint. The other elements of the sound mix—the music, effects, voice-over, etc.—are then recorded on audiotape and, to each tape, time code is added. Now a set of audio edit lists is prepared, one for each track. The purpose of this set of lists is to enable a sound engineer to take an eight-track cassette, put the video master time code on track 8 and the sync sound on track 1, and then put up to six more audio sources in correct alignment on each of the other six tracks. This kind of track alignment is illustrated in Figure 10.5.

Figure 10.5: Segment on an 8-track tape with time code and audio for video.

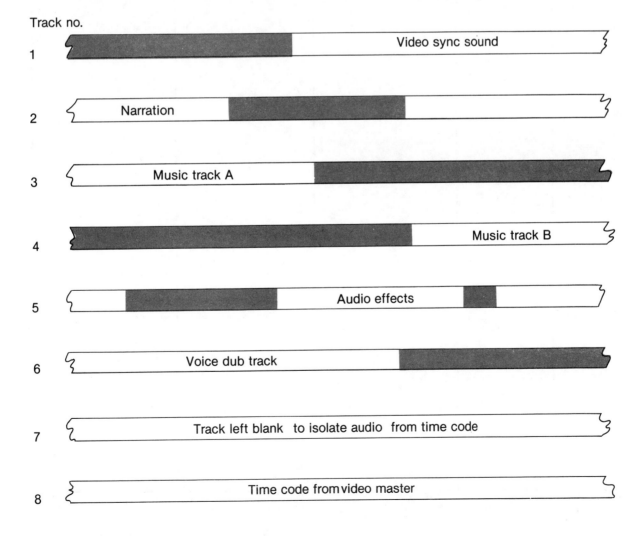

Form 10.2: Audio track line-up sheet.

Title _____		Track No. _____		Type _____
Audio Seg. No.	Video Time Code Location	Audio Source Information		
		Audio TC Start	Audio Content	Audio TC End

The Audio Track Lineup Sheet

A form for an Audio Track Lineup Sheet is provided in Form 10.2. As video forms go, it is relatively simple. For any audio element that needs to be mixed (except for the sync sound), a separate sheet, or set of sheets, is prepared. For example, the narration would arrive on its own audiotape with its own time code track, and a sheet for it would be prepared as follows.

The first column simply numbers all the narration segments that will be used. The second shows the time code of the point on the video master where that segment of narration should start. The "Audio TC Start" gives the time code of the point on the narration tape where this segment starts. The next column provides some reference information about the segment, and the last provides the end point for the segment. This list will include as many pages as necessary to indicate where each narration segment should go. A list is prepared for each audio element: music, effects, voice dubs, etc.

Using these lists, the audio engineer lays down each audio element in its own track at optimum audio level, until the audiocassette contains all the audio elements that the program will use, in their correct time relationship to the video. The beauty of this system is that the engineer and the producer can check the alignment of each track as it is being recorded—as well as later, as it is being mixed—because the videotape and audiotape can be run in sync on their respective machines, using the matched time code.

The Final Audio Mix

Once each audio element in the program is located in the right place, the mixdown to a single track can begin. (Recording for stereo requires that all tracks be duplicated and balanced for right and left audio.) Since all the audio is at one level, it must now be mixed so that each element comes in at its correct level. This is normally done on the fly by the audio engineer, with the producer present to check the mix at each point.

If the mix is too complex to do all at once, selected tracks can be combined in a preliminary mix. This "sub mix" can then be used as if it were a single track. Alternatively, a computer-driven mixer can be used. In this case, the level for each track is rehearsed and memorized by the system. Then, all the tracks are mixed simultaneously by the computer, using the memorized data to maintain correct levels.

At each point, the mix can be corrected. For example, if an effect or the music obscures the dialog, if an audio cue is missed, or if an audio fade was too abrupt—whatever the problem—the tape can be backed up and the mix run again until the correct balance is achieved. The result is a finished audio track (or pair of tracks) that is then recorded on the audio workprint of the videotape and on a separate audiotape with the video time code. The mixed-down audio is dubbed directly on the audio track (or tracks) of the video master.

CONCLUSION

With the development of sophisticated offline EDL processes that speed and simplify the online session, finished programs can now be produced with less online editing time. Today the online editing stage can merely be one of "compiling" the finished program rather than making editing decisions. With proper planning, a clean EDL, and an understanding of the online process, a producer will make the best use of his energy, equipment and his funds.

11 Post-Production Effects, Graphics and Fixers

Graphics, digital effects and other fixer types of devices are included under post-production because, with the proliferation of single camera and on-location shooting, this is where they are usually applied in the program building process. However, the basic rules also apply if these devices are used during live productions.

TITLES AND GRAPHICS

Common methods for generating titles and graphics for television fall into two basic categories: board based and computer generated. Both methods are used to create full-screen charts or graphics such as drawings, text and diagrams, or text and graphics that are superimposed over other video images.

The graphic, no matter how it is produced, must conform to the 3:4 aspect ratio of television. In addition to adhering to the "safe title area" (see Figure 11.1), it is important to use strong, bold lines and to avoid very fine detail. Color can be used to enhance the graphics message. It is a good practice to review finished graphics on both color and black-and-white monitors. This procedure will indicate any changes in the graphics (such as contrast, separation of tone, letter height and colors) that may be needed.

Board-Based Graphics

Despite the development of sophisticated graphics generators, board-based graphics continue to be used as a course of graphic images for video. This traditional method uses a camera to capture the images from "art cards" positioned on an easel, graphics stand or animation table, as shown in Figure 11.2. The degree to which such graphics can be animated depends on the type of setup used. If the camera is on a tripod, the operator can pan, tilt and zoom to create movement; on the animation table, highly controlled and complex camera moves can be performed and memorized by computer-controlled drive circuits.

Graphics cameras are usually dedicated high-resolution black-and-white cameras, which have several advantages. They provide sharp images, they are relatively inexpensive, and they are small and therefore easy to handle. However, a dedicated camera is not necessary to use, and depending on the setup selected, a studio or ENG camera can be used instead.

Even with a minimal camera setup a good switcher in the hands of an inventive operator can create many graphics with the verve and elegance of computer generated material. Figure 11.3 shows how a graphics camera is tied into an editing

Figure 11.1: Relative proportions for TV board graphics. The safe area for superimposed titles and graphics provides extra space around them so that their edges do not disappear into the monitor frame.

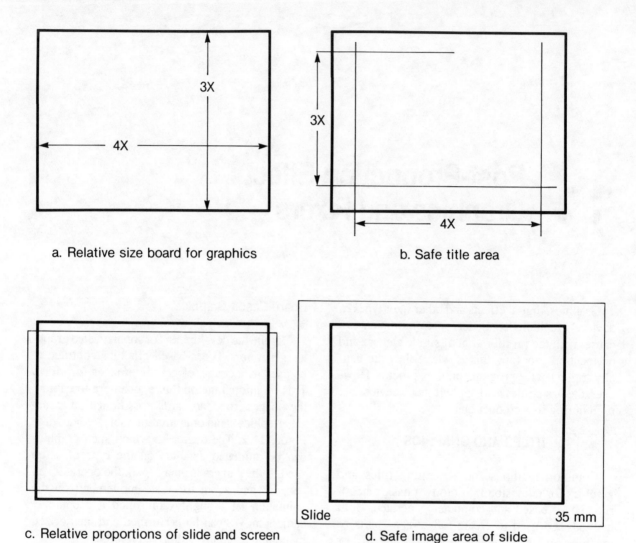

a. Relative size board for graphics

b. Safe title area

c. Relative proportions of slide and screen

d. Safe image area of slide

system through a switcher which genlocks the camera to the source deck. (The camera gets its black burst from the switcher, unless a separate sync generator is driving the whole system.)

This setup makes it possible to record the graphics with any transition of which the switcher is capable. For example, a title or other graphic can be super-imposed over the video during an edit. It can be keyed in over another taped or graphic image, or over a matte background generated in the switcher. Effects can be created with any of the wipe patterns with which the switcher is equipped. It is also possible to go from a taped edit

to the graphic and back with any of these effects. The more features the switcher has, the more varied the possibilities are for video animation. The basic features needed are some interesting wipes and some means of keying. Still better features include a chromakey, a variety of wipes and double re-entry.

Techniques for Board Graphics Animation

The first step of the process is to create top-quality art and title cards, drawn with good clarity and contrast, creative and appropriate to the job at

Figure 11.2: Setups for graphics cameras.

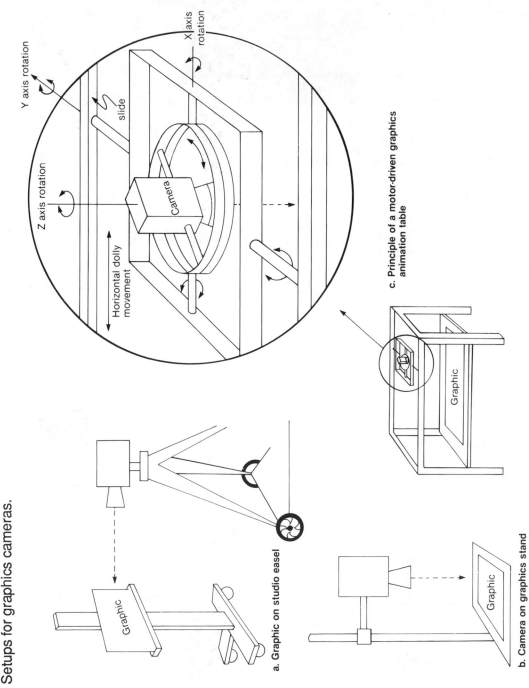

a. Graphic on studio easel

b. Camera on graphics stand

c. Principle of a motor-driven graphics animation table

Figure 11.3: Editing system for board graphics insertion.

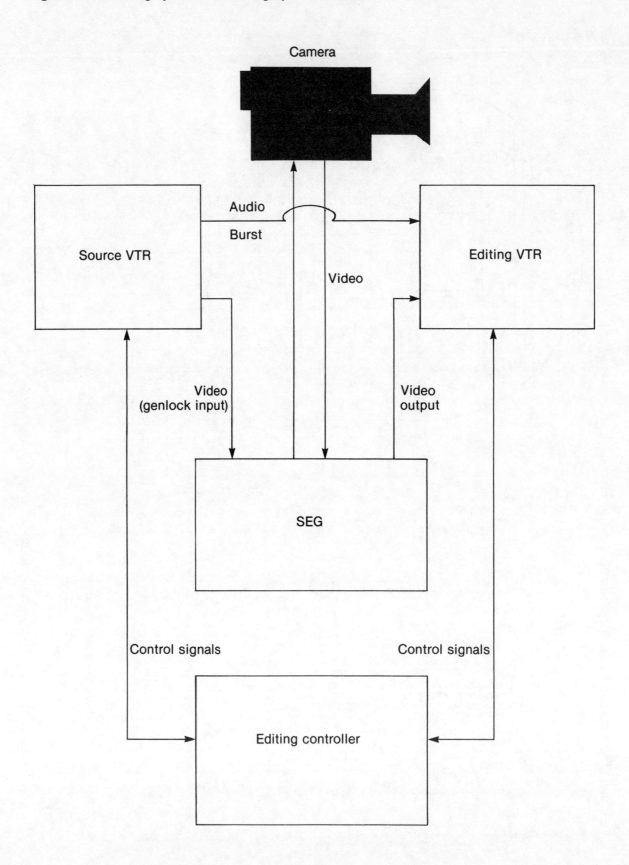

hand. If the material will be superimposed over non-video backgrounds, then the quality of the background graphics and their suitability to the broad graphics must also be considered. While the primary graphics are specific to the program, background graphics can be obtained from a number of outside sources, such as photographic libraries and government agencies (NASA's satellite photographs and tapes are, for example, available for a mailing had handling fee).

Before the material is gathered, the producer should have a good idea of what he wants to do with it. The simplest way is to shoot each graphic head on and insert it as footage in the appropriate place in the program. But a little ingenuity, time and a good camera person can give the producer a lot more latitude. Even three-dimensional graphics can be simulated from board art by using just the basic editing system. An example is shown in Figure 11.4. It involves using three-dimensional letters drawn in deep perspective, for example, a two-word title, such as that shown in the Figure, can be put on two lines. The upper line can be drawn so that it appears to be seen from the bottom; the lower, so that it appears to be seen from the top. The depth for both words can be tapered so they appear to zoom out of the center. Then, by superimposing them over a star background, we can appear to zoom toward and between them, into the stars—or into the next edit.

Figure 11.4: Board-based title card with dimensions.

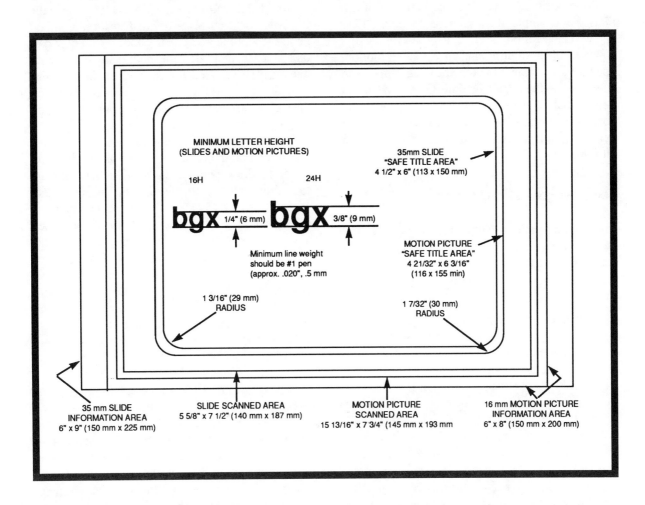

Wipe Animation

Wipes provide an enormous range of ways in which to frame and sequence images. Soft wipes on a bright image make it appear to "glow." With wipe-plus-rotation capability, an image can not only be brought in from different parts of the screen, but it can be unfolded, folded up, contrasted or expanded. For example, if the switcher has a circle wipe, the zoom into the starscape between the two words "Video Visions", described above, can be a "starburst." That is, as the zoom moves into the center, the image is wiped in as a small, soft-edged central "star." As the wipe is flashed open, the viewer feels as though he continues to zoom forward, straight into the next image.

Wipe rotation enables the user to bring any image in circularly—such as in the "clock wipe," where the edge of the wipe moves like the hands of a clock to bring in the next image.

Wipe positioning yields a large number of options. For example, if a logo has a dot on an "i" or "j," we can position the circular wipe over the dot, zoom in on it slightly, and in the same motion, open the circle rapidly so that the image appears to have been in the dot all the time. Or, the talent can hold a small object in his hand and the wipe can be positioned over it. If the object is central to the next edit, this can be a very effective way to introduce it.

Computer-generated Graphics

Computer-generated graphics are produced using character generators (CG) and graphics generators that are either dedicated units or based on a personal computer (PC) platform.

Character Generators

A character generator, is an example of a "dedicated" digital computer, whose program is actually built into its operating system. It is basically a word processor, designed to create letters and to permit the letters to be placed in different positions on the screen and recorded in NTSC format by a VCR. Specialty features include selectable font styles, size, color and storage capability (see Figure 11.5). These additional features are directly correlated to the unit's price. Whatever features are offered, CGs are typically connected as shown

in Figure 11.6. The video is routed directly through them, or, if a switcher is used, the CG is connected between the switcher and editing deck.

Digital Graphics Generators

Digital graphics generators can be dedicated units or they can be graphics programs based on personal computers. In either case, the user can create his own forms to a considerable degree of detail. While they are primarily used to create sophisticated and expressive charts, diagrams and logos, they may also be used to create entire pictures, both representational images and abstract designs.

The complexity of the images that a graphics unit can generate depends on the size of its "pixel"—the number of horizontal units into which each line of video is divided. A horizontal resolution of 1023 (2^{10}) pixels (discrete picture elements) is provided on most broadcast graphics units, with the color of each pixel defined in three components—red, blue and green. Since each color can take at least eight different shades, any one of 512 hues can be selected for each pixel. Some units provide a palette of tens of thousands of colors for the well dressed pixel. But color is only the beginning.

Each pixel can be individually defined, or it can be part of a border or an area. To make such a unit easier to draw with, a digitized tablet with an electronic stylus is often used. With this, the video graphics artist can create shapes while watching the screen. He can specify the color of each line, or area, or create a borderless area by making the border and the area color the same. Even on less sophisticated units (relatively speaking) the color of an area can be specified and filled in automatically within the boundaries. To take full advantage of this process, bounded areas of graphics can be "magnified" so that each pixel can be individually colored and "shrunk" (negative magnification) back to its original size.

Although most CGs and graphics generators offer enough solid-state memory to save several pages of text, this information is normally lost when power to the CG or graphics generator is turned off. Outside storage mediums such as floppy disks or magnetic cassette tapes can greatly improve the effectiveness of the graphics system. Battery backup power should be available in case of momentary power failure.

Figure 11.5: Character generator with storage device.

(photo courtesy LAIRD Telemedia Inc.).

PC-based Units

Today many facilities are using PC-based units rather than a dedicated character and graphics generator. PC-based generators are configured to the user's requirements by installing the appropriate software and video boards which allow for composite video out. While they offer great flexibility and some cost savings, great care must be taken with setting up a PC-based system. Unlike dedicated CG and graphics generators, system integration and interfacing for PC-based systems are the responsibility of the user and getting support can sometimes be difficult.

Recently there has been a move toward merging CG and graphics generators together to form graphic workstations. These workstations provide both CG and graphics capabilities in one unit.

Again, these workstations may be dedicated or PC based. Many of these systems are compatible with component digital equipment, and Ethernet and RGB signals. It is important for the producer to note that while these workstations appear to have similar capabilities, each manufacturer's unit has unique features; only through careful investigation and demonstration can educated decisions be made.

The choice between using computer- or board-based graphics may be a practical matter. If there are a lot of graphics and/or little time, a computer-based system is the obvious choice. On the other hand, if a completely customized look is required, title cards may offer the best solution. Board art also provides access to previously produced graphics and charts.

Figure 11.6: Editing system with character generator.

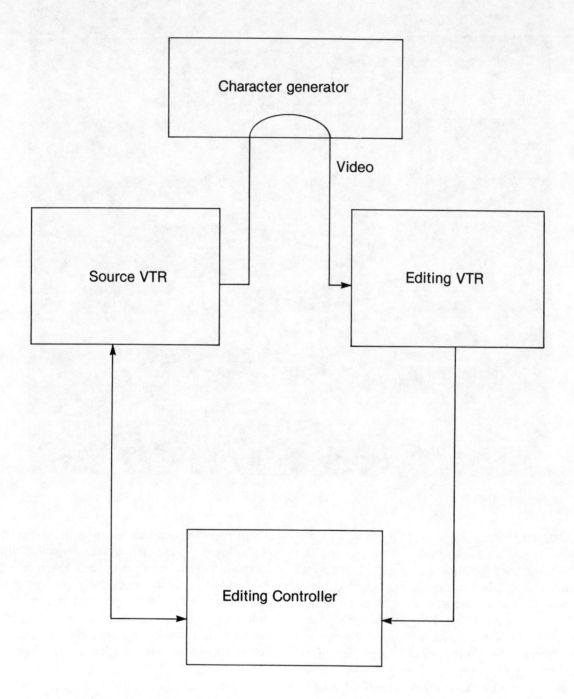

DIGITAL VIDEO EFFECTS

Complex computer graphics can be created from single frames of video, including those picked up from photographs or other art. This is done by digitizing the image—giving a digital value to each pixel's position, color and shade and manipulating that information. And that brings us to the next development in image handling—digital video effects.

Digital effects units are dedicated computers that store the image frame by frame, and manipulate the image to make it appear to move and change shape in many ways. Apparent 3D motion is created by generating a series of perspective views of the graphic object that represent the object as it moves around a selected hypothetical vertical (Y) axis. Once these views are defined, this Y axis can be tilted or rotated in any direction so that the object or form appears to twist or tumble. However, when we speak of tumbling or rotating a shape in any way, we are implying that the shape is separated from its background—and indeed, it is.

Video graphics are generated in "layers." There is a foreground, a background, and often, additional layers in between. A "matte" effect is a colorized background layer. Each layer can be colored and defined separately. In some units, the foreground and background layers can be combined at the borders to form a matte, and they can be "faded" into each other.

Digital Frame Stores

Graphic video images other than those that colorize or "posterize" video cannot be created in real time. With a horizontal resolution of 1024 pixels, we are dealing with about half a million pixels in every frame—or over 15 million pixels in 30-frame second—far too much for broadcast TV's seven-megahertz bandwidth to handle. But that is not all. Each pixel must also be defined as to its brightness, hue and chroma, and information about the position of each pixel on X and Y coordinates must also be supplied. That is why completely digital television can potentially use a bandwidth of some 30 megahertz, to avoid storing and manipulating such vast amounts of information in digital form. Digital effects devices create their effects one frame at a time. These units, accordingly, include a "frame store," in which the information for one frame of the image to be manipulated is held. The operator then gives the device the appropriate instructions to manipulate that particular frame, using magnification, positioning, rotation and other programs that have been built into the system. For example, a magnification-plus-positioning program will take a frame of video and "squeezoom" it into or out of infinity.

However, all of this must be initially designed frame by frame. When we see a moving video image integrated into a graphic—as when the bad guys in a science fiction epic are sent protesting into outer space on the side of a hypercube, or a presidential visage zigzooms out of the center of an "O" into full frame—we are looking at a KEY into an existing graphic. Nevertheless, the graphic in which the real-time image is set was created frame by frame.

TYPICAL VIDEO EFFECTS DEVICES

Video effects devices designed for professional video production include the Squeezoom™, Kaleidoscope, Apex Digital Optics (ADO) System, Video Toaster, and IMPACT Variable Image transformer.

Squeezoom™

The Squeezoom, a trademark of Vital Industries Inc., was the first commercially available multi-channel digital effects system. It's operational features include manipulation of the image on the vertical and horizontal axes; freeze frame; zoom from zero to eight times normal size; and manual programming of effects as well as more than 100 pre-programmed effects.

Kaleidoscope

The Kaleidoscope digital effects system, manufactured by Grass Valley Group, Inc. has most of the capabilities of the Squeezoom™, and it also provides dimming, shadowing and contrast effects, as well as mosaic picture cropping and drop shadow to the standard selection of video effects.

ADO

The Ampex Digital Optics (ADO) System was the first system to offer image perspective—the illusion of depth in the two-dimensional image. (See Figure 11.7.)

The ADO system relies on software to achieve its flexibility. The system operator manipulates the video image by activating the proper key on the control panel and positioning a joystick lever to achieve the desired change. These changes are stored in the system memory for subsequent recall.

Each entered video change on the ADO system is called a keyframe. Since any effect requires both a start point and a stop point, an effects sequence actually requires the programming of at least two keyframes.

The ADO system can handle up to 24 keyframes per effect sequence (24 changes of video size,

Figure 11.7: The ADO 100 is designed for smaller broadcast, post-production and corporate video facilities.

shape or position in a continuous sequence). In addition, 36 separate effects sequences can be individually stored on each mini-floppy disk.

The ADO's ability to achieve true image perspective and to give apparent depth to a moving effect is accomplished by moving images along the so-called Z-axis—the axis that adds a feeling of apparent depth to the TV picture. Previous devices could control image motion only along the horizontal and vertical axes.

Video Toaster

The Video Toaster, by New Tek Inc., is actually more than just a digital effects device. It is more accurately referred to as a video workstation. Designed as a high quality, low cost professional video production device, the Video Toaster provides many features including:

• a video production switcher that performs cuts, fades, chroma keys, standard soft edge wipes and "organic" wipe shapes input by using any of the seven video input sources;

• a still store/frame grabber that freezes frame images from any video source, then allows them to be used with any other video toaster features;

• a DVE generator that features hundreds of digital effects including: flips, spins, tumbles, page peel, warp, trajectories, curtains, analog trains, and digital trails;

• a character generator that produces smooth, true-color gradient backgrounds and over 40 standard fonts, with 16.8 million variations of color fonts including brass, chrome and rainbow. Semitransparent shadows with linear key are also standard as are variable-speed crawling and text scroll;

• a computer graphics generator that can model, render and animate video in full broadcast resolution;

• a video paint system that provides the ability to rub through, blur, colorize, variable transparency. It also includes a frame store that can composite two or more images, and alter and blend images captured either from live sources, or from other sections of the workstation;

• a real-time color processor that allows the user to alter all aspects of brightness, contrast and color of a live video image.

IMPACT

The IMPACT Variable Image Transformer, from Microtime, is also a video workstation that includes all the standard video effects such as rotation, perspective, expansion, compression, and so on, but in addition allows the user to perform real time video mapping of genuine 3D objects. This is accomplished by dividing the image into a variable number of polygonal patches, each of which can be manipulated in real time. Some additional features include: three video sources on the screen simultaneously; creation of a cube in a single pass; a library of 3D objects such as the wave, spiral, page turns, cylinder, shards, a 20-sided icosahedron and many more shapes that can be added through a "software update program"; defocus; and sparkles, trails and multilayering.

Other Aspects

Currently the digitized video output of DVE units must be returned to composite or analog format to be recorded on a VCR, transmitted and viewed. This will be no longer be necessary when digital recording becomes more available.

Digital effects units have quickly gone form being the exclusive tool of broadcast level post-production facilities to an affordable tool for the non-broadcast producer. Nevertheless, their use requires considerable special training and time, so the cost of a skilled operator must be added to that of the equipment, leaving it a valuable but still a fairly expensive adjunct to the post-production process.

While DVE's are best known for their ability to rotate, change perspective and zoom images with dazzle and flash, they can also be high-priced but excellent tools for touching up or repositioning video images. For example, a wide shot that has too much headroom may be tightened with the use of a DVE zoom program. But this function belongs to the domain of another type of video equipment—the "fixers."

FIXERS

"Fixing it in post" generally refers to correcting a videotape during post-production. It may be as simple as replacing a faulty camera move with a cutaway, or it may be as complex as restabilizing a technically defective image. The first is within the realm of realistic expectation, the second often belongs to the category of wishful thinking. Whichever category, the amount of improvement depends on the capabilities of the sophisticated video processing devices available, one of these being a time base corrector.

Time Base Correctors

A time base corrector (TBC) corrects the timing of the video signal—primarily the time that each line starts, lasts and is blanked. To do this, a TBC stores one or more lines of video at a time, comparing the timing of the blanking and sync for each line to a correct reference interval. For example, if a line is a microsecond early compared to the reference time, it is delayed one microsecond and then released. If late, the line will be delivered earlier. (A line can be delivered "earlier" relative to its previous line, which was also delayed.) A functional block diagram of a TBC is shown in Figure 11.8.

Time base correctors are digital devices that digitize each line they store. That is, they assign each point in a line of video a set of specific values that completely define it. The comparison of line timing to a timing standard is entirely a computerized operation. When it is completed, the line of video is returned to its analog state.

The ability of a TBC to correct time base error is limited by the relative size of its "window of acceptance" (line-storage capacity) and the magnitude of the error. Most time base correctors can only deal with one or more horizontal lines at a time. Only the most sophisticated TBCs can deal with an entire frame of video, including the vertical interval.

As digital devices, some TBCs are also able to provide random-noise reduction and image enhancement. They can sometimes reduce image noise created by line-timing errors. Incorrect line timing causes the lines to shift slightly in relation to each other from frame to frame. When the line timing is corrected, each line starts at the same point and the image detail lines up at its original position.

Time base correctors also provide manual adjustments for hue and chroma, adjusting color phase and chroma level. However, since color is affected by time base error, some improvement in color occurs automatically with time base correction. Manual adjustments therefore need not be made until the unadjusted output is observed. Video

and pedestal level can also be adjusted at the TBC. In an editing system, all these adjustments are made at the output of the source deck, to correct the source video. In a multi-machine system, the output of the source decks are supplied with its own time base corrector, and the TBCs are driven from a common sync source.

TBCs were originally designed to provide a final correction to the time parameters of television signals for broadcast transmission. They were created when videotape machines were introduced into the TV production process, to correct for small variations caused by quad tape wow and flutter. The capacity of TBCs to correct for errors introduced in small-format TV production was an unexpected bonus. Today, they are standard peripherals in fine-cut editing systems.

Processing Amplifiers

If there is a gross timing error (such as may result from a gyroscopic effect in portable VTRs) that causes an entire frame to be destabilized, a TBC may only make the situation worse while it hunts for a horizontal line to time. Unless the producer has access to a more sophisticated TBC with a sufficiently large window, tapes with frame-size timing errors are often hopeless. But some unstable images may suffer less from time base error than from weak horizontal sync or poor vertical sync. Such cases may be helped by a separate processing amplifier, or "proc amp."

These are devices designed to strip all the sync and color burst from the composite video and correctly regenerate them. Time base correction may still be necessary, because the sync is regenerated on the existing time base. Most TBCs incorporate some sort of proc amp, but usually at the output, rather than at the input, to the TBC. As a result, if the sync is too poor for the TBC to "see" the point where a line of video starts, the video will not get to the point where the TBC proc amp can deal with it. However, if the video is put through a separate proc amp first, then the overall signal may be good enough to get timed correctly by the time base correction circuitry.

Noise Reduction

At its worst, video "noise" appears as if microscopic flecks were swarming over the video image. Similar to white audio noise, which sounds like hiss, video noise is entirely random and diffi-

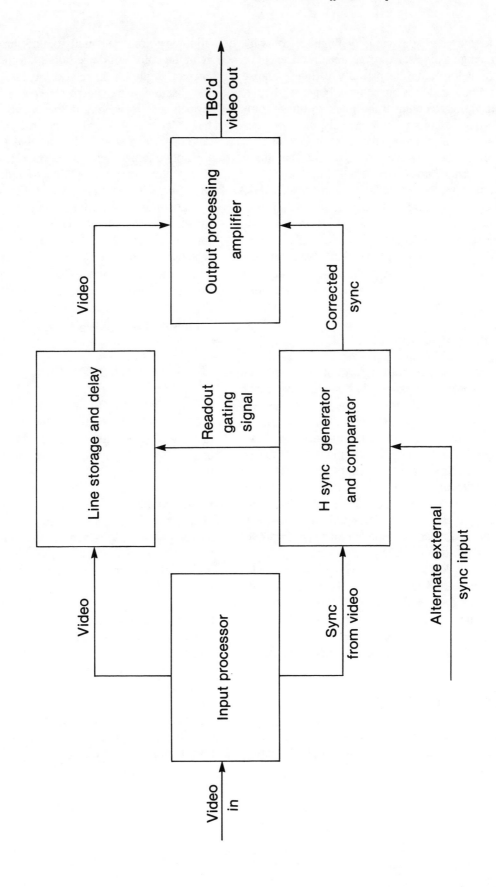

Figure 11.8: Functional block diagram of a TBC.

cult for automatic devices to distinguish from rapidly changing pixels. However, noise reducers have been developed that can partially distinguish noise from video, and they are constantly getting better. Using various techniques for image-to-image comparison and random-event analysis, these devices can significantly reduce the level of video noise. However, the producer must realize that these devices reduce noise, but do not eliminate it.

In the process of reducing the noise, subtle elements of texture and shading are lost, giving the video a "cartoon-y" look. There are no hard-and-fast rules for deciding whether noise reduction devices should be used and at what level they should be operated. The producer should keep in mind that the best defense is quality in production; "fixing it in post" is a poor second best.

Image Enhancement

Image enhancement is a form of "contour correction" provided by most professional video cameras (see Chapter 2). Image enhancement devices allow some improvement to be made on a poorly defined video image. Like contour correction, these devices deal with the "edges" of the images (places where the color or gray level of the image changes) such as the edge of a figure against a wall, or the edge of a tie against a shirt. By amplifying video signals at these points—making the whites whiter and the darks darker—image enhancers improve image definition and sharpness.

As these devices are improved, they are able to retain more and more detail. However, as with noise reducers, detail is generally lost as the image is redefined. And, as the amount of enhancement increases, the image looks more and more like a cartoon. Accordingly, image enhancers should be used sparingly.

Color Correction

When only the color phase is off, a single control on a time base corrector can fix it. In that case, all three colors are equally out of phase alignment with the color reference burst, but they remain in correct alignment in relation to each other. (See the discussion of vectorscopes in the Technical Appendix.) However, if the white balance has been incorrectly recorded, then the phase relationship of the colors to each other is not correct, and the only alternative is full color correction.

A color corrector is able to reduce a video image back into its fundamental color components and position them at the correct angle relative to the color burst. In addition, a color corrector permits adjustment of color gain, or chroma level, which controls saturation of foreground colors; of color black level, which determines color saturation; and of gamma, which, when off, can change the effective gray scale for each color and make the image appear tinted.

CONCLUSION

To deal effectively with the possibilities of post-production, producers need a broad understanding of the techniques that can be used to create titles, graphics and effects and the nature and capabilities of the equipment that is available to provide them. These aspects of video program creation should not be an afterthought, but should be part of the overall program design, considered during pre-production. Only then can the full potential of their possibilities be realized under the time and budgetary constraints under which all producers work.

The problems of post-production, on the other hand, cannot be planned for, although the professional producer will be able to avoid many pitfalls that less experienced makers of video programs encounter. Nevertheless, when problems inevitably arise, it is important to know the capabilities and limitations of the fixers available, and to have skilled personnel to operate these devices. Experience is still the best predictor of success in all aspects of production.

12 Summary Production Budgets

Few producers have (or want) the leisure to review the production they have just completed to see all the elements that were involved. Most would rather be working on the next production and let the previous one take care of itself. In this book, however, we can overlook the production perspective by examining an overall production budget that takes a program from development through to distribution. While this is a perspective that the producer needs from the beginning of a project, it is last in this book because it cannot be used until all the other aspects of production are understood. As we have reached that point, let's start at the beginning of this budget—Form 12.1—with "Program Development."

• *Program development* involves everything that it takes to get an idea for a program into production. Since few producers are independently wealthy, most—even those who work for producing and other organizations—have to submit their ideas in the form of a written proposal. To write it, they have to do research and sometimes consult with others, who may charge a fee, usually on a consultation or per-diem basis. At some point, a script has to be prepared. Occasionally, travel—to check a location, interview a potential host, do some research, convince an investor, etc.—is involved. On some occasions, likely prospects have to be entertained.

When the funds and other aspects of the project are in place, the nuts and bolts of the production need to be assembled. Production planning involves meetings, interviews, studio and location scouting and equipment evaluation. There is a great deal of communication: phone calls, letters and more meetings (some in coffee shops and restaurants), and endless exchanges of papers, signing of contracts, agreements, releases and the like. All these activities are covered under "Program Development."

• *Casting* covers a wide range of activities. It may simply involve a few phone calls to find a moderator, host narrator or panelists. On the other hand, the producer may need to assemble a cast of professional actors. In that case, a casting director may become a necessity.

A casting director is someone who spends his or her days and nights seeing every showcase, play, film, soap opera and night club act in town, as well as attending general auditions given by agents. Unlike agents, casting directors are not committed to individual actors and so have a wide range of available performers to choose from. If there is a perfect person for a role, a good casting director usually knows who it might be.

Casting directors seldom cost more than they are worth. They normally work on a per-diem basis, and this fee is usually negotiable. The number of days is usually the days of auditions. However, the casting director may pre-audition talent for the particular show and that time is also billed. The negotiability of a fee, as with other professionals, does not only relate to the budget. Other, less tangible factors can enter in, such as the visibility of the credit (a credit on national TV is worth something). The merit of the show can cut the fee. Two days of casting a teleplay of a Samuel Beckett piece may cost considerably less than casting a commercial.

If auditions are held, a space may have to be rented. The producer may also want to videotape the auditions to see how the talent comes across on tape and to give him or her time to think about it. All this is budgeted under "Casting."

• *Talent and staff* fees cover the entire cost of each individual for the entire production. If their fees for studio, remote and post-production have been figured, these figures are added for each individual and entered here, as is any time not covered under those categories. The producer's time for program development and casting, for example, needs to be added, as does his time spent arranging audio recording, rights or distribution. If, however, anyone's fee is based on a percentage of the cost of a production, the production cost should be calculated without this fee, and the fee then added. On the other hand, if (for example) the executive producer owns the show outright, then he may not take a fee but opt for a cut of the profit.

• *Studio and remote production* figures should be taken from the subtotals in their respective budgets. Of course, with some extra figuring, these numbers can be assembled right on this form to estimate the overall cost of production.

• *Audio recording* may be an entirely separate operation, and if so, this is the place to cost it out. If there is a narrator, his fee and the cost of taping him are entered here. The cost of the director's time is part of his overall fee, as the cost of the narrator's script is covered under program development. Other voice-over recordings can also be covered here, as is effects recording.

Music recording may involve fees not only to the performing musicians, but also to a composer who provides an original score. If the musicians belong to a union, their fees, like the talent fees,

may involve a mandatory benefit payment of up to 10% into their union fund, and this amount should also be added to the fee total.

• *Post-production* figures can be taken directly from the post-production budget, or entered here.

• *Professional services* such as insurance and lgal and accounting assistance are often required for a production. Although the program may not require the services of six-figure legal minds and Wall Street accountants, it will probably need a lawyer to write up or check a letter of agreement or a talent contract. It may also involve an accountant at tax time, if at no other. And it will probably involve an insurance policy, if only for equipment. All that can be entered here.

• *Rights* were discussed in Chapter 1. Rights to music may be to the recording, in which case they are obtained from the recording company. If they are rights to play and record the music, the publisher is the source. On the other hand, if an original composition is used, and the composer chooses to be paid in royalties instead of (or in addition to) a fee, only the fee is entered here.

Text rights are to written material, such as plays and books which are pretty much used verbatim. Story rights, however, are just that—the rights to tell a particular sequence of events. This may also involve the right to use the story of a real event, in which case the rights to the "story" have to be obtained from the persons involved—and here, especially, the legal fees from the previous section may come into play.

• *Videotape* is one of those items whose cost is often neglected, but it invariably creeps up on a production. Any estimates that were included in the studio, remote or post-production budgets can be pulled out here. To those figures should be added tape used for auditions and for distribution, including screenings. After the estimates are made, they should be padded. There is always a need for extra copies of a program.

• *Initial distribution* involves only the first stages of getting a program out. What is allowed for in this budget is sending the tape to those exhibitors and distributors who may be interested in showing or handling the program. This may involve screening, mailing and some travel and entertainment. The item of duplication may or may not involve the cost of videotape; the duplicator may include the tape in his fee. However, the cost should not appear both here and under videotape.

• *Totals* give the direct cost of the production. But the producer's real expenses do not end there. Even if his operation is quite small, numerous overhead costs—those that are not specific to a specific production operation—are incurred. Telephone, heating, cooling and electricity costs may have been incurred. Even if a separate space is not rented, a rent expense may be attributable to the space in which the business is conducted. Stationery may be printed, and advertising may be taken out that is not specific to this production. If there are people like receptionists, secretaries and maintenance persons who are hired not only for this production, their cost is part of the overhead. There are no hard-and-fast rules for setting overhead, but a realistic estimate is important. Obviously, the lower the overhead, the lower the price of a production can be, and the greater the advantage for the producer. Whatever the amount, overhead is usually expressed as a percentage of the cost of a project.

Profit is taken on the total of the direct plus the indirect (overhead) cost. Again, there are no standard profit margins for television production. They vary by sectors of the industry (industrial productions usually have smaller margins than commercials), by the prestige of the producer, by the size of the production, and by the degree to which profits are deferred in favor of future income from distribution.

The final price is always more than everyone expects and often less than the production will really cost. However, it is the mark of the professional producer that the disparity—if any—is small, and the final product is worth every penny.

CONCLUSION

This book has discussed the process of television production from concept to finished program in considerable detail. It is not a substitute for production experience, but it will make sense of that experience and fill in the dozens of gaps that experience often leaves. It is written as a useable handbook for both students and people who are active in the field, providing both practical considerations—the nuts and bolts and how-to of production—as well as a fairly substantial dose of technology.

Starting with program development and script preparation, the book presented a series of important considerations involved in proposing and casting a program, as well as preparing treatments and different kinds of scripts. The book then took the reader into the studio starting with a detailed look at equipment and then, through several chapters, moving through the entire studio production process. The same was done for shooting in the field, providing fairly detailed information about portable equipment and production techniques.

The last third of the book deals with editing the produced material into a finished program, including concepts, equipment and techniques. The rough cut, editing decision lists, fine cut and graphics were dealt with, providing discussions, illustrations and examples designed to help the producer move through the hazardous process with a good chance of success.

Thoughout, the book provides forms for all aspects of the process: from talent release to editing lists, and for budgets at all stages of production, including the summary production budget that provides an overview of the entire process in one long form. For those who want to take their understanding of technology a step further without taking an engineering degree, a Technical Appendix has been provided.

Yet the actual process of production is beyond this book. Every working producer will be presented with unique problems that he will have to use ingenuity and perseverance to solve qualities that no book can provide. And the element of professionalism is always central. What separates the professional producer from someone with "professional" equipment is the ability to use his skills under fire to produce a program that is creative, within his budget and a joy to watch—both for the people who made it and the people it was made for.

Form 12.1: Summary production budget.

Item	Item per day	No. days	Item total	Total
PROGRAM DEVELOPMENT				
Consultation				
In-house				xxxxxxxx
Other				xxxxxxxx
Research				xxxxxxxx
Treatment				xxxxxxxx
Script writing				xxxxxxxx
Production planning				xxxxxxxx
Travel				xxxxxxxx
Entertainment				xxxxxxxx
				xxxxxxxx
				xxxxxxxx
Development subtotal		xxxxxx	xxxxxxxxxxxxxxx	$
CASTING				
Casting director				xxxxxxxx
Location				xxxxxxxx
Recording				xxxxxxxx
Other				xxxxxxxx
Casting subtotal		xxxxxx	xxxxxxxxxxxxxxx	$
TALENT FEES				
				xxxxxxxx
				xxxxxxxx
				xxxxxxxx
				xxxxxxxx
				xxxxxxxx
				xxxxxxxx
				xxxxxxxx
				xxxxxxxx
				xxxxxxxx
Talent subtotal		xxxxxx	xxxxxxxxxxxxxxx	$
STAFF				
Executive producer				xxxxxxxx
Producer				xxxxxxxx
				xxxxxxxx
				xxxxxxxx
Director				xxxxxxxx
Assistant director				xxxxxxxx
				xxxxxxxx
				xxxxxxxx
				xxxxxxxx
Staff subtotal		xxxxxx	xxxxxxxxxxxxxxx	$
Page Subtotal xxxxxxxxxxxxxxxxxxxxxxxxxxxxxxxxxxxxxxxxxxxxxxxxxxxxxxxxx				$

Title _____

Form 12.1: Summary production budget (cont'd).

Title _____	Item per day	No. days	Item total	Total
Balance carried forward xxxxxxxxxxxxxxxxxxxxxxxxxxxxxxxxxxxxxxxxxxxxxxxxxxx				$
STUDIO PRODUCTION				
Studio fees & equipment _____	_____	_____	_____	xxxxxxx
Additional equipment _____	_____	_____	_____	xxxxxxx
Crew total _____	_____	_____	_____	xxxxxxx
Local travel _____	_____	_____	_____	xxxxxxx
Supplies _____	_____	_____	_____	xxxxxxx
Commissary _____	_____	_____	_____	xxxxxxx
Sets _____	_____	_____	_____	xxxxxxx
Props & graphics _____	_____	_____	_____	xxxxxxx
Costume _____	_____	_____	_____	xxxxxxx
Makeup _____	_____	_____	_____	xxxxxxx
_____	_____	_____	_____	xxxxxxx
_____	_____	_____	_____	xxxxxxx
Contingency _____	_____	_____	_____	xxxxxxx
Studio subtotal		xxxxxx	xxxxxxxxxxxxxxxx	$
REMOTE PRODUCTION				
Location rental _____	_____	_____	_____	xxxxxxx
Equipment _____	_____	_____	_____	xxxxxxx
Supplies _____	_____	_____	_____	xxxxxxx
Props, graphics _____	_____	_____	_____	xxxxxxx
Costume _____	_____	_____	_____	xxxxxxx
Makeup _____	_____	_____	_____	xxxxxxx
Crew total _____	_____	_____	_____	xxxxxxx
Travel _____	_____	_____	_____	xxxxxxx
Air/train _____	_____	_____	_____	xxxxxxx
Local _____	_____	_____	_____	xxxxxxx
Food _____	_____	_____	_____	xxxxxxx
Lodging _____	_____	_____	_____	xxxxxxx
Location permits _____	_____	_____	_____	xxxxxxx
_____	_____	_____	_____	xxxxxxx
_____	_____	_____	_____	xxxxxxx
Contingency _____	_____	_____	_____	xxxxxxx
Remote subtotal		xxxxxx	xxxxxxxxxxxxxxxx	$
AUDIO RECORDING				
Narration _____	_____	_____	_____	xxxxxxx
Fees _____	_____	_____	_____	xxxxxxx
Recording _____	_____	_____	_____	xxxxxxx
Music _____	_____	_____	_____	xxxxxxx
Fees _____	_____	_____	_____	xxxxxxx
Recording _____	_____	_____	_____	xxxxxxx
Effects _____	_____	_____	_____	xxxxxxx
_____	_____	_____	_____	xxxxxxx
Audio recording subtotal		xxxxxx	xxxxxxxxxxxxxxxx	$
Page Subtotal xxxxxxxxxxxxxxxxxxxxxxxxxxxxxxxxxxxxxxxxxxxxxxxxxx				$

Form 12.1: Summary production budget (cont'd).

Item	Item per day	No. days	Item total	Total
Title _____				
Balance carried forward xxxxxxxxxxxxxxxxxxxxxxxxxxxxxxxxxxxxxxxxxxxxxxxxxx				$
POST-PRODUCTION				
Workprint (TC & Trans) _____	_____	_____	_____	xxxxxxx
Catalog _____	_____	_____	_____	xxxxxxx
Editing script _____	_____	_____	_____	xxxxxxx
Graphics _____	_____	_____	_____	xxxxxxx
Board _____	_____	_____	_____	xxxxxxx
Slide _____	_____	_____	_____	xxxxxxx
Other _____	_____	_____	_____	xxxxxxx
Slide/Film transfer _____	_____	_____	_____	xxxxxxx
Rough-cut _____	_____	_____	_____	xxxxxxx
Fine-cut _____	_____	_____	_____	xxxxxxx
Audio mix _____	_____	_____	_____	xxxxxxx
_____	_____	_____	_____	xxxxxxx
_____	_____	_____	_____	xxxxxxx
_____	_____	_____	_____	xxxxxxx
Post-production subtotal		xxxxxx	xxxxxxxxxxxxxxxxxx	$
PROFESSIONAL SERVICES				
Insurance _____	_____	_____	_____	xxxxxxx
Production insurance _____	_____	_____	_____	xxxxxxx
Equipment insurance _____	_____	_____	_____	xxxxxxx
Liability insurance _____	_____	_____	_____	xxxxxxx
Special policies _____	_____	_____	_____	xxxxxxx
Legal _____	_____	_____	_____	xxxxxxx
Contracts _____	_____	_____	_____	xxxxxxx
_____	_____	_____	_____	xxxxxxx
Accounting _____	_____	_____	_____	xxxxxxx
Budgets _____	_____	_____	_____	xxxxxxx
Payroll _____	_____	_____	_____	xxxxxxx
Taxes _____	_____	_____	_____	xxxxxxx
_____	_____	_____	_____	xxxxxxx
Professional services subtotal		xxxxxx	xxxxxxxxxxxxxxxxxx	$
RIGHTS				
Music _____	_____	_____	_____	xxxxxxx
Recordings _____	_____	_____	_____	xxxxxxx
Publishers' _____	_____	_____	_____	xxxxxxx
Other _____	_____	_____	_____	xxxxxxx
Text _____	_____	_____	_____	xxxxxxx
Story _____	_____	_____	_____	xxxxxxx
_____	_____	_____	_____	xxxxxxx
_____	_____	_____	_____	xxxxxxx
Rights subtotal		xxxxxx	xxxxxxxxxxxxxxxxxx	$
Page Subtotal xxxxxxxxxxxxxxxxxxxxxxxxxxxxxxxxxxxxxxxxxxxxxxxxxxxxxxxxxxxxxxxxxxxxxxxxxxxx				$

Form 12.1: Summary production budget (cont'd).

Title _____				
Item	Item per day	No. days	Item total	Total
Balance carried forward xxxxxxxxxxxxxxxxxxxxxxxxxxxxxxxxxxxxxxxxxxxxxxxxxxx				$
VIDEOTAPE				
Studio Production _____	____	___	_____	xxxxxxxx
Remote Production _____	____	___	_____	xxxxxxxx
Workprints _____	____	___	_____	xxxxxxxx
Rough-cut _____	____	___	_____	xxxxxxxx
Fine-cut _____	____	___	_____	xxxxxxxx
Dubs _____	____	___	_____	xxxxxxxx
1-in _____	____	___	_____	xxxxxxxx
3/4 in _____	____	___	_____	xxxxxxxx
_____	____	___	_____	xxxxxxxx
Videotape subtotal	xxxxxx	xxxxxx	xxxxxxxxxxxxxxxxx	$
INITIAL DISTRIBUTION				
Duplication _____	____	___	_____	xxxxxxxx
Screening _____	____	___	_____	xxxxxxxx
Mailing _____	____	___	_____	xxxxxxxx
Travel _____	____	___	_____	xxxxxxxx
Entertainment _____	____	___	_____	xxxxxxxx
_____	____	___	_____	xxxxxxxx
Distribution subtotal	xxxxxx	xxxxxx	xxxxxxxxxxxxxxxxx	$
Cost subtotal	xxxxxx	xxxxxx	xxxxxxxxxxxxxxxxx	$
Overhead (%)	xxxxxx	xxxxxx	xxxxxxxxxxxxxxxxx	$
Cost plus overhead subtotal	xxxxxx	xxxxxx	xxxxxxxxxxxxxxxxx	$
Profit (%)	xxxxxx	xxxxxx	xxxxxxxxxxxxxxxxx	$
Total project price	xxxxxx	xxxxxx	xxxxxxxxxxxxxxxxx	$

Technical Appendix

The following appendix covers the color processing system used as the American television standard, some television camera parameters and the uses of television test equipment.

NTSC TELEVISION COLOR CONSIDERATIONS

Television color is an ingenious simulation of real color. In the United States, it is based on the NTSC standard, created in the 1950s by the National Television Standards Committee of the Federal Communications Commission (FCC). The NTSC was given the job of devising a color television system (for the U.S.) that would be compatible with the then-existing black-and-white television standard, so that monochrome sets would not be made obsolete.

The NTSC system is based on a standardized concept of color vision developed by the International Commission on Illumination (usually referred to by its French initials, CEI). The CEI standards were based on extended studies of the color perceptions of thousands of willing subjects. The CEI concept was modified, as noted here, to create the NTSC format. To make it compatible with black-and-white—or "luminance-based"—television, the NTSC made color phase-dependent and therefore sensitive to color error due to phase shifting. That is why the NTSC standard is sometimes referred to by irate video engineers as "never the same color."

Television Color Parameters

The image viewed by the camera passes through the lens of an optical system that divides it into its three "primaries"—the color components: red, green and blue. Each primary is given a specific CEI wavelength for international standardization. (One of the differences in the American system is that our TV primaries vary slightly from the international standard to make them compatible with the characteristics of the color phosphors used in television receiver screens.)

A "map" of the color perception standard, a "chromaticity diagram" (shown in Figure A.1), is used to specify television color. For every color there is a pair of x, y coordinates, and therefore a specific location. At the boundaries of the curved figure, the hues are saturated; they are at their maximum intensity. As we move toward the center of the figure, representing daylight "white" with a color temperature of 6500°K, the colors become paler—progressively mixed with white—until they all become "white."

Color Temperature

The white used is specified because all colors are seen in relation to the "color temperature" of the source of light. Color temperature is a simple, much-misunderstood concept that relates to the color radiated by a "black body" at different tem-

Figure A.1: CEI graph of the television color spectrum.

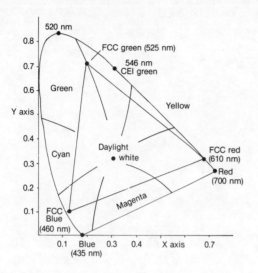

peratures, measured in "degrees Kelvin." The Kelvin scale is just a centigrade (or Celsius) scale that sets °K at "absolute zero," or –293°C. (Therefore, 0°C equals 293°K.) A black body is a theoretical construct of a chunk of matter that reflects nothing, but radiates when heated. As it is heated from absolute zero, this material emits visible radiation related to its actual temperature in accordance with a theoretical model—on which the CEI map is based, and which defines the color temperature standard used in television and elsewhere. By this standard, incandescent lights are yellowish and therefore are 2700° to 3500° on the Kelvin scale. White fluorescents are about 4300°K. Daylight, as noted earlier, registers as a blue-white between 4200° and 6500°K.

However, what we *perceive* as white covers a wide range of "whiteness." A white shirt assumes different shades in different settings (becoming bluish outdoors, yellowish in lamplight), but we unconsciously compensate and see one white. The television camera does no such thing, yet the picture on the screen must fit our perceptual expectations. Accordingly, in videoland, all colors are seen under perpetual tungsten lights, as if bathed in 3200°K illumination. Since we also shoot under other color temperatures, we provide each camera with a set of compensating filters that shift the wavelengths of the incoming light in the 3200°K direction. However, as such filters can only pro-

vide a gross correction, we also have a "white balance" adjustment that sets the primaries in the perceptually correct relation to one another.

White Balance

White balance describes the relationship of the three primary colors to each other and to a specific source. As discussed in a following section on the vectorscope and in Chapter 11, adjusting the white balance sets each primary at a specific phase angle to the color subcarrier. This corrects for differences in the color temperature of the light coming into the camera.

The importance of white balance adjustment is illustrated in Figure A.2. Let's say that we have a green that can be located on the graph at x = 0.12, y = 0.57. If we draw a (solid) line from our daylight white source point through the color point, we find that the wavelength of the color in approximately 508 nanometers (nm), making it a true green. However, if we illuminate the color with the light of a 3200°K tungsten lamp, we find that its wavelength (as seen by the camera) has shifted five nanometers toward the blue, so that the green on our monitor screen has a slightly blue cast. (Note that, unlike optical color, television

Figure A.2: CEI map showing color shifts under tungsten.

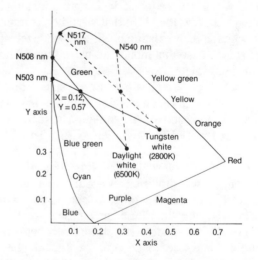

color shifts toward blue as the light source becomes cooler and yellower.)

However, as Figure A.2 also shows, the amount of this shift is different for each color. If an image includes a yellow-green (540 nm for daylight white), the tungsten illumination will shift that color 23 nm toward the blue (illustrated by broken lines) so that it looks more like a true green. As each color shifts a different amount under the 3200°K light, it is not easy to correct for the wrong white balance.

To correct white balance, two of the primaries—normally, the red and the blue—must be moved in relation to the third and to each other. This can be easily done at the camera head or control unit. Where the color filters in the camera provide a coarse correction, white balance adjustments provide a fine correction for the color temperature of the production situation. In some cameras, white balance is manually adjusted, but in most it is automatically set by activating an auto white balance circuit. This is a digital circuit that measures the balance of the primaries and makes the necessary fine correction. It should be noted that once incorrect white balance is recorded, only an expensive color correction process will make the color recorded on a videotape right again.

Color Encoding

In recording and transmitting the color image according to the NTSC standard, it is first necessary to extract the luminance—the element of the picture that records as a black-and-white image. (The higher the luminance of a point in an image, the higher the video level at that point and the whiter the point is on the screen.) Thus separated, the luminance is designated the Y signal, and the color, or chrominance, is generated as two combination signals, I and Q.

To obtain the correct luminance value from each of the primaries, we again return to the CEI standard. According to this, we find that the human eye sees different colors of the same brightness as having *different* brightness, or luminance.

If we look at equal color patches of the three primaries that reflect exactly the same amount of light—i.e., have the same brightness—we nevertheless see the green as if it were significantly brighter than the red or blue patch. Therefore, when luminance is determined in the television camera, different proportions of each of the three primary colors are extracted for each image point.

These proportions are: 59% of the green, 30% of the red and 11% of the blue—just as the human eye would see it. The total extracted from each of the primaries is added together to give the luminance signal value for that point.

Luminance and chrominance are separated into discrete electronic signals by matrixes—electronic circuits that perform the necessary mathematical operations, shown in block-diagram form in Figure A.3. While all three primaries are used to determine luminance, only the blue and the red signals are color-encoded, for reasons that will be noted later. We can see that both R and B—as well as their luminance-subtracted values (R-Y and B-Y)—are processed in their respective matrixes to yield two "transmission primaries," I and Q. These will modulate the color subcarrier. (The I stands for In-Phase Subcarrier and the Q for Quadrature-Phase Subcarrier.)

The calculations performed in the matrixes are at the high school algebra level and are given here for the perusal of interested readers who can follow how these encoders make it possible to get both monochrome and color information from the same signal. The relationship between color and luminance is most clearly illustrated when we have a white image element, which, as in nature, comprises each of the three primaries equally (R = G = B). Then both I and Q equal zero (I = 0.60 − 0.28 − 0.32 = 0; and Q = 0.21 − 0.52 − 0.31 = 0), and no color information is generated; only luminance information remains.

The other interesting aspect of this configuration is that the amount of green at each point of the image is implicit in the I and Q signals, and therefore green need not be encoded. To find out how much green was at the original image point, a decoding matrix at the receiver or recorder can obtain G from the Y, R and B information as: G = 0.51(R-Y) − 0.19(B-Y).

CAMERA PARAMETERS

The camera pickup tube transforms an image into an electrical signal that records the luminance value of the image as a varying signal on a series of "lines." The image is focused on the target of the pickup tube. The target is a photoconductive surface that changes its electrical resistance at each point in proportion to the amount of light falling on it. As the scanning electron beam generated at the back of the tube falls on each point,

Figure A.3: A Y/I Q encoder block diagram.

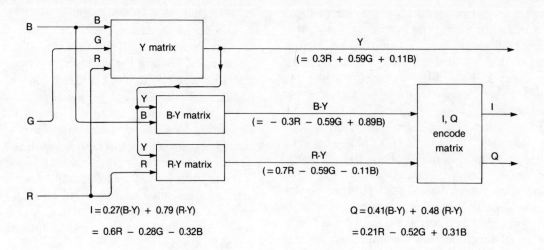

beam current is drawn in proportion to the illumination at that point. If the illumination is high, more beam current is drawn, the output resistance falls as the beam passes that point and the level of the video signal rises. At a darker point in the image, less beam current is drawn, the output resistance is higher and the video level is lower.

Controlling Video Levels

In the camera, the "white level" is controlled by the iris, the lighting on the scene or set, and by camera controls. The lower "black level" is controlled primarily within the camera, or in a remote camera control unit (CCU).

• *White, or video, level:* The auto-iris in a video camera controls the aperture to maintain the overall video signal at one volt peak-to-peak. The basic purpose is to prevent the level of the video signal from exceeding (or falling below) a predetermined maximum (or minimum). Some cheaper cameras, when overdriven, will compress the whole signal, including sync, resulting in weak sync with high video levels. It is important, therefore, when using a cheaper camera, to be particularly careful not to exceed the prescribed video level of 100 IEEE. (See also sections on the waveform monitor, below.)

The auto-iris is designed to respond to rapidly varying lighting conditions which occur when a camera is used on location, or when there are zooms—for example, from a wide-angle shot of a well-lit, darkly dressed group to a closeup of a pale face. The video signal that would then exceed 100 IEEE units on a waveform monitor is clamped at slightly less than 100 IEEE. However, since the iris closes down as the camera moves to the pale face, the maximum video level and the overall balance of video level is maintained.

In professional cameras, white level can be controlled at the camera head. The video level for the brightest surface in a scene is set to 100 IEEE, so that all other levels for the shot will remain below this. In such controlled lighting situations as a studio offers, the problems of balanced illumination can be dealt with by correct lighting. In the field, the camera operator is warned of excessive light levels by such in-camera indicators as "zebra" (or "tiger") stripes: bright diagonal lines that appear on the video image in the camera viewfinder when excessive video level is generated.

• *Black or pedestal level or setup:* The black (or reference black) level is the level below which so little light is reflected from an image point that it does not affect the electrical conductivity of the target. As far as the camera is concerned, such a point is black. Therefore, the IEEE level below the lowest level which does register an image defines the black level. In multi-camera shoots, matching the black levels of the cameras is an important element of camera balancing. The terms "setup" and "pedestal" refer to the difference in IEEE level between the blanking and the black level.

Resolution and Beam Sharpness

Since the maximum vertical resolution of television is fixed by the number of lines in a picture, improved resolution results from more definition in each horizontal line (how small a detail in brightness or color can be distinguished). Horizontal resolution in a camera is a function of a number of factors, including bandwidth. Bandwidth determines how many information elements can be transmitted each second, and therefore determines the number of elements per line. The other major factors relate to electron beam sharpness (see also "Aperture Correction," following), to color registration (or the number of color-filter stripes in a single-tube camera), and noise.

The electron beam contributes to resolution to the degree that it can be focused. Just as a finer line can be drawn by a finer pen, the size of the smallest detail that can be read out of a camera tube is a direct function of the degree to which the beam is focused. Resolution is usually given in two figures: a higher figure for the center area, and a lower one for the corners of the image. This is because the beam arrives at the corners at an angle and, therefore, with a greater cross-section. This is mitigated to some extent by various forms of automatic beam control, which narrow and intensify the beam when it approaches a corner.

Comet-Tailing and Lag

Comet-tailing occurs when a highlight—a small, intense reflection—is so intense that the beam cannot discharge the target at that point in one pass. The beam is normally set to discharge the imaging surface only up to about 200 IEEE. Even as the spot moves, the area is still being discharged, giving the spot a track like a comet's tail. With "dynamic beam control," the white level is constantly monitored, and the beam intensity is adjusted to compensate for these hot spots.

Lag—the ghost-like traces momentarily left by the paler parts of moving images—is a related effect. This effect is greatly reduced by the use of *bias lights,* small LEDs in the imaging tubes that shed a low-level illumination over the imaging surface. Since lag occurs as the light level gets lower and the retention of the imaging surface increases, raising the bias, or black level of the output, reduces the lag.

Aperture and Contour Correction, Image Enhancement

• *An aperture correction* adjustment circuit makes it possible to "sharpen" the electronic signal for each element of the image, to improve image detail by making the peaks higher and sharper and the valleys lower and steeper. The effect is the same as if the scanning electron beam in the tube were more sharply focused, so that the cross-section of the beam—the aperture—was smaller. The result is improved resolution.

• *Contour correction* is a form of aperture correction in which the output of the green channel is "sharpened" and then fed into the red and blue, as well as back to the green channel, to sharpen all three color video signals in phase. This reduces the possibility of registration errors.

• *Image enhancement* sharpens transitions at the edges of image areas, such as the line of a shoulder against a background. Delay lines are used to hold the previous line (for vertical enhancement), or the most-previous image point—about one nanosecond—(for horizontal enhancement). The two lines or neighboring points on a line are then compared, and if there is a significant difference in luminosity, that difference is "enhanced." For example, the edge of a gray suit is made darker, and the white wall behind it is made whiter, at their common border. However, if enhancement is excessive, the image gets a flat, "cartoony" look.

Gamma Correction and Shading

The gamma characteristic of a pickup tube is its response to the range of tones from black to white. Left to themselves, pickup tubes stretch blacks and compress whites, making the blacks (and dark grays) darker and the whites paler than they really are. Since pickup tubes "see" only luminance information, the output of each tube must be subjected to gamma correction. This is done by taking the video signal from each tube, changing the video level to compensate for the error inherent in the tube. Then the information each tube generates about the level of the color it "sees" will be correct. In the camera, circuits adjust the output of each tube to provide full gamma correction of up to 1.0 (unity) for each step in the EIA gray scale (see Glossary). Where manual gamma correction is provided, it ranges from 0.45 to 1.0.

Shading involves adjustment of the camera tube's uneven response to even illumination over its surface. This is done by means of sawtooth and parabolic test signals provided for that purpose. Adjusting these parameters requires expertise. If one adjustment is changed, others must also be altered.

Registration and Geometry

Registration is the alignment of the three color images from the three pickup elements in a multi-element camera. As in multicolor printing, the color image from each tube is superimposed on the others when the image is regenerated on a television screen. Like resolution, registration is best in a center circle that covers 80% of the tube height. In a good camera, center registration error is less than 0.1%, increasing to no more than 0.25% at the corners. Lesser cameras may manage close to 0.1% at the center, but their registration falls off rapidly to as much as 0.5% in the corners. Registration is achieved by moving the red and blue images horizontally and vertically in reference to the green image, until all three color images coincide. On professional cameras, registration controls are available as "red and blue horizontal (RH, BH) and vertical (RV, BV) centering."

Geometric distortion, sometimes confused with registration, is the tendency of cameras to splay the image at the edges, so that the same thing assumes different proportions when it appears in different parts of the picture area. This factor can be evaluated by focusing the camera on a grid, to see that the squares at the edges are as square and of the same size as the squares at the center. In a professional camera, the change in geometry from the center to the corners should be less than 2%.

Figure A.4: S/N voltage ratio on a logarithmic curve.

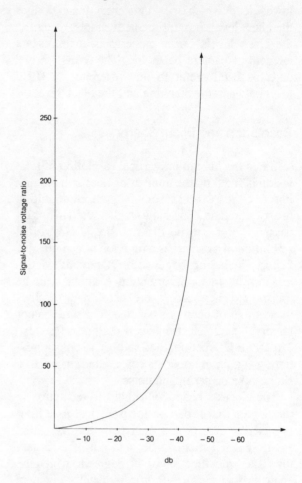

Signal-to-Noise Ratio

The signal-to-noise (s/n) ratio is the ratio of the amplitude (voltage level) of the video signal to the amplitude of the electronic noise (unwanted random voltages generated in the circuit), and it is expressed in negative decibels (– db). However, decibels are a logarithmic, rather than a direct, function of the relationship between voltages, as shown in Figure A. 4.

As a result, a change of 1 db in the higher end of the curve, say near –50 db, indicates a much larger improvement in signal quality than a 1 db increase in the –40 db range. As a result, a camera with a –50 db s/n ratio produces a picture with about three times less noise than a camera with a – 40 db s/n ratio.

Although there is no written industry standard for measuring the signal-to-noise ratio in a television camera, it is generally measured for a specified level of illumination (such as 20 footcandles) on a surface of specified reflectivity (such as a 60% reflective surface).

COMPOSITE VIDEO AND INFORMATION DISPLAYS

The encoded Y, I and Q information, combined with the appropriate blanking and synchronizing signals, constitutes "composite video." The following material deals with the video signals and introduces some of the equipment used to monitor them. But we should note that the following is not intended to serve as how-to instruction; it is designed to give the reader a frame of reference for understanding those video signals that are so central to the success of a production. By combining instructions from the equipment manuals with the information given here, a great deal can be accomplished.

Before going further, it helps to remember that video comprises solely horizontal lines. Although we refer to "vertical" sync and blanking, these too are recorded on horizontal lines. In video, all verticality is created by the stacking of horizontal lines, and the only vertical movement of the beam is its movement from line to line (horizontal retrace) and from the bottom to the top of the image at the end of each field (vertical retrace). But during these intervals, the trace is "blanked": it is not visible, and is not "video."

Reading Horizontal Video on the Waveform Monitor

Since the basic element of video is the horizontal line, control of the line quality will result in good video. Figure 3.5 shows a horizontal trace on a waveform monitor. (The configuration of the graticule on the waveform monitor is described in Chapter 3.) The trace shown includes all the 262½ lines from each of the two fields of a frame, superimposed on each other (the first field is on the left, the second on the right). Between the video from the two fields is the horizontal blanking interval, in which the horizontal sync and color burst signals are included.

Checking Video and Pedestal Levels

The video level, or image brightness, looks like silhouettes or ragged grass when shown on a wave-

form monitor. The peaks of this "grass" represent the brightest parts of the image. The amplitude, or height, of the grass is therefore a measure of luminance. For a good video image, the highest peaks should not exceed 100 IEEE units (marked on the left of the scale), with the monitor's setting switched off. Should the video level exceed 100 IEEE, there is too much light on the scene, the camera aperture is too wide or, if recorded video is being measured, the record level of the deck may be too high.

The video can also be checked for clipping. Clipping makes the video appear like a trimmed hedge, because it looks as if a section of the top (white clipping) or the bottom (back clipping) of the video information were cut in a straight line. The effect may be controlled by adjusting the f-stop or the lighting. However, it may also be a symptom of an electronic problem within the camera or deck.

The pedestal level, or setup, is the bottom of the actual video level, the lowest amplitude of picture information (reference black). Accordingly, when checking pedestal, it is essential to provide a nonreflective black area on the set. The broadcast standard for pedestal is 7.5 plus or minus 2.5 IEEE, but it is better to work at the higher end because the pedestal separates and, in effect, protects, the blanking reference level from being disturbed by picture information.

Checking Horizontal Blanking, Sync and Burst

The horizontal blanking interval falls between the lines of video. Figure A.5 shows that the horizontal sync signal that triggers the horizontal retrace should bottom at –40 IEEE, and the color burst signal should center on the blanking and be set between –20 and +20 IEEE. By adjusting the waveform monitor for an expanded display, shown in Figure A.5, more details of the horizontal blanking signal can be read.

Each horizontal graticule division on the expanded display measures one microsecond (μsec). The full blanking interval (specified by FCC regulations) must fall between 10.5 and 11.4 microseconds (nominal, 11.1 μsec). Other aspects of the horizontal sync configuration should also follow Figure A.5. The sync signal is preceded by a short interval known as the "front porch," which must fall between 1.27 and 1.72 μsec (nominal, 1.59

Figure A.5: Horizontal blanking interval on expanded display.

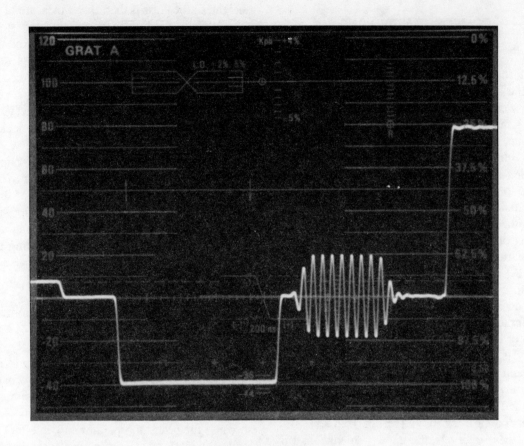

a. Actual expanded display

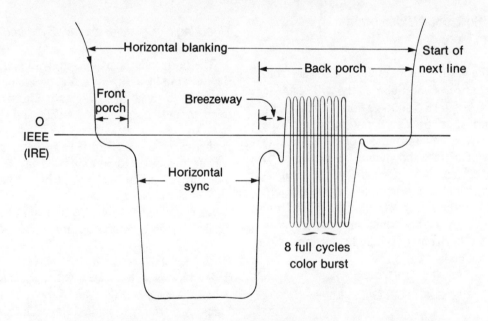

b. Elements of expanded display

Figure A.6: Configuration of the vertical blanking interval.

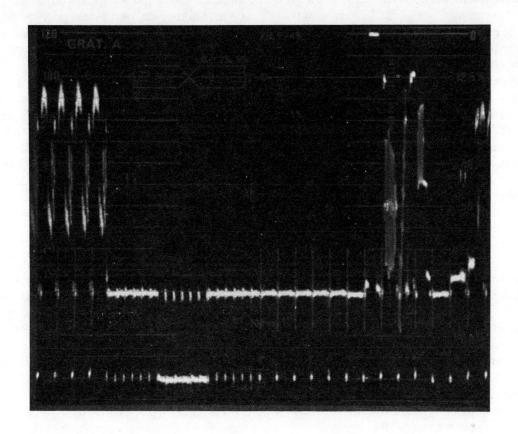

a. Actual vertical interval waveform

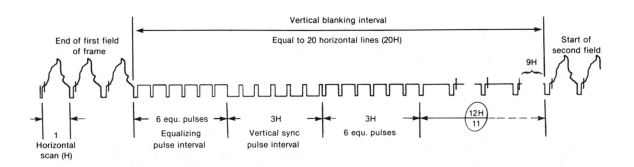

b. Detail of vertical interval

μsec). The sync is followed by another interval before the color burst comes along. This is known as the "breezeway" and must fall between 0.39 and 0.64 (nominal, 0.56) μsec. Finally, the breezeway, the burst and the interval between burst and next video is called the "back porch," which falls between 4.15 and 5.72 μsec (nominal, 4.76 μsec).

The width of the horizontal sync must not be less than 4.44 or more than 5.08 (nominal, 4.76) μsec. The color burst occupies nominally 2.24 μsec. It can be wider—up to 2.55 μsec—but not narrower. The burst signal should be a full eight cycles with eight peaks in either direction, symmetrically above and below the blanking level of –10 IEEE.

Checking Chroma Level

Chrominance can be checked by setting the response switch to CHROMA on most waveform monitors. This will display the chrominance component of the video fields, separated by the horizontal blanking interval with color burst. Chroma level should be well within the standard of +20 and –20 IEEE. If it is recorded at a higher level, it will tend to give trouble in later generations of small-format recordings and is difficult to correct without losing other aspects of image quality.

Checking Vertical Sync

The last 19 to 23 lines of each field are devoted to vertical blanking. Figure A.6 shows the configuration of an entire vertical interval as it appears on a waveform monitor. At the left and right are several horizontal lines, shown before, separated by horizontal blanking and burst. Remembering, again, that the vertical interval consists of horizontal lines, it can be seen that it starts with a "line" of video that is divided into two periods, or two "equalizing" pulses. The next two lines are the same, so that the first three lines of the vertical interval consist of six equalizing pulses.

The next three lines carry the actual vertical sync in the form of a single sync pulse, three lines long, marked by six "serrations"—two per line. This sync interval is followed by three more lines of six equalizing pulses (like the first three lines), making a total of nine lines. For the balance of the vertical interval, which may be from 10 to 14 lines long, the system generates horizontal lines, with sync and burst, but with the "video" at a constant amplitude: the blanking level. (These normally unused lines of blanking can be used to store digital information, such as teletext, providing that the information is properly encoded and modulated so as not to interfere with the timing of the picture information.)

The duration of the vertical blanking interval is set by the FCC at 21 plus or minus 2 lines. However, in production, blanking is normally set at 20 lines, because video recording systems tend to add lines of blanking rather than picture. It is much more difficult to add lines of picture information to replace excess blanking than it is to add lines of blanking to replace excess picture lines.

Reading a Vectorscope

To read a vectorscope, it is necessary to understand that the video signal is transmitted not only through the air, but through most video systems on a carrier, a 6-megahertz signal. Since color capability was added to the basic monochrome signals color information rides on a "sideband" or "subcarrier" frequency of 3.58 MHz in the NTSC standard.

The video signal can be thought of as a line flowing through the center of a thick-walled pipe, where the pipe is the color signal. A vectorscope displays a cross-section of this "pipe," with the luminance coming at the viewer from the center on a "Z" axis, and the chrominance in a circle around the center, as shown in Figure A.7. The chrominance amplitude (also termed chroma level or saturation) determines the radius of this "pipe," and the chrominance phase (or hue) determines the pattern of distribution of the color around the center.

The subcarrier, or color burst frequency, is shown on vectorscopes as a 180° radius from the center to the left. Since the subcarrier is the reference frequency by which the frequency of each color is determined, all colors are displayed on the vectorscope at specific "phase angles" in relation to the burst radius, whose position never changes.

For each color there are two markings. One is a small, cross-hatched box where the color should be located for a precise, electronically generated waveform, such as color bars. However, when the signal comes from a camera image, the color cannot be so precisely located. In that case, there is a larger box for each color, and if the color is within

Figure A.7: Vectorscope display.

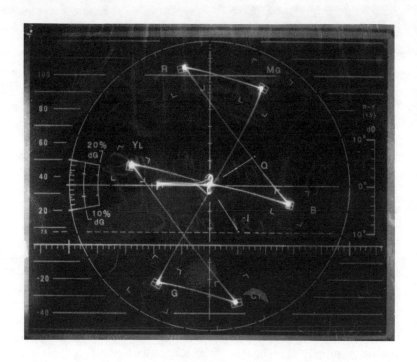

a. A vectorscope display

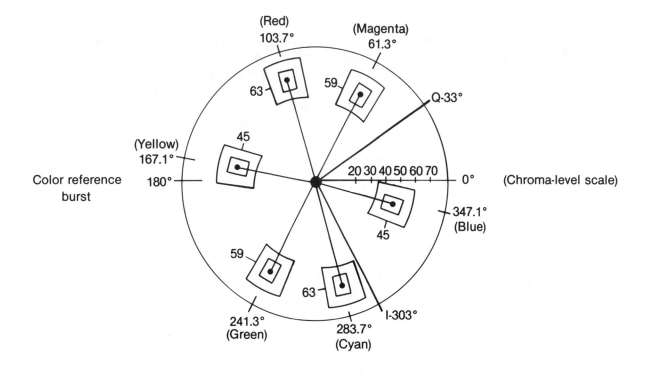

b. Vectorscope display parameters

Figure A.8: Image from a cross-pulse monitor.

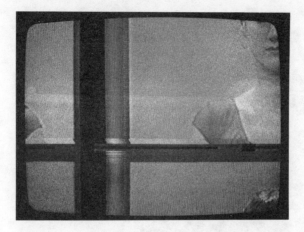

the larger box, the color is correct in both hue and saturation.

In use, the vectorscope is initially set with an electronically generated color bar signal, which is displayed as the zig-zag shown in Figure A.7. Reading burst at 180°, the color positions are marked in a counter-clockwise direction as:

Magenta	(Mg)	at	61°
Red	(R)	at	104°
Yellow	(Y1)	at	167°
Green	(G)	at	241°
Cyan	(Cy)	at	284°
Blue	(B)	at	340°

To use the vectorscope to color-match two cameras, the video output of both cameras is put into the two video inputs of the vectorscope. The output of each camera is then carefully adjusted for optimum color alignment on the scope. If the vectorscope has only a single display mode, the displays from the two cameras are rapidly switched. When the apparent "flicker" is at a minimum, the cameras are color-matched to the degree possible.

In post-production, the vectorscope is also used to check color. Primarily however, it is used to check the color setting of the color bars at the head of the tape, which should be the color bars used during production and recorded at the head of each tape before it is used. The color bars will

indicate precisely how much color-phase adjustment is necessary in making the master. In dubbing, the vectorscope can be used to check the color bars on the master to make a correct color dub, if color phase adjustment is available.

Using a Cross-Pulse Monitor

Another item a producer will need is the cross-pulse (also called pulse-cross) monitor. As explained in Chapter 3, this provides a video image with the horizontal and vertical blanking brought to the center of the raster, so that the four quadrants of the picture appear in their diagonally opposite corners, as shown in Figure A.8. This viewing configuration is a switchable option on many professional monitors that also display a regular image. On the most sophisticated units, the vertical sweep can be expanded so that the lines of the vertical interval can be examined more closely.

Figure A.8 identifies the various elements of blanking and sync information shown on this monitor for an NTSC color image. The horizontal blanking interval appears as a double vertical stripe, black (or dark gray) on the left, and yellow on the right. The gray column is formed from the stacking of all the horizontal sync pulses (bordered by the front porch on the left and by the breezeway on the right) from all the lines on the raster. The yellow column is formed by color burst signals, similarly stacked. (These are the waveforms shown in Figure A.5.)

The structure of the vertical interval is illustrated more clearly in Figure A.9. The interval begins with the six short equalizing pulses (see waveforms in Figure A.6), followed by six long sync pulses separated by short serrations (the blank space after the sync pulses). These are followed, in turn, by six more equalizing pulses, and finally, by the remaining lines of blanking.

It is particularly useful to combine the information of Figures A.6 and A.9, because this clearly illustrates how the electrical information of the waveforms is translated into horizontal lines, and how these are distributed among interlaced fields. As can be seen, each equalizing pulse and each sync pulse from one field alternates with the same equalizing and sync pulse from the next field.

If a cross-pulse monitor with an expanded display is available, its face can be calibrated to check not only the number and interlace of the vertical blanking, but its timing. To make the

Figure A.9: Cross-pulse monitor blanking information layout.

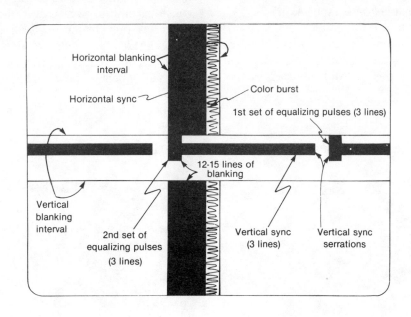

a. Blanking and sync information

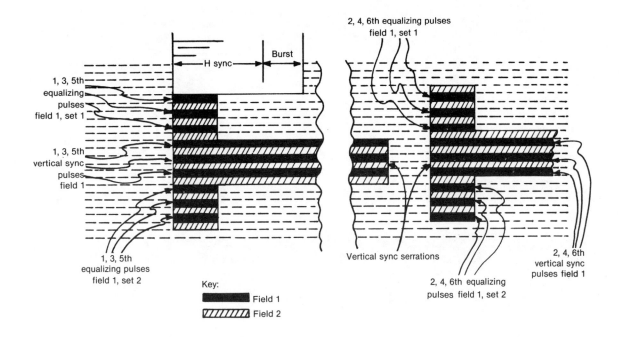

b. Detail of vertical sync

calibrations, all that is necessary is that a tape with perfect composite video be played on a properly adjusted deck, and that the correct widths and positions be marked on a graticule—a piece of transparent acetate film marked with a suitable grid.

The point at which the column of horizontal blanking signals breaks for the vertical blanking interval is very useful in setting the SKEW control. Movement of this control permits adjustment of tape tension during editing and dubbing to optimize video output from the source. Since tapes are almost always recorded and edited on different machines, small differences in tape tension can cause instabilities that reduce the quality of the master or dub. If severe, these instabilities can cause the top of the image to "flag" (to wave to the left or right). The image from a tape before and after adjustment is shown in Figure A.10.

Figure A.10: Skew adjustment on the cross-pulse monitor.

Glossary

All terms used within a definition that are defined elsewhere in this glossary appear in italics.

A/B roll editing: Using two video sources during editing to create *effects transitions* in the finished videotape.

above-the-line: A production management term describing indirect costs and the salaries and fees of administrative and creative personnel involved with the production.

address code: See *SMPTE time code*.

address track: Any track on video- or audiotape used exclusively for cueing or location information. On 1-inch equipment, it is a separate track on one edge of the tape. On some ¾-inch equipment, it refers to the location of *time code* information in the *blanking*.

ambient: Describes any condition found at a production site: ambient light, ambient sound, ambient noise. See also *room noise*.

amplitude: The strength of an electrical signal in terms of volts.

amplitude modulation (AM): *Modulation* of a *carrier* so that the *amplitude* of the carrier varies with the amplitude of the modulating signal. See *frequency modulation*.

analog: An electrical signal or other output that varies continuously in proportion to the parameter that it represents. Example: The *analog* audio signal varies with the level of the sound. See *digital*.

aperture: The ratio between the width of a lens opening and the focal length of the lens, designated in "f stops." With the focal length as 1.0 unit, aperture is designated as f/n or fn, where n is the ratio. Example: An f/1.4 lens.

aperture correction: The "sharpening" of the video signal in the camera, so that peaks are sharper and steeper and lows are deeper, thus improving the effective *resolution*.

APL: Average Picture signal Level with respect to *blanking* level, during active picture scanning time. Expressed as a percentage of the difference between the blanking and *reference* white levels.

aspect ratio: The ratio of picture width to picture height. In television, the aspect ratio is four units wide by three units high.

assembly editing: Recording a video segment with audio as a *hard cut,* so that existing video, audio and control track are erased and replaced with the new material.

attenuation: In electronic technologies, a decrease in the electrical signal *amplitude*.

audio cue: A sound that is used to tag or denote an upcoming production event.

audio dub: Recording sound without disturbing the existing video.

audio level: The *amplitude* of the audio signal. The higher the audio level, the louder the sound produced.

audio mix: The result of balancing all the audio sources used for a program and mixing them onto a single track on an audio- or videotape.

auto-assemble: Generation of an edited master by a video or audio-for-video edit controller using an existing edit decision list.

auto-iris: An automatic iris, or aperture control on a lens, that opens or closes in inverse proportion to the amount of light available.

automatic gain control (AGC): A circuit used to maintain video or audio levels automatically within certain specified limits. Also called automatic level control (ALC).

back porch: A portion of the signal generated during the horizontal *blanking* interval, between the trailing edge of the horizontal *sync* pulse and the start of the next *line* of *video*.

background audio (BG): Sound, usually including music, recorded as part of the final mix, under the *sync sound*.

background light: Illumination of the background of a set or setting.

backlight: Illumination of the subject from behind and usually, but not necessarily, from above.

backtime: To determine the amount of time left in a program by subtracting the present program time from the total program time. Also used with regard to edit point calculations.

balanced line: Carries audio between inputs and outputs designed to be symmetrical with respect to ground. When these arrive at an input, amplitude differences due to induced hum and random noise are removed, leaving only the original audio signal. Requires an *XLR* type of connector. See also *unbalanced line*.

basic: See *black burst* and *crystal*.

beam control: Any form of electronic control of the electron beam in the camera *pickup tube*. Examples: dynamic beam control, in which the intensity of the beam is momentarily reduced for intense sources to maintain video level under 100 *IEEE,* and automatic beam control, in which the beam focus is increased at the edges of the *target* to compensate for the beam's tendency to spread there.

below-the-line: A production management term describing the direct costs of a production, including the wages of all personnel who are paid on an hourly or daily basis—primarily technical personnel. See *above-the-line*.

bias light: An *LED* within a television camera *pickup tube*, used to reduce *lag*.

bite: The *sync sound* of an on-camera person (such as a news reporter) that is continued under other, related video. Also called a "sound bite."

black body: A theoretical object that is totally non-reflective, so that any radiation coming from it is entirely due to its own properties.

black burst: A recording made to the *NTSC* standard, with horizontal and vertical *sync, burst* and *control track,* but with all video recorded at *black level*. Also called basic and *crystal*.

black level: The amplitude of the video signal at which the beam of the picture tube is extinguished, so that there is no trace on the face of the tube. Black level is set by the FCC at 7.5 + 2.5 *IRE*. See *setup*.

blanking: A period at the end of each *line* of video (horizontal blanking) and at the end of each *field* (vertical blanking), in which the electron beam in the *pickup tube* is turned off (blanked), so that no trace is recorded during *retrace*. In the *picture tube,* however, the beam is only blanked during the *sync* pulse, and is visible at just above *black level* during the rest of the blanking period.

bleed: The unwanted transfer of information from one track of video or audio to a neighboring track. Also, the tendency of the color, especially the reds in latter-generation *low-band* videotapes to smear from one area of the image into the next.

blocking: The *talent* and camera movements specified by the director for each scene.

BNC: A self-locking *UHF* connector for video cable connection.

boom: A manually or mechanically operated arm or pole from which a camera or microphone is hung above the talent to obtain a favorable angle.

breezeway: Part of the horizontal *blanking* interval, between the trailing edge of the *horizontal sync* signal and the *color burst* signal. It is set by the FCC at 0.56 usec, +0.08, -0.17.

brightness: See *luminance.*

broad: A flood lamp of 1000 watts or more, used to create "flat" lighting.

broadcast quality: A specific term applied to *pickup tubes* of any type—*vidicon, plumbicon,* etc.—which are without flaws and meet broadcast standards. Also, an ambiguous term for equipment and programming that meets the highest technical standards of the industry, such as *high-band* recorders. See *industrial quality.*

burn-in: Informal term for *time code* which has been converted to video so that the numbers are superimposed on each frame of video for rough cut and edit list processing.

burst: A color reference signal used to synchronize recorded color information (*hue*). The signal is made up of 9 + 1 cycles of the 3.579545 *MHz subcarrier,* and appears during each horizontal *blanking interval,* after the *sync* and before the video. Its *amplitude* is 40 IRE peak-to-peak, or 20 IRE above and below the *blanking* level. also called "color burst."

bus: A group of contacts with a common ground. In television, especially used to describe a bank of contacts that perform a single function for different inputs on a special effects generation (*SEG*). Example: the *preview* or *program* bus.

B-Y: Color difference signal obtained by subtracting the luminance signal from the blue camera signal. On a vector diagram, it is plotted on the 0 deg–180 deg axis.

C-mount: A threaded lens mount.

cable compensation: A phase correction made for errors in video signal phase caused by excessive cable length, as between a camera and VTR in *EFP* situations.

cameo: Lighting by which an individual is set against a dark, unlit background. See also *limbo.*

camera head: The part of the camera that includes the optics, *pickup tube, viewfinder, preamplifiers* and other camera circuits.

cannon plug: See *XLR connector.*

capstan: A motor driven shaft in a videotape recorder that controls tape speed. The tape is held against the capstan by a pinch roller.

capstan servo: A *servo motor* driving the *capstan.*

cardioid: A microphone sensitivity pattern with maximum sensitivity in front (less at the sides) and maximum rejection in the rear.

carrier: A higher *frequency,* selected for the transmission bandwidth, that is modulated by electronic signals of a lower frequency. The carrier permits the information to be transmitted through the air or other medium. At its destination, the information is *demodulated* and used. See *modulation.*

CCU: Camera control unit.

character generator: A dedicated digital computer designed to generate and format alphanumeric characters and deliver them as *NTSC* standard video. A character generator normally accepts a *genlock* input over which the alphanumeric information can be superimposed.

chip chart: A *gray scale* that produces a standard waveform on a *waveform monitor* when the *white level* in a camera is correctly adjusted. Also called an "EIA gray scale."

chroma: The *chrominance* or color portion of the television signal. See *hue.*

chroma level: The degree of *saturation,* or intensity, of the color in a television signal or image. See also *hue.*

chromakey: A process of keying one image into another by using a color background as a keying reference. The keyed person or object is shot against a "chromakey color" background, and the image from the other source appears in the area of the chromakey color.

chrominance: The portion of the television signal that carries the color information. See also *transmission primaries, chroma* and *hue.*

coax: Coaxial cable and connectors: The type of *UHF* cable used to carry video information. Also, the term applied to a screw-on barrel-type connector, now generally supplanted by *BNC* connectors in professional equipment and *RCA* connectors in consumer equipment.

color bars: A standard test signal that appears as a series of vertical color bars by which the *chrominance* and *video* levels of a camera output or recorded signal can be checked. See also *full-field* and *split-field color bars.*

color burst: See *burst.*

color correction: A process by which the amplitude and phase relationship of individual *hues* to the *color subcarrier* are corrected.

color lock: A VTR circuit that stabilizes *hue* during playback. Also, a condition in which both *burst* timing and *color phase* are correct.

color matte: A solid color, usually adjustable, generated by a *colorizer* in an *SEG,* used as a border or inserted into a chromakey *window.*

color phase: The phase relationship between the video signal for any *hue* and the *color burst* signal.

color subcarrier: The 3.579545 *MHz subcarrier* that carries the *chrominance* information of the television signal.

color temperature: An international standard for measuring the color of light in reference to the *hue* of the radiation emitted by a *black body*—a nonreflecting source—as it is heated from 0° *Kelvin* to higher temperatures. Example: *tungsten* lights have a color temperature of about 3200°K.

colorizer: A device or circuit that generates *NTSC* colors and provides controls, so that the user can blend them and use them to "colorize" an existing television image.

comb filter: A notch filter with a response pattern designed to improve *resolution.* A *luminance* comb filter has maximum response at harmonics of the TV line frequency; a *chrominance* comb filter has maximum response at harmonics of half the TV line frequency.

comet-trailing: An image defect created in the *vidicon* when a bright image source—such as a reflected highlight—is moved across a darkened ground, leaving a comet-like trail across the image.

component video: A video signal in which the *luminance* and *chrominance* are generated, handled and recorded on separate, alternate tracks that include *horizontal* and *vertical sync* and *burst.*

composite video: A video signal including both *luminance* and *chrominance,* as well as *horizontal* and *vertical sync* and *burst.*

condenser mic: A microphone that generates an audio signal by measuring the varying electrical capacitance between a metalized diaphragm and a conductive plate, as the sound waves cause the diaphragm to vibrate.

confidence heads: A separate *head* (or heads) on the *head drum* of some VTRs, positioned after the *record head* (in the direction of rotation), that reads video as it is being recorded so that it can be checked. (Otherwise, the video displayed during recording is actually *E-to-E* so that, for example, tape defects cannot be observed.) See *head*.

conforming: The process of assembling alternate segments of footage on A and B (and C) rolls to facilitate making *effects transitions* during the fine-cut.

contour correction: Enhancement of the contours of the video signal in the green channel to improve the definition and sharpness of the image, and the subsequent addition of this information to the red and blue channels. Also called "contours-out-of-green."

contrast: The *gray scale*—a range of light to dark values, from *black* to maximum *white level*. A standard gray scale for television has 10 steps from black to white. The contrast ratio is a measure of the number of gray scale steps present. If too high, the median steps are missing; if too low, the ends of the scale are not represented.

control track: A track on videotape, recorded by a fixed control track *head,* that contains a pulse for each frame on the videotape. Used to measure and control the rate of movement of the tape.

cover shot: A shot taken to "cover" a technical or performance problem in a previous take, or in anticipation of such a problem, or to avoid the possibility of a *jump cut*. See *cutaway*

crawl: Movement of alphanumeric characters across the screen from the left to right. Also, the apparent movement along diagonal edges of a *chromakey* insert, usually due to excessive *enhancement*. See *roll*.

cross-fade: A *dissolve* to black, immediately followed by a fade-in.

cross-pulse monitor: A monitor on which the *horizontal* and *vertical blanking* are centered and displayed so that they appear to cross while the image appears in the four quadrants created by the *blanking*. It is used to examine both blanking in-tervals and to check tape tension. Also called "pulse-cross monitor."

crosshatch: A test pattern consisting of vertical and horizontal lines used for converging color monitors and cameras.

crosstalk: Interference which occurs in audio or video recording, when the recording from one track bleeds into the recording on a neighboring track. Example: Crosstalk from the *time code* on the audio track.

CRT: Cathode ray tube. The generic term for any television *pickup* or display tube, such as is used in a television camera or monitor, which has an electron beam that is generated by the emission of electrons from a heated cathode element.

crystal: See *black burst*.

crystal sync: Any synchronizing information generated from a stable source. Especially *sync* generated from a piezo-electric crystal transducer, which vibrates at a fixed frequency depending on its thickness when subjected to an electrical voltage.

cue track: A track along the edge of videotape designed to hold *time code* or other information that identifies the location of a segment. An audio track is also used for this purpose. See also *address track*.

cut: A direct video transition without an effect. In the studio, it is from one camera or other video source to another. In editing, it is from the last frame of one segment to the first frame of the next, also called a "butt edit." See *match cut*.

cutaway: A *cover shot* of material pertinent to the action, but not of it.

cyc: Short for "cyclorama," a continuous background, usually of fabric, running around two or three sides of a studio.

dB or decibel: A logarithmic measure, usually used in television and audio as a measure of relative sensitivity or intensity. Originally used to specify sound pressure, and inherited from audio electronics. Example: The camera has a *signal-to-noise ratio* of -53dB.

definition: A visual measure of the apparent sharpness of detail in a television image. See *resolution*.

demodulation: The process of extracting the original signal from a modulated *carrier*.

dichroic: An optical element, especially a mirror, that will reflect one wavelength (or color) of illumination and pass another. Dichroic mirror systems are used to separate colors in three-tube cameras.

digital: A term describing any binary system of signal encoding. In electronics, it describes any varying signal that is represented by a series of discrete binary values, expressed in 1s and 0s, and recorded as a set of positive or negative pulses for each value. Also, any device that uses digital circuitry or logic. See *analog*.

dimmer board: A switcher/fader for a lighting system. Term refers to old-fashioned theatrical wooden boards containing an electrical dimmer for each light. Modern "boards" may be computer-controlled.

dissolve: An *effects transition,* in which one segment fades out as the next segment fades in. Called a *cross-fade* when used for audio.

distortion: Any unwanted change in the amplitude or frequency of an audio or video signal.

dolly: Any wheeled platform on which a camera or its tripod may be mounted for smooth camera movement. Also, any camera movement requiring the use of a dolly (a dolly shot).

double re-entry: Capability of an *SEG* to take the output of one mix/effects system and *re-enter* it into another effects system (within the SEG) for further image manipulation.

downstream keyer (DSK): A keyer within an *SEG,* located just before the SEG's output, that can be used to key into the output of a mix/effects *bus* "up-stream" of the keyer.

drop-frame time code: *SMPTE time code* generated so that two *frame* numbers are removed each minute (except the tenth), to compensate for the extra frame numbers generated at the less-than-30-per-second frame rate of contemporary *NTSC* color television.

dropout: Loss of small elements of the video image due to damage to the oxide coating of the videotape, appearing as random white spots or lines on the image.

dropout compensation: Capability of a VTR to correct *dropout* by replacing lines in which dropout occurs by substituting video from the previous line. This can only be done on the tapes with original dropout.

dub: To copy the material recorded on a video- or audiotape onto another video- or audiotape. Also, the copy made.

dub up/down: To *dub* from a lower/higher to a higher/lower format. Example: To "dub up" from 3/4-inch to 1-inch tape. Also, to "bump up/down."

DVE: Digital video effects.

dynamic mic: A microphone that generates an electrical audio signal by using the pressure of sound waves to move a coil of wire in a magnetic field.

edger: Capability of a *character generator* or *switcher* to provide border or edge effects on characters or inserts. Such effects can be normal, shadowed or colorized, including black.

E-to-E: In VTRs, this describes the mode in which the image from any source—VTR, camera, etc.—is routed through the recording deck for display on a monitor, except when the recording VTR is operating in either playback or record with a video *confidence head.* Stands for "electronics-to-electronics."

edit: Any point on a videotape where the audio and/or video information has been added to, replaced, or otherwise manipulated.

edit list: A record of all the edit decisions to be made in creating a video program. This list can take the form of a printed copy, floppy disk or paper tape and serves many functions such as providing the list for automatically assembling the program, making revisions or allowing for exact program timing. also known as an "edit decision list" or "EDL."

edit points: The beginning and ending points of a selected event within a program being assembled on magnetic tape. Often called "edit-in and edit-out" or "in and out" points.

edit programmer: A digital storage device used to store an edit list and operate an editing system automatically, usually the edit points stored.

EDL: See *edit list.*

effects bus: Any *bus* in an *SEG* that outputs to a mix or effects system in the SEG, as opposed to a *preview* or *program* bus.

effects transition: Any transition between edits other than a *hard cut* such as a mix, wipe or *key.*

EFP (electronic field production): Field productions using portable equipment (like *ENG*), but involving multiple cameras and *switchers.* Sports, concerts and public events are produced as EFP rather than ENG.

EIA: The Electronics Industries Association, which sets international standards for electronic equipment, from rack-mounting dimensions to *sync* signal parameters.

EIA gray scale: See *chip chart.*

electret condenser mic: A *condenser mic* in which the metal coating on the diaphragm is permanently charged so that less battery power is used in operation.

encoder: The logic circuits in a television camera that organize the RGB output of the *pickup tubes* into *luminance* and *chrominance* in accordance with the requirements of the *NTSC* format.

ENG (Electronic News Gathering): Field productions using portable cameras and decks, usually on battery power, in which the immediacy or inaccessibility of the situation and the mobility and flexibility of the crew are paramount.

enhancement: Any manipulation of the video to improve the technical and visual quality of the image, especially in terms of *contour* and *aperture correction.*

equalizing pulses: A series of short pulses generated during the first three lines and the 7th, 8th and 9th lines of the *vertical interval,* that precede and follow the *vertical sync* signal.

erase head: A *head* used to erase audio or video information recorded on magnetic tape.

fax sheet: Facilities sheet. A list of all the equipment required for a shoot.

fader: Any control used for the linear adjustment of video, audio or lighting intensity.

feedback: Looping a portion of a signal back into its generating circuit as a means of correction or distortion. When the feedback is added to the signal to reinforce it, it is called "positive feedback." When the feedback is inverted so that it can be subtracted from the signal to correct it, it is called "negative feedback."

field: Half of a video *frame,* consisting of 262½ odd or even lines of the 525-line frame, at 60 fields per second. Field 1 ends at the bottom on line 262½ and the retrace runs vertically up to start Field 2 at the center of the line. Field 2 ends at the bottom right, and the retrace runs diagonally to the upper left to start Field 1 of the next frame. See *interlace.*

fill: Lighting used to reduce, or "fill," shadows. Any lamp used for this purpose is a "fill light."

film/slide chain: Any system used to transform film or slide images into video images. Also called "telecine" system.

fishpole: A lightweight, handheld *boom.*

flag: The transient instability occurring when an edit falls between two odd or two even *fields.* In the first case, the trace must jump from the center of line 262½ that ends Field 1 to the start of the full line that begins a *frame.* In the second case, it must jump from the start of Line 1 to mid-line, where the second half of the 262nd line starts Field 2. Also called "whip edit."

flagging: A "flagging" of the top of an image due to improper tape tension, which can be corrected to some extent by using the *skew* control available on some decks.

flare: Enlargement of the image of a light source on the screen, due to the excessive video level generated by the source.

floodlight: Broad, unfocused illumination, or the lamp that provides it. Also called a *broad*.

floor manager: The person in charge on the floor of a studio or set during a multi-camera shoot, when the director must be in the control room. He acts as the director's agent on the floor during production and cues the talent.

flying erase head: An *erase head* on the *head drum*, positioned before the *record head* in the direction of rotation, so that any information already on the videotape is erased, re-randomizing the oxide particles on the tape to improve recording quality.

footcandle (fc): The intensity of light on a 1-square-foot white surface illuminated by a standard candle placed one foot away. See *lumen* and *lambert*.

format: A particular type of videotape system, defined by its tape width and applicable recording specifications. Examples: the Type C 1-inch format, the 3/4-inch format, and the 1/2-inch industrial format.

frame: One full 525-line *raster* of video, generated 30 times per second, consisting of two *interlaced* 262½-line *fields* (under the American *NTSC* standard).

framestore: A digital device that stores a full *frame* of video for the purposes of image manipulation, *graphics* generation or *sync* and *blanking* correction.

frequency modulation (FM): The modulation of a *carrier* so that the carrier frequency varies in proportion to the modulating signal. *High-band* and *low-band* frequency modulation is used in videotape recording technology, and for the trans-

mission of the audio portion of the television signal. See *amplitude modulation*.

fresnel: A crude lens with concentric ridges, used to focus a *floodlight* to create a *spot*.

full-field color bars: *Color bars* that include only the seven color references—white, yellow, cyan, green, magenta, red and blue. See *color bars* and *split-field color bars*.

gaffer: The person in charge of lighting. A gaffer is *below-the-line,* while a lighting designer is *above-the-line*.

gain: Any amount of amplification of a video or audio signal.

gamma: A measure of the relation between the original light level and the video signal level in both the *pickup tube* and the television *picture tube*. Ideally, the gamma (light-to-video signal output) of the pickup tube multiplied by the gamma (video signal-to-light output) of the picture tube equals unity (1.0). As TV picture tube gamma is usually 2.2, pickup tube gamma is usually set at 0.45.

gel: A colored, heat-resistant plastic sheeting, used in front of lights to color or filter the illumination.

generation: Refers to the relationship of a *dub* to the *master*. A "first generation" dub is made directly from the master. A "second generation" dub is made from a first generation dub and so on. The image and audio quality of a dub decreases as the number of generations increases.

genlock: A system that uses, or "locks to," the *sync* from a video source to synchronize all its elements, as when a studio system genlocks all cameras to the video from a VTR.

geometric distortion: Distortion around the center of a camera image, detected by shooting a rectangular grid consisting of equal squares. When distortion exists, the outer squares are skewed to some degree.

gobo: Any device used to block light, including a black cloth, screen or sheet of material. Also used to describe a foreground element that frames a shot, and some pattern projectors. Used by technicians to describe a sudden, momentary drop in *white level.*

graphic: Any element other than an image generated from live action that is used in a program, including alphanumeric characters, drawings and electronically generated images.

gray scale: See *EIA gray scale.*

guardband: A space between adjacent tracks of recorded video or audio on tape, provided to minimize the possibility of *crosstalk.*

hard cut: A cut (a transition without an effect) in which the last *frame* of the previous edit butts the first frame of the next edit. Also called a "butt edit."

HDTV (high definition television): A format using significantly more lines per *frame* than the current 525-line *NTSC* American standard or the 625-line *PAL* or *SECAM* standards.

head: An electromagnetic *transducer* that records a video or audio signal by magnetizing the particles coating magnetic tape in proportion to the strength and direction of the signal. On playback, the head "reads" the particles and regenerates the original signal. See *flying erase* and *record heads.*

head drum: The rotating drum on which the video *heads* in a *helical-scan* system are mounted, and around which the videotape passes.

headroom: The amount of space left above a subject when its video image is displayed on a television screen. Also, the range in audio level above the normal level set for a mic or *line,* before audio distortion will occur.

helical-scan: The primary method of videotape recording in use, whereby the video information is recorded in a series of parallel tracks laid down in sharply angled diagonals on the tape, which is wrapped around one or more rapidly rotating video *heads.* See also *type A, B or C.*

hertz (Hz): A unit of frequency, given in cycles per second. 1.0 Hz = 1.0 cps.

high-band: Refers to any television recording that carriers both *luminance* and *chrominance modulated* over a 3-MHz bandwidth, ranging from 7 to 10 MHz of the 10-MHz carrier used for high-band recording. See *low-band* and *frequency modulation.*

highlight: A small, usually reflective source in a scene that generates a short, sharp peak in *white level,* which may be permitted to exceed 100 *IRE.*

horizontal interval: The *blanking* interval between each line, occurring at 15,750 Hz, during which the *horizontal sync* and *burst* are generated. *See blanking.*

horizontal sync: The 15,750-Hz, synchronizing pulse that triggers the *pickup* or *picture tube* to generate the next horizontal line.

hue: Any of the primary colors (red, green, blue) and their mixtures (yellow, magenta, cyan). See also *chroma level.*

IEEE: A unit of *amplitude* measurement used for television signals, formerly called an IRE unit. 140 IEEE = 1.0 volt. On this scale, *blanking* is at 0 IEEE, and *reference white,* the maximum *white level,* falls at 100 IEEE. (IRE stood for Institute of Radio Engineers, now part of the Institute of Electrical and Electronics Engineers, thus IEEE.) IEEE is now correct, but IRE is still used.

image enhancement: Electronic manipulation of the image to improve detail and sharpness.

image retention: Any failure of the camera tube or *picture tube* to remove traces of the image from previous *fields.* See *lag.*

impedance: Electrical resistance to the flow of current. For a signal to flow undistorted from one piece of equipment to another, the impedances of the output and the input must be matched. In TV production, impedance is significant for audio, where low-impedance mic inputs and high-impedance line inputs (for example) must normally be matched by the output impedance of the audio equipment.

industrial quality: A specific term used to identify *pickup tubes* of all types, which have a nominal number of microscopic flaws that will not interfere with performance, but will not meet broadcast standards. Also, a somewhat ambiguous term designating equipment not designed for broadcast use, but more sophisticated and of better quality than consumer video equipment. See *broadcast quality.*

initialization: System startup, or setting equipment and circuits to their beginning positions and values.

inky: A very small *spotlight,* often mounted on the camera, used to brighten a subject or to add sparkle to the eyes.

insert: Any effect that is keyed into a defined area. Also, any edit in which video and/or one or more audio tracks are recorded, using existing *control track.*

interlace: The relationship between the first and second *field* of a television *frame,* in which the 525 lines of a frame are scanned alternately to prevent the image from flickering. Adjacent lines belong to alternate fields: 262½ even-numbered lines (2,4,6) form the first field, and the 262½ odd-numbered lines (1,3,5) form the second field.

interlock: To run sound and picture together in perfect *sync* from separate film and/or tape transports.

inverse square law: The fact that the amount of radiation received from a source varies as the inverse square of the distance from the source: I = c/d, where I is illumination in *footcandles;* c is intensity of the source in candles; d is distance from source.

IQ signals: See *transmission primaries.*

IRE scale: Oscilloscope scale that applies to composite video levels. 140 IRE units = 1 volt. Also see *IEEE.*

ISO reels: Multiple reels of tape on which the same subject has been recorded simultaneously by different VTRs through different cameras.

isocam: Shooting a production with one or more cameras so that each camera records its output on its own deck, as opposed to using a video *switcher.* Also called "film style."

jam-sync: The process of locking a *time code* generator to the time code recorded on an existing tape in order to recreate or extend the time code on the tape. This is necessary because time code may disappear or degenerate after a few *generations.*

jog mode: Standard function available on broadcast quality VTRs equipped with dynamic tracking. In this mode, the VTR may be moving fast forward, fast reverse, slow forward, slow reverse or be in stop frame and the picture can be viewed and used for editing.

jump cut: A *hard cut* between two parts of a single shot, giving it the appearance of missing frames.

kelvin (K): A temperature scale, measured in Centigrade-equivalent degrees, but with 0°K equal to –273.16 C. Used to define *color temperature.*

key: A video effect, in which one image is electronically inserted into another. See *chromakey* and *luminance key.*

key light: The primary light source on a scene, simulating the apparent source, such as the sun or a lamp.

kilohertz (KHz): A frequency of 1000 cycles per second.

lag: *Image retention* occurring when the bright portions of a moving subject or object in a video image leave a gradually diminishing trace on the screen.

lambert: A measure of brightness. One foot lambert = *11 footcandles.*

lavalier: A small microphone worn by the talent. The term was once used for mics worn around the neck, but is now also applied to small mics designed to be clipped or pinned to lapels or other pieces of clothing.

layback: The process of rerecording (laying back) and synchronizing sound that was previously separated from its image onto videotape.

LED: Light-emitting diode. A small light source requiring minimal current, used to create alphanumeric readouts, such as *control track* readout on editing decks.

light plot: The floor plan, showing locations and functions of all luminaires.

limbo: A lighting situation in which the subject appears in a gray or neutral background without an apparent back surface. Similar to a *cameo*, in which the background is black.

line: One line of the 525 lines in a television *frame*. Also, a relatively high-*impedance* source or input for a video or audio signal (as opposed, for example, to a low-impedance mic input or output).

line pairing: The uneven spacing between lines from different *fields* due to improper *interlace*.

linearity: In television, this describes the straightness of the rise of the horizontal and vertical *sawtooth* signals that cause the electron beam to sweep across each line and move down to the next. This determines how evenly the picture elements and lines are distributed on the *raster*. Perfect linearity is unity, as the rise in voltage for each unit of time is constant, and equal to 1.0.

lip sync: Any synchronization of spoken audio with the lip movements of a subject.

location: A *shoot* or production that takes place in a setting outside of a television studio. Also called a "remote."

looping: Taking a signal from the output of one device to input it into another, as when two *monitors* are looped together, taking the input to the second from the "video out" connector of the first. See *termination*.

low-band: Describes any television recorder or recording that carries *luminance* over a 2.5-MHz bandwidth and *chrominance* over a 1-MHz bandwidth, using the 4.3- to 6.8-MHz band of the 7-MHz carrier used for low-band recording. See *high-band*.

lumen: The amount of light illuminating a surface lit by one standard candle.

luminance: The brightness of the video image. Therefore, the *component* of the video signal that carries information about the intensity of illumination at each image point. Symbol: Y.

luminance key: A *key* in which a *luminance* level, normally white, is used to determine where the second image will appear.

lux: A measure of illumination, approximately equal to 0.1 *footcandles*.

master: An original recording (used with a qualifying term).

master, duplication or dubbing: Can be the edit master or a copy of the edit master made specifically for the duplication process.

master, edited: The first generation of a fully edited videotape with continuous program material and time code from beginning to end.

master, field: The raw, original program footage on videotape containing original time-of-day and shoot time code identification (if applicable) and original field audio (also known as a "camera/source master").

master, film-to-tape: The first generation tape recording from a film.

master, multi-track: Unmixed original multi-channel recording.

master, music: The mixdown of a multi-track music recording or edited version, such that it becomes a master in its own right.

master, original: A first generation recording (usually the camera master).

master, production: The finished recording, ready for duplication. Often used to describe shows that are live—switched and do not require editing.

master, protection: Preferably called a safety. A copy of a master to be used if the working master is damaged.

master, sub: A partially mixed or edited recording used to create a master.

match cut: An edit made in the middle of a scene, where the scene is reconstructed so that the edit is invisible. Used as a starting point for an *A/B-roll edit,* or to reconstruct an edit on a *master.*

matrix: In logic design, a network of circuits performing one or more logical functions.

matte: A solid tone or color (*color matte*) generated (matte generator) in an *SEG,* to be used as a background or to fill a border or a *key.*

megahertz (MHz): A frequency of 1 million cycles per second. Example: the color *subcarrier* is set at 3.5797 MHz.

mini: An audio plug characterized by a single pin without a sleeve. See *RCA* and *XLR.*

mix bus: Any *bus* in an *SEG* that is connected to a *fader.*

modulation: In radio and television, varying the *amplitude (amplitude modulation—AM)* or frequency (*frequency modulation—FM*) of a *carrier,* in proportion to the amplitude or frequency of the modulating signal. In television, the video is AM, the sound is FM. See also *frequency* and *amplitude modulation.*

monitor: A television set that accepts and displays unmodulated video.

monochrome: Black-and-white television, using *luminance* without *chrominance.*

multiplexer: The remote-controlled mirror/prism assembly in a *film/slide chain* that permits the camera in the chain to view the images from different projectors on command.

ND filter: A neutral density filter, used over the lens or on the camera's filter wheel to reduce excessive illumination in location situations.

nano: A prefix meaning one billionth.

newvicon: A type of *pickup tube* that has good sensitivity in low light.

noise: Any electrical interference in the video or audio, especially random or "white noise."

NTSC: National Television Standards Committee, the official body that sets television standards for the Federal Communications Commission (FCC). Therefore, the American television standard—including the number of lines per *frame,* frame rate, carrier frequencies, etc.—is NTSC. See *PAL* and *SECAM.*

octopus: Any cable with multiple connectors at either or both ends.

offline: Describes any secondary editing system, or any editing done on such a system, to produce a *rough-cut.* Such an edit is usually performed with *workprints.* At broadcasting stations, any system that is not used *online* to play video and audio for transmission.

offline editing: Preparation that is done to produce an edit decision list later used in the *auto-assemble* online process. A videotape may be produced as a by-product of offline editing and is often called a "worktape." The offline process usually does not include the generation of complex effects or graphics.

omni: Omnidirectional: The *polar pattern* of a mic that is equally sensitive to sound from all directions.

online: Describes any primary editing system, or any editing done on such a system, to produce a *master.* At a given facility, it is the best editing system available. In a broadcast facility, online refers to any equipment used to play video or audio for transmission. See *offline.*

online editing: EDL-based computer editing that is done to produce a finished program *master.* Often denotes an edit session that includes the complex graphics and special effects.

on-the-fly editing: Choosing edit points while the tape is moving at play speed.

open-ended edit: An edit without a defined outpoint. The system will record until the record or stop button is depressed.

pad: Additional video placed at the end of an edit to provide overlap for the start of the next edit, to avoid blank *frames* if the edit comes in one or more frames late. Also, additional video placed on the front of an *A/B roll* edit so that significant audio or video will begin after the start of the effect.

paint system: A hardware and software package which enables the operator to generate freehand images on a video screen by direct manipulation of a frame buffer. Paint systems usually consist of a computer processor, video screen, storage devices, frame buffer, digitizing pad and stylus or mouse.

PAL: Phase alternation line. A 625-line television standard, operating on a 50-Hz line frequency, used in most European and other countries.

pantograph: A folding ceiling mount for a light that permits it to be easily raised, lowered or angled to any position within its range of extension.

parabola: A waveform used to correct *shading* error at the center of the screen.

patch board: A frame holding an array of video (video patch board), audio (audio patch board) or lighting connectors which provides a central location at which all related equipment is connected, and which can be used to facilitate their interconnection by means of patch cords.

pedestal: See *setup*.

phase: A stage in the development of a cycle of a frequency, from 0° to 360°. For a signal to be "in phase" with another, both must have the same frequency and their positive and negative peaks must occur at the same time. Example: the *color burst* must be in phase with the color *subcarrier*.

phone plug: An audio plug with a 1/4-inch wide connector shaft.

phono plug: See *RCA*.

phosphor: The picture element of a *picture tube*, which is coated with one or more substances that phosphoresce when energized by the electron beam, to produce the television image.

pickup tube: The cathode ray tube in a television camera that is designed to translate an image into electrical signals. See *vidicon, plumbicon, newvicon* and *saticon*.

picture tube: The cathode ray tube in a television monitor or receiver that transforms the video information into a television image.

pixel: The smallest discernible element of an image.

plumbicon: A *pickup tube* using a lead oxide compound for its photoconductive surface, that is widely used in television broadcast cameras because of its high *sensitivity* and low *lag*. Available in *broadcast* and *industrial quality*.

polar pattern: A polar "map" of the sensitivity of a microphone, with the head of the mic at the center, facing the 0° point.

polarity reversal: Reversing the *gray scale* of an image electronically so that a "negative" image is generated.

portapak: A registered Sony trademark for its earliest portable VTRs. Now used as a generic term for small portable recorders.

preamp: Preamplifier; the first amplifier in any system that amplifies a newly generated signal. In television, preamps are used to shape up and amplify the video output of a camera *pickup tube* and the audio output of a mic's pickup element.

preroll: The period between tape start and an edit, needed to bring all tapes up to the correct speed for accurate ending.

preview: The display of an image or effect during production or editing before the image or effect is put *online* or recorded.

proc amp (processing amplifier): Any device used to correct the *blanking sync* or other aspects of the *composite video* signal.

program: Any circuit or monitor used during production or editing to handle or display an image or *effect* for transmission or recording. Also, to set up an organized sequence of *effects* or operations on a switcher, editing controller or other device, including a computer. Also, any organized and completed television material prepared for presentation.

pulse-cross monitor: See *cross-pulse monitor*.

quad (quadraplex): A video format, once dominant in broadcast television, that uses a four-head, *segmented* recording system and 2-inch videotape. (Note: technology specific only to this format is not covered in this book.)

quad split: A *wipe* in which four separate images appear in the four quadrants of the screen.

quartz lamp: A form of *tungsten* lamp commonly used for television lighting, that maintains a constant color temperature throughout most of its life.

ramdom access: The ability to retrieve video, audio, or data from any point on the tape, disk, or solid state memory device.

raster: The area of the 525-line screen illuminated by the *modulated* or unmodulated *beam;* the picture area.

RCA: A type of connector characterized by a pin with a $\frac{1}{4}$-sleeve. Used as an audio connector (see also *mini* and *XLR*) on some professional video equipment and as a video connector on consumer video equipment.

re-entry: The capability of an *SEG* to accept the output of a *mix* or *effects bus* and use it as an input to another effects bus. See *double re-entry*.

reaction shot: A *cutaway* in which a subject shows an emotional reaction to the event shown in the previous shot.

real time: A *sequence* or *program* that takes place in the same amount of time as the event shown.

rear-screen projection: A slide or film projection on a semi-transparent screen, usually for use as a background.

record head: A *head* used to record video or audio information on magnetic tape.

reel number: The number assigned to an audio or video reel or cassette to be used in an edit session; used for identifying each reel or cassette on the *edit list* for the final assembly or for future revisions.

reference black: See *black level*.

reference white: See *white level*.

registration: The correct alignment of the three color television signals from the *pickup tubes* to produce a single, coherent chromatic image.

remote: A *location shoot*. Also, a term describing any control device, such as a camera control unit, that is located at a distance from the unit controlled.

resolution: The number of *pixels* into which a horizontal line of video can be resolved, ultimately limited by the *bandwidth* of the recording or transmitting equipment used. Defined as "lines of horizontal resolution." Cameras may resolve as much as 800 lines; *high-band* recorders can resolve a maximum of 650; *low-band* recorders and consumer TV receivers, a maximum of 325 lines.

RF (radio frequency): The entire band of frequencies used for transmission of audio and video information, ranging from 10 KHz to 300,000 MHz. Also, any random *noise* within the RF range.

RF adaptor: A device that adapts the video output from a videotape recorder so that it looks like a regular antenna input and can be delivered directly to the antenna input of a standard television receiver.

riser: A platform, usually covered with carpeting, used in studios to elevate talent to minimize the amount of camera tilt required.

rock focus: To change the focus of the lens during a shot in order to shift the attention of the viewer to a different element of the image.

roll: Movement of alphanumeric characters on the screen from bottom to top. Also, unwanted vertical roll of the image, indicating unstable *sync*.

room noise: Any recording of *ambient* sound made on *location* for later use to lay under audio recorded elsewhere or to fill in audio gaps.

saticon: A *pickup tube* with a complex selenium compound forming its photoconductive surface, with low *lag,* good *sensitivity,* stability, long life and median cost. Available in *broadcast* and *industrial quality*.

saturation: The intensity of a color.

sawtooth: A sawtooth-shaped signal with a linear rise (or fall) and a sharp return (or rise) to its base voltage level. Used in television to control *scanning,* with one 15,750-Hz sawtooth per horizontal *line,* and one 60-Hz sawtooth per *field.* Sawtooth signals are also used to control *shading.*

scanning: Movement of the electron beam across the *target* of a *pickup tube* or the *phosphor* of a *picture tube* to form the *raster.*

scoop: A *floodlight.*

SCR: Silicon-controlled rectifier. A type of power *dimmer* used on lighting boards.

scrim: Any translucent material or screening, used to soften *ambient* or studio lighting.

SECAM (Sequential Couleur a Memoire): The television standard used in France and The Commonwealth of Independent States (formerly the U.S.S.R.), in which the primaries are recorded sequentially on separate lines.

SEG (Special Effects Generator): A device that permits the operator to create *effects transitions* between one shot and the next. Often referred to as a *switcher.*

segmented scanning: Any video recording system that scans less than a full *field* with each pass of a *head,* so that it is not able to produce a *still frame* without an auxiliary storage device. See *quad* and *type B.*

segue: To make a smooth transition from one segment to the next, particularly in audio (pronounced seg 'way).

sensitivity: A measure of the minimum level of input, such as of light or sound, at which a *transducer,* such as a camera or mic, can produce an acceptable output.

sequence: A series of related shots or *takes* that is intended to be viewed as a whole.

servo: Any electromechanical device that uses *feedback* to control movement, such as the servomotor that controls the *capstan* in editing decks.

setup: The difference between the *blanking* level and the *black level.* Set by the FCC at 7.5 +2.5 *IRE.* Also called *pedestal.*

shading: The process of correcting errors in the level of *pickup tube* output when a given level of scene illumination causes one side or the center of the screen to be darker than the rest. Shading errors at the sides, top and bottom are corrected by adjusting horizontal and vertical *sawtooth* generators, and center-screen errors by *parabolic* waveform generators in the camera control unit.

shoot: Any production in process, in a studio or on location. Example: a three-day shoot.

shooting ratio: The amount of tape recorded relative to the amount of tape actually used.

shot sheet: A complete list of all the shots planned for a production day in the order in which they are to be done. Also, a list of the shots to be done by each camera, given to each cameraperson each production day.

shotgun: A *supercardioid* microphone, designed to pick up sound within a narrow forward angle over relatively long distances, widely used in *ENG* situations.

signal-to-noise ratio: The relationship between the level of the signal to the level of *noise* in a circuit or system, measured on a logarithmic scale.

single-tube camera: A color camera with a single *pickup tube* using a striped three-color filter to separate the image into its component primaries, and thus provide full color recording.

skew: A measure of videotape tension. See *flagging.*

slip rings: Conductive rings on a rotating device through which spring-loaded contacts, called brushes, deliver electrical signals to circuits within the device. Example: slip-rings on the *head drum* conduct video information to and from the *heads.*

small-format video: Any videotape *format* smaller than the current *broadcast* standard, including ¾- and *industrial* ½-inch, and the equipment designed to be used with such formats.

SMPTE time code: An eight-digit *address code* that identifies each recorded *frame* of video on a tape, providing each frame with a unique hour, minute, second and frame number. Developed by SMPTE, the Society of Motion Picture and Television Engineers.

snoot: A hood for a light, to reduce its *spread*.

soft key: Any *key* on which the edges can be diffused, so that the transition between the ground and keyed image is softened. On many *SEGs*, the softness of the edge can be varied over a range from hard to soft.

soft wipe: A *wipe* with the characteristics of a *soft key*.

softlight: A *floodlight* with a larger reflector that diffuses the light evenly over a wide area.

sound perspective: The relationship between sound level and the apparent distance of the source on the screen, as when the level drops as a speaker moves away from the camera.

spill: Excess *spread,* which can be cut by the use of barn doors, *scrims, shoots* and *gobos*.

split edit: A type of edit transition in which the audio or video of the source is delayed for a given period of time.

split screen: A horizontal (vertical) *wipe* stopped in mid-screen, so that the right (top) half of the right (top) image and the left (bottom) half of the left (bottom) image are shown simultaneously.

split-field color bars: *Color bars* for which the screen is split horizontally so that the seven color reference bars—white, yellow, cyan, green, magenta, red and blue—are displayed at the top, while a pure white is displayed at the bottom, together with reference tones for the I and Q signals.

spotlight: A focused light; a "spot." Also, an effect available on some *SEGs,* that raises the *white level* of an area on the image. It can also be used to create highlights.

spread: The area covered by a light.

staircase: A video test signal containing several steps of equal *amplitude* at increasing luminance levels. The staircase signal is usually *amplitude modulated* by a subcarrier frequency and is useful for checking amplitude and phase linearities in video systems.

still frame: A single *field* of video, continuously rescanned so that it appears completely stable.

storyboard: A comic-book-like series of illustrations that shows the action in each shot or sequence, with the dialog underneath each "frame," used in advertising and by some feature directors as a working script.

strike: To take down a set or remove props that are no longer needed.

subcarrier: Any *carrier* inserted into the video frequency passband to carry additional information. In television, refers primarily to the *color subcarrier*.

submaster: A copy made directly from the *master* for use as a dubmaster, so that the master need not be used for all *dubbing*.

super (superimposition): An effect in which two images are combined, using either a mix or an effect, but especially one that involves the superimposition of text over picture.

supercardioid: A *cardioid* microphone with a highly directional *polar pattern* and exceptional rejection of sound at the sides and back. See *shotgun*.

sweeten: To improve the video (video sweetening) or the audio (audio sweetening) of a videotape, audiotape or film sound track.

switcher: Any device that routes video from one source to another. A *vertical interval* switcher does so only during the vertical *blanking* interval so that the transfer occurs in *sync*. Also, a common informal term for an *SEG*.

sync: A synchronizing pulse that controls timing. In television, the *horizontal sync* pulse starts the horizontal retrace, while the *vertical sync* pulse starts the next *field*.

sync-board: A board, usually a plug-in unit, that adapts the output of one equipment to the input of another, so that the two operate on the same type of synchonizing signal. In video, this is typically used to adapt the output of such equipment as PC graphics units for use in video systems requiring composite sync. Usage of sync-boards can be found in many popular multi-track audio recorders.

sync sound: Any sound that was produced when an image was shot (including *background audio,* as well as speech, music and other sounds made by the subjects) and is synchronous with the video. See *lip sync.*

system timing: Two or more video signals that should coincide in time, *amplitude,* and *subcarrier* phase. An example is the mix/effect amplifier in a production switcher.

take: A director's instruction to the technical director to put a source *online* during a multi-camera production. Also, a shot sequence on tape, logged for editing on a "take sheet."

talent: Anyone who appears on camera.

tally: Any part of the system of lights on cameras or on a *SEG* that indicates which camera is currently *online.*

target: The image-forming element of the *pickup tube.*

TBC (time base corrector): A device designed to correct time-base errors in a television recording.

td (technical director): The person, during production, who operates the *SEG* and supervises the technical aspects of a production.

tearing: Ragged horizontal disturbances in an image, which may be due to interference, timing errors, defective cables and other problems.

telecine: See *film/slide chain.*

teleprompter: A generic term for any device that systematically displays text for talent to read while he or she is on camera. Also, the trademark of the Teleprompter Corp. for their version of such a device.

termination: A load resistance that must be present at the end of a transmission line to prevent wave reflection. In television, this is usually 75 ohms, and is provided as a switch position on many monitors that have *looping* capability.

test tone: A tone, usually at 1000 Hz, generated within professional audio recording systems to establish a reference for recording during equipment setup.

tight shot: A shot in which there is little or no *headroom* or other space around the subject.

time base error: Any error in the timing of the horizontal or vertical *sync* and *blanking,* including both starting time and duration.

time code: See *SMPTE time code.*

track: A linear area on an audio- or videotape which contains audio, video, *control track* or *time code* information.

tracking: The alignment of the movement of a video *head* with the *track* it is reading, so that it picks up the maximum *RF* signal. When a head does not follow a track correctly, the result is "tracking error." A tracking adjustment control is provided on most VTRs.

tracking shot: A *dolly shot* or a pan in which the camera is moved so that it keeps pace with (tracks) a moving subject.

transducer: Any device used to convert energy or information from one form to another, such as a *pickup tube,* a mic element or an antenna.

transmission primaries: These are: *Y,* or *luminance,* and two *chrominance* primaries. The chrominance primaries are: I, the "in-phase" *subcarrier,* and Q, the "quadrature phase" subcarrier.

treatment: A proposal for a production in summary, indicating the story line or main sequence of events, characters, settings and the manner in which it will be shot.

triax (triaxial cable): A lightweight cable with low energy loss, favored for *EFP* situations.

trim: To adjust lights to control *spill*.

tungsten: In television production, tungsten/halogen and quartz/iodide lamps are used because they maintain a 3200°K *color temperature* over most of the lamp life. Generally, the term refers to any incandescent lamp with a tungsten filament.

two-shot: Any shot in which two persons are included.

two-to-one interface: Describes the *EIA* standard for the *interlace* of the two *fields*. See *line pairing*.

type A, B or C: 1-inch *helical scan* formats. Type A is an obsolete single-*head*, nonsegmented format; Type B is a dual-head segmented format used by Bosch-Fernseh, but accepted as a *SMPTE standard;* Type C, the primary SMPTE standard used in the U.S., is a nonsegmented format with one head for video information and another head for the vertical *blanking* information.

UHF (ultra-high frequency): The transmission band from 300 to 3000 MHz. Also, any cable and connector used to carry video signals. See *BNC* and *coax*.

U-Matic: A Sony trademark for its ¾-inch videocassette machines, often used generically to describe all ¾-inch VTRs.

unbalanced line: Audio inputs and outputs designed with one side connected to ground. Describes two-wire lines and connectors, such as *RCAs*. See also *balanced line* and *XLR*.

underscan: A special monitor display in which the video is compressed so that the *blanking* around the image is visible. Used to examine the borders of the image for timing defects.

vectorscope: A special oscilloscope with a radial pattern designed to check *hue* and *chroma* in relation to *color burst*.

vertical interval: The vertical *blanking* interval. See *blanking*.

vertical sync: The synchronizing signal occurring during the *vertical blanking interval* after each *field* of *video*, that initiates the vertical retrace.

video: The image information in the video signal, between the end of one horizontal *blanking* interval and the beginning of the next.

video level: The strength, or *amplitude* of the video signal, from the low of the *black level* to a maximum of 100 *IEEE* for the *white level*.

vidicon: Specifically, a *pickup tube* with an antimony trisulphide target, characterized by median *sensitivity,* durability and *lag*. Available in *broadcast* and *industrial* version. Also used as a generic term for all pickup tubes that use a vacuum tube and photoconductive target configuration.

viewfinder: The small television monitors provided on cameras to show the image being generated by the cameras.

voice-over: Any speaking voice that is recorded over video, where the speaker is not on camera. Used primarily for narration and for documentary segments.

VU meter: A meter that indicates the strength of any audio or video signal. "VU" stands for "volume units"—units of volume, or signal *amplitude*.

waveform monitor: An oscilloscope designed to show basic television waveforms on standard *IEEE* scales, including the *horizontal* and *vertical intervals*. Used to set up and check video equipment.

white balance: The point at which the output of the *encoder matrix* is balanced for the particular illumination in use, performed by exposing each camera to a white source and adjusting a white balance circuit accordingly.

white level: For camera setup purposes, it is the adjusted 100 *IEEE* level for the *video* generated from the white chip on an *EIA gray scale*. Also, describing the television picture, it is the highest level of video signal for any point on an image.

wild: Describing nonsynchronous video or audio recorded for later use as *background* or *cutaways*.

window: A specified range within which a piece of equipment will operate. Example: the *TBC* has a one-line window; i.e., it will store and operate on one line at a time. Also, an *effects* window, created by a *SEG*—an area within which other images may be inserted, as a "*chromakey* window."

windscreen: A windproof screen—usually of plastic foam—molded to fit over the head of the mic, so that wind pressure will not record as audio. See *zeppelin*.

wipe: An *effects transition* that occurs at the edges of a preset pattern stored in an *SEG*, so that one image is brought into the existing image along those edges. Example: in a "circle wipe," the new image appears at the center and is enlarged as the diameter of the wipe increases.

wipe code: A two or three digit numeric code used to identify a wipe pattern. Used with a production *switcher* and/or edit controller.

wireless mic: A microphone that incorporates a transmitter, with the receiver located at the audio console or video deck, freeing the *talent* from having to deal with a mic cable.

workprint: A copy of original footage, usually made on $\frac{3}{4}$- or $\frac{1}{2}$-inch tape, to be used to work out the exact sequence of shots and *effects transitions* in a rough-cut in preparation for the fine-cut.

XLR: A three-pin, grounded, lockable audio connector, designed for use on a *balanced line* and therefore used on professional audio equipment.

Y: The symbol for *luminance*.

zeppelin: A thick *windscreen* in the shape of a dirigible, used to cover a microphone completely for use outdoors.

Selected Bibliography

TELEVISION TECHNOLOGY

Benson, K. Blair and Jerry C. Whitaker. *Television and Audio Handbook: For Technicians and Engineers.* New York: McGraw-Hill, Inc., 1990.

Grob, Bernard. *Basic Television and Video Systems.* New York: McGraw-Hill Book Co., 1984.

Heller, Neil. *Understanding Video Equipment: Design, Operation and Maintenance of Videotape Recorders and Cameras.* White Plains, NY: Knowledge Industry Publications, Inc., 1989.

Ingram, Dave. *Video Electronics Technology.* Blue Ridge Summit, PA: TAB Books, Inc., 1983.

Krupnick, M.A. *The Electric Image: Examining Basic TV Technology.* White Plains, NY: Knowledge Industry Publications, Inc., 1990.

Pohlmann, Ken C. *Principles of Digital Audio.* Indianapolis, IN: Howard, W. Sams & Co., 1989.

Smith, C. Cecil. *Mastering Television Technology: A Cure for the Common Video.* Richardson, TX: Newman-Smith Publishing Co., Inc., 1988.

TELEVISION TECHNIQUES

Alten, Stanley R. *Audio in Media,* 3rd ed. Belmont, CA: Wadsworth Publishing Co., 1990.

Alkin, Glyn. *Sound Techniques for Video & TV.* Cambridge, UK: Butterworth & Co., Ltd., 1989.

Anderson, Gary H. *Video Editing and Post-Production,* 2nd ed. White Plains, NY: Knowledge Industry Publications, Inc., 1988.

Armer, Alan A. *Directing Television and Film.* Belmont, CA: Wadsworth Publishing Co., 1990.

Bartlett, Bruce. *Introduction to Professional Recording Techniques.* Indianapolis, IN: Howard W. Sams & Co., 1987.

Compesi, Ronald J. and Ronald E. Sheriffs. *Small Format Television Production,* 2nd ed. Needham Heights, MA: Allyn & Bacon, 1990.

Bensinger, Charles. *The Video Game.* Indianapolis, IN: Howard W. Sams & Co., Inc., 1982.

Burrows, Thomas and Donald Wood. *Television Production.* Dubuque, IA: William C. Brown, 1982.

DeLuca, Stuart M. *Instructional Video.* Stoneham, MA: Focal Press, 1991.

Fuller, Barry J., et al. *Single-Camera Video Production.* Englewood Cliffs, NJ: Prentice-Hall, 1982.

Huber, David Miles. *Audio Production Techniques for Video.* Indianapolis, IN: Howard K. Sams & Co., 1987.

Iazzi, Frank. *Understanding Television Production*. Englewood Cliffs, NJ: Prentice-Hall, 1984.

Kennedy, Thomas. *Directing Video*. White Plains, NY: Knowledge Industry Publications, Inc., 1988.

Lazendorf, Peter. *The Videotaping Handbook*. New York: Harmony Press, 1983.

Letourneau, Tom. *Lighting Techniques for Video Production: The Art of Casting Shadows*. White Plains, NY: Knowledge Industry Publications, Inc., 1987.

Medoff, Norman J. and Tom Tanquary. *Portable Video: ENG and EFP*. White Plains, NY: Knowledge Industry Publications, Inc., 1986.

Oringel, Robert. *The Television Operations Handbook*. Boston, MA: Butterworth, 1984.

Robinson, Richard. *The Video Primer*. New York: Perigee Books, 1983.

Schihl, Robert J. *Single Camera Video: From Concept to Edited Master*. Boston, MA: Focal Press, 1989.

Soifer, Rosanne. *Music in Video Production*. White Plains, NY: Knowledge Industry Publications, Inc., 1991.

Utz, Peter. *The Video User's Handbook,* 3rd ed. Englewood Cliffs, NJ: Prentice-Hall, 1989.

Utz, Peter. *Today's Video*. Englewood Cliffs, NJ: Prentice-Hall, 1987.

Wershing, Stephen and Paul Signer. *Computer Graphics and Animation for Corporate Video*. White Plains, NY: Knowledge Industry Publications, Inc., 1988.

Whittaker, Ron. *Video Field Production*. Mountain View, CA: Mayfield Publishers, 1989.

Wurtzel, Alan. *Television Production*. New York: McGraw-Hill, 1983.

Zettl, Herbert. *Television Production Handbook,* 5th ed. Belmont, CA: Wadsworth Publishing Co., 1992.

WRITING FOR TELEVISION

Brady, Ben. *The Keys to Writing for Television and Film*. Dubuque, IA: Kendall-Hunt Publishing Co., 1982.

Coopersmith, Jerome. *Professional Writer's Teleplay/Screenplay Format*. New York: Writers Guild of America, East, 1983.

Goodman, Evelyn. *Writing TV and Motion Picture Scripts that Sell*. Chicago, IL: Contemporary Books, 1982.

Struczynski, J. Michael. *The Complete Book of Scriptwriting*. Cincinnati, OH: Writers Digest Books, 1982.

Swain, Dwight V. and Joye R. *Scripting for the New AV Technologies,* 2nd ed. Stoneham, MA: Focal Press, 1991.

Vale, Eugene. *The Technique of Screen and TV Writing*. Englewood Cliffs, NJ: Prentice-Hall, 1982.

Van Nostran, William. *The Scriptwriter's Handbook: New Techniques for Media Writers*. White Plains, NY: Knowledge Industry Publications, Inc., 1989.

Zettl, Herbert. *Television Production Handbook,* 5th ed. Belmont, CA: Wadsworth, Inc., 1992.

OTHER ASPECTS OF TELEVISION

Bergman, Robert E. and Thomas V. Moore. *Managing Interactive Video/Multimedia Projects*. Englewood Cliffs, NY: Educational Technology Publications, 1990.

Gayeski, Diane M. *Corporate & Instructional Video*. Englewood Cliffs, NJ: Prentice-Hall, 1983.

Hansell, Kathleen J. *The Teleconferencing Manager's Guide*. White Plains, NY: Knowledge Industry Publications, Inc., 1989.

Iuppa, Nicholas V. with Karl Anderson. *Advanced Interactive Video Design*. White Plains, NY: Knowledge Industry Publications, Inc., 1988.

Marlow, Eugene. *Managing Corporate Media,* 2nd ed. White Plains, NY: Knowledge Industry Publications, Inc., 1989.

Miller, Philip. *Media Law for Producers*. White Plains, NY: Knowledge Industry Publications, Inc., 1990.

Perlmutter, Martin. *Producer's Guide to Interactive Videodiscs*. White Plains, NY: Knowledge Industry Publications, Inc., 1991.

Sneed, Laurel. *Evaluating Video Programs*. White Plains, NY: Knowledge Industry Publications, Inc., 1991.

Wiese, Michael. *Film & Video Financing*. Studio City, CA: Michael Wiese Productions, 1991.

Index

American Society of Composers, Authors, and
    Publishers (ASCAP), 4
Animation. *See* Graphics
Art Director, 87
Aspect ratio, 153
Assistant director, 87
Associate producer, 78
Audience, defining the, 3-4
Audio
    mix, 137, 140, 147-149, 151
    patchboard, 52
        See also Studio equipment

Bandwidths. *See* Helical-scan videotape
    recording
Boom operator, 79
Broadcast Music Inc. (BMI), 4
Budgets, 6
    editing, 136, 138-139
    field production, 104-105, 108-109
    production, 167-173
    studio production 61-63

Camcorders, 93-94
Cameos, 64, 70
Cameras, 23-27, 29-30
    filters, 26
    optics, 24, 26
    perspective, 180 rule, 10
    pickup tubes, 26-28, 29
        See also Portable cameras

Camera operators, 79
Capstan servo. *See* Helical-scan videotape
    recording
Casting director, 78, 167-168
Character generators, 23, 39, 158, 160
Charge-coupled devices (CCDs), 26, 27, 29
Chromakey
    effects, 154
    space, 64
Chrominance, 32, 34, 42
Color adjustment, 29-30
Color correction, 166
Control track, 123, 129
    See also Helical-scan videotape recording
Cycloramas, 65, 66

Directors, 79-80, 83, 85, 87, 119-120
Direct Broadcast Satellite (DBS), 4

Editing concepts and equipment, 121-125
    basic operations, 125-126, 128-130
    controllers, 123, 125, 128
    offline, 121
    online, 121, 137
    time code, 121, 123, 132
Editing preparations and budgets, 131-140
    budgeting, 136
    cataloging, 132-134, 135
    editing script, 134, 136
    rough-cut, 121, 134, 136, 137
    time code and workprints, 132, 136

See also Fine-cut editing, Audio mix
Equipment. *See* Studio equipment, Field equipment
Executive producers, 77

Field equipment
  audio equipment, 95-97
  ENG, 89
  EFP, 89
  lighting, 97, 98
  portable cameras, 89-90, 93-94
  portable special-effects generators, 95
  portable videotape recorders, 94-95
  power, 97
Field production
  budget, 104-105, 108-109
  checklist, 102-103, 104, 106-107
  lighting, 105, 110-115
  recording audio, 115-118
  scouting the location, 101, 104
  staff, 119-120
Film/slide chain, 23, 39, 56, 57
Fine-cut editing, 121, 141-151
  A/B rolls, 141-145
  edit decision list, 137, 145-147
  systems, 147
Fixers, 163-164, 166
Flags, 54
Flats, 65, 66
Flow charts, 17-19

Gobos, 54, 114
Graphics
  board-based, 153-154, 157
  digital generators, 158-159
  editing systems, 156, 160

Helical-scan videotape recording
  bandwidth, 32
  capstan servo, 31-32
  control track, 31
  tracking, 31

Image enhancement, 166
Intercom systems, 53-54

Keys, *See* Special-effects generators

Lighting designer, 85
Lights, 23, 54-56, 97, 98
  See also Field equipment, Field production, Studio equipment, Studio production

Limbo, 64, 70
Line producers, 78
Low-Power Television (TV), 4
Luminance, 30, 32, 34, 42

Mattes. *See* Special-effects generators
Metal oxide semiconductors, 29
Microphones, 23, 49-51, 95, 96
Monitors, 23, 56

National Television Standards Committee (NTSC), 23, 29
Newvicons, 26, 27
Noise reduction, 164, 165

Photography director, 87
Plumbicons, 26, 27
Portable cameras, 89-90, 93
Producer, the, 78
Production assistants, 78
Production coordinators, 78
Production managers, 78
Program development, 1-6, 167

Releases and rights, 4-6, 168
Risers, 65, 66

Saticons, 26, 27
Scripts
  editing, 134, 136
  elements of, 6-9, 10
  formats, 10-19
  treatments, 1-3
Script supervisions, 78
Set designers, 87
Shot formats, 7
  transitions, 9-10
Society of Motion Picture and Television Engineers (SMPTE), 123
Special-effects generators (SEGs), 10, 23, 39, 41, 42
  key and mattes, 42, 44
  portable, 95
  switching, 23, 39-40, 42
  time base considerations, 39
  wipes, 9, 23, 42, 158
Storyboards, 6
Studio equipment
  accessories, 52, 54
  audio mixer, 23, 51-52
  audiotape recorders, 23, 52

helical-scan videotape recorders, 31-35
lighting systems, 54-56
luminaires, 55
phase shifters, 23
microphones, 23, 49-51
special-effects generators, 23, 41
television cameras, 23-30
videotape recorders, 23, 30-31
video test equipment, 44
See also Lights, Microphones, Monitors,
  Special-effects generators, Vectorscope,
  Videotape recorders, Waveform monitor
Studio production
audio recording, 70, 72-76, 168
basic budget, 61-63
lighting, 65, 67-70, 71
planning a shoot, 59-91
sets, 64-65, 66
Switcher, *See* Special-effects generator

Sync generator, 23, 39

Technical director, 78-79
Time base corrector (TBC), 39, 164, 165
Tracking, *See* Helical-scan videotape recording

Vectorscope, 23, 45-47
Videotape, 36, 38, 168
Video effects devices, 161-163
Videotape recorders, 30-31, 34-36, 39, 125
  operator, 79
  portable, 94-95
    See also Editing concepts and equipment
Vidicons, 26, 27

Waveform monitor, 23, 44-45
Wipes, *See* Special-effects generators
Workprint, 132
Writer's Guild of America, 10

About the Authors

Ingrid Wiegand was a senior engineering writer on a number of early high-tech space projects and video presentation systems. She wrote and produced several industrial films, through which she first developed shooting and production techniques. But in the early '70's, when the first professional video equipment became available, she started working in video.

She has produced numerous video documentaries and educational and industrial programs. As a Fellow of the Rockefeller Foundation, she traveled widely in India and produced a program on contemporary culture in that country. Her programs have been exhibited on PBS, on various cable stations and at the Berlin Film Festival.

She has lectured and conducted workshops on television technology and scriptwriting at the New School, the City University of New York, and at universities throughout the United States. Her articles on video have been published in a number of periodicals and included in several books. Currently, she is a founder and vice president of Media for the Arts, Inc. Her biography appears in "Who's Who of American Women" and "Who's Who in Entertainment."

During the last fifteen years, Benjamin L. Bogossian has held managerial, technical and production positions in the video industry. Currently he is the manager of producer services for a major southern California video dealer. Ben has a strong background in corporate video having participated in every aspect of the industry from bench technician to producer. He has published articles dealing with video system maintenance and staff management issues in *E-ITV* magazine and ITVA newsletters, and he is a popular presenter of technical seminars for Knowledge Industry Publications, Inc., at IMAGE WORLD/VIDEO EXPO sessions.